The Franciscan Journey

Catch

Me A

Rainbow

LESTER BACH OFM Cap

IMPRIMATUR: George O. Wirz ... Auxiliary Bishop of Madison, WI
Vicar General ... January 10, 1990

IMPRIMI POTEST: Kenneth Reinhart OFM Cap ... Minister
Provincial ... January 16, 1990

The author acknowledges these publishers for their permission to reprint texts from their publications. Permission is granted for a limited edition of *Catch Me A Rainbow*.

+ Quotations from the Revised English Bible – Copyright *Oxford University Press & Cambridge University Press* – 1989 ... Reprinted by permission.

+ *Franciscan Herald Press* for quotations from:
Omnibus of sources – Marion Habig OFM – 1973
Golden Words, sayings of Brother Giles of Assisi
    – Ivo O'Sullivan – 1966
Rule of the Secular Franciscans – 1978

+ *Paulist Press* for quotations from:
Francis and Clare, the complete works
    – Ignatius Brady OFM & Regis Armstrong OFM Cap – 1982

+ *Miss D.E. Collins* – A.P. Watt Ltd, literary agents
St Francis of Assisi – G.K. Chesterton – 1924
Published in USA by IMAGE BOOKS

Reproduction of any quotation from the above copyright holders is forbidden without their written consent.

Published by
National Formation Commission
of
Secular Franciscans

Ron Pihokker, SFO, Chairperson
377 Rutherford Boulevard
Clifton, NJ 07014

Marilyn Friga, SFO
Rt. 6, Box 3015
Gloucester, VA 23061

Matthew L. Gaskin, OFM
63 Bartholdi Avenue
Butler, NJ 07405

Diane Halal, SFO
11741 Cherry Street
Los Alamitos, CA 90720

Camillus MacRory, OFM Cap.
453 Miller Avenue
South San Francisco, CA 94080

Violet Tipotsch, SFO
1420 East Tilden Street
Roswell, NM 88201

Mary Lou Young, SFO
110 West Santa Fe Street
Olpe, KS 66865

Printed by
Barbos' Printing
Lindsborg, KS

Table of Contents

Introduction

Revising *Catch Me A Rainbow* has been a delight for me. It offered me the opportunity to incorporate fresh ideas into the book. There is much new material in the new edition. May you gain delight from using this book. May it guide you to greater faithfulness to the gospel.

Catch Me A Rainbow is frequently used by the Professed Secular Franciscans as well as by those in initial formation. In order to assist the Professed in using this book I have added REFLECTION QUESTIONS for them.

> These questions appear in "boxed-in" sections such as this one. They are meant primarily for the professed, but others may use them if they wish. They should help both personal reflection and group discussion.

When using this book for initial formation, I suggest this process:

1. All participants read the entire chapter. Then answer, in writing, the questions on the page headed – QUESTIONS. Everyone comes to the formation session prepared to share.

2. At the formation session people share their answers. This sharing offers a wider understanding of the chapter. With each sharing different insights emerge.

3. Take time to reflect on the <u>SCRIPTURE reading/reflection</u>. It may help to have someone read the scripture text out loud before sharing ideas. The proclamation of the word has its own power. This is prayerful time.

4. End the session with common prayer. People can take turns leading this portion of the session. The prayer will naturally reflect the sharings of the session. Prayer time should not be too long but a gentle way to conclude the formation session.

Our common call to follow the gospel in the spirit of St Francis is a privilege. May you enjoy the privilege every day of your life!

SHALOM

Lester Bach OFM Cap

CHAPTER 1

THE INNER JOURNEY

Anticipating an event often out-runs its reality. A celebration of friendship, a trip to the dentist, confronting a difficult situation – all bring a variety of feelings to awareness. Quite often, the reality does not match our anticipation of the event.

Francesco Giovanni Bernadone, also known as Francis of Assisi, experienced the difference between anticipation and reality. He anticipated that his knightly foray into battle would be filled with glory. Fighting against the Perugians was going to be a glorious adventure for the bold young knight. Reality brought defeat and imprisonment in Perugia. Far from glory, Francis found himself in the awful misery of prison.

In some of his gloomier days in prison, Francis remembered his rides in the hills around Assisi. The fresh air and sunshine were delightful. How he longed for those days of freedom. But time dragged on in prison. Sickness took its toll on the body of Francis. When he finally returned home a year later, he was a sick young man.

When he was strong enough to ride, the hills did not play the same music as before. The old ways seemed boring and lifeless. Once again. reality did not match the anticipation of his "rememberings."

The way of "self-discovery" is often like that. We find that the things we anticipated with joy give but little return in reality. The journey of self-discovery reveals both hidden fears and unknown gifts in our hearts. Reality offers a taste of things that were unknown in the time of anticipation.

Fear can move us to "do a Jonah" i.e. seek ways of escaping the reality of God's call. We develop defenses against the surprises of life. Rigid opinions and authoritarian ideas help us avoid a reality that would expand our horizons. Excusing ourselves because of human weakness or denying human weakness blinds us to reality. We create idols that replace God in our lives. We idolize material wealth. We idolize the products of technology. Computers and fax machines have equal value with God in our lives. As we examine what (who) we trust, we find that God is not always in first place. We have many "strange gods" that we worship, almost unconsciously.

Much of our absorption in these "gods" gives us a sense of being "in charge". We think that we are in control. We avoid surprises and make choices that protect us from spontaneity. Planning and programming allow us to predict how things will be for us. We anticipate marvelous things as our power and wealth grow.

Once again, reality does not always fulfill the anticipation. Loneliness, un-ease, hidden fears begin to crop up in our hearts. Just when every-thing should bring happiness into our lives, a crisis dashes our hopes. Things we were going to do for loved ones "some day" are still undone – and the loved ones are gone. The inner search for reality will not be stilled by either busyness nor idols. It is difficult to stifle the heart's search for reality.

The journey to the reality-of-the-gospel is, for the Christian, a complex one. Honest searching brings both the ecstasy of discovery and the agony of a sense of loss. Reality can be both difficult and energizing, fearful and exciting, full of sudden insights and long waiting periods. Sometimes our discoveries are precious and private. At other times they absolutely shout to be shared with others. Our journeys are similar to others' journeys – yet retain a personal uniqueness. YOU are the final authority who determines the direction you choose to follow.

Francis And Franciscans:

People who choose to follow St Francis of Assisi will also choose to follow the path of self-discovery. Openness to the Spirit of Jesus is a common quality in Franciscans. It will be touched with the fingerprints of our uniqueness, but has common elements with others on the journey. St Francis' way was right for Francis. But each of us has our own name and a way that God calls us to follow. For me, I will be Lester Bach, not Francis of Assisi. Francis shows me what can happen when I am open to the Spirit of Jesus. He reveals the real inner joy that comes when God's reality is accepted with a loving heart. I discover what sensitivity can do in my life. I understand the pain of surrender. I begin to experience the peace that comes when Jesus' Father becomes my Father in reality. My situations and experiences are not the same as those of Francis. Yet the same gospel ideals are present to me. My calling is to give flesh to the qualities of Christ-centeredness, surrender to the Father, spontaneity, and the Capuchin-Franciscan ideals. Each of us is given a personal invitation to respond to God's call. Our best and only gift is our "self." It is the most precious gift we have. It is the unique gift that we offer to God.

Gathering Information On The Journey:

God, in creating people and a world for them to live in, did it with love. God shared goodness with creation. We are made in the image of this God. We have within us the source of goodness. The wonders of the world can touch us with delight and joy. Take a look at the care with which your fingers bend, with just enough skin to allow for bending at the joints. Read about the wonders of the brain at work, with hundreds of cells co-operating to accomplish ordinary tasks. There is wonder and goodness all around us and within us. We are not a problem to be solved, but a mystery to be discovered!

When we discover weakness and brokenness, we also discover God's desire to touch us with strength and healing. God knows us inside out. Recognition of weakness makes us more vulnerable to God's desire to save us. The words of Scripture remain always true:

> So it was; and God saw all that he had made, and it was
> very good.
>> **Genesis 1: 31**

To accept ourselves as good does not mean we are perfect.

We can mis-use good gifts and choose destructive ways of action. We can choose paths other than the gospel way of life. Our false self can disguise our basic goodness with doubt and denial of goodness. Constant put-downs and criticism can make us feel inferior. Such false-self developments do not negate our basic goodness, but it can make it seem non-existent. Growing up in a dysfunctional family can make self-love even more difficult to achieve. But the reality remains – we are good because of God's gift of life to us.

Think of the ways we have been convinced we are not so good. Important people in our lives tell us we are no-good. We choose a lifestyle that is destructive. Then we tell ourselves we can't possibly be good. We have only mediocre accomplishments, so we can't really be good. We have grown selfish and unconcerned, so goodness cannot reside in our hearts. Reflection on such negatives convinces us that we are really bad people. Any opinion about our basic goodness is a fairy-tale.

Some folks stereotype us as useless and boring. Our marriage is nothing like we anticipated. We feel trapped in a life that has no open doors. We may even lash out at people and the world in defiance and self-righteousness. But inside, we easily believe that we are no-good.

Living in such an atmosphere makes it difficult to hope that we can change. It is nonsense to talk about our goodness when we feel useless and clumsy. What St Francis of Assisi offers is hope. Francis tells us that Jesus came to save sinners. Jesus came to bring freedom from the trap of hopelessness and helplessness.

We begin to understand that we are imperfect people called to be faithful to the gospel. Left to ourselves, such a way of life would be impossible. With Jesus, all things are possible. Of equal importance, we travel this road of conversion TOGETHER – with Jesus and one another.

Kermit the Frog, of Sesame Street fame, sings a song that reflects what happens to many people. He finds himself not liking being green. It seems like such a dull color. It doesn't dazzle people like so many other colors do. So Kermit would like to be some other color. But the longer he thinks about it, the more he comes to consider the fact that "being green" may not be so bad. It has its own set of beautiful elements about it. So he finally decides that being green is what he really wants to be. It is but another way of saying, "being your real self is all you need to be." Trying to be someone else is a losing struggle.

4

Being who I am will do fine.
I'm beautiful, and I want to
be me!

We, too, often complain about the hand that fate deals us. As we reflect on reality, however, we begin to accept being "green" and find we like it. There is peace in such acceptance. The reality is: "I" is all I have and it is enough.

Influences That Shape Us:

Self-pity and moping are not unknown among us. "Isn't it awful that I am who I am!" "If only ..." We decide that we would really be happy if we were like Mabel or Joshua or Maria or Bill. They do things so well. I am so ordinary and common and not worth much to anyone. We downgrade ourselves until we are convinced that what "we think" is reality. Life becomes an imitation of others, trying to capture their goodness for ourselves. But we wind up unhappy and feeling less competent. It isn't easy being who I am...

Sometimes the price-tag of conversion seems too high. There is agony and struggle as we deal with our limitations. Sometimes others expect us to be more than we can be. Sometimes our brokenness is hard for others to accept. Sometimes we hate to acknowledge brokenness and limitations. We act as though we have everything in control. At other times we deny our gifts because of the responsibilities such an acknowledgement would bring.

Jesus tells us that brokenness can be healed. Jesus tells us that our gifts can be enhanced. Step by step we can change and become our real self. I am me and it will do fine. I am beautiful – and it's what I want to be.

Society provides obstacles in our search for self-acceptance. It gives us an "image" of how successful people ought to look. It requires us to dress a certain way, follow a certain lifestyle, possess certain things as necessary on the road to self-acceptance. It puts a high focus on externals. Toothpaste and mouthwash are vital to success. Having the right car or the latest computer is vital to advancement. Instant escape from pain is the norm and any need to wait for things is insufferable. TV plots solve intricate puzzles in one hour or less, with the hidden implication that successful people can do the same.

We bring these ideas to our Christian life. We ought to be able to convert in a hurry. Perfection requires us to be efficient. There are to be no blemishes on holy people. Perfectionism makes it impossible to achieve any lasting satisfaction. Instant gratification must be given by God or it is a sign that God doesn't love us. Problems and pain are to be solved instantly or something is wrong with us. All in all, society does not support God's way of doing things.

Closer to home, family, friends and job also influence us. Important people expect us to accept their ideas and attitudes without question. Our job may demand a lifestyle quite contrary to the gospel. Marriage partners may make demands that we cannot meet. Death of a loved one can devastate our world. Economic recessions and unpayable bills can push us into the hole of depression. Joblessness and unconcern by others make us feel useless. On the other hand, we are touched by joyful celebrations and renewed by relaxing vacations. We are touched by compassion shown by people. We are amazed at people who accept us in our brokenness with beautiful love. Both positive and negative influences come from people we deal with each day.

Life does not stand still even if we want it to. We are called to change. The years make a difference in our view of things. Sickness pricks our balloon of invincibility. Past solutions become today's problems. Little wonder that we need a solid community of friends to walk with us. Our common sharing on the journey gives us hope and binds us together. New attitudes develop. They influence the way we deal with the reality of life. The Spirit of Jesus continues to create a new spirit within us.

> ...For were you not told of him, were you not as Christians taught the truth as it is in Jesus? – that, leaving your former way of life, you must lay aside that old human nature which, deluded by its lusts, is sinking toward death. You must be made new in mind and spirit, and put on the new nature of God's creating, which

shows itself in the just and devout life called for by the truth.

The gospel calls us to be "made new in mind and spirit." Francis of Assisi was well aware of this call. He also knew the difficulties involved. Even when the call is clear, the "way-to-do-it" takes a lot of learning. Francis quickly realized the value of the model that Jesus gives. Jesus became the focus of Francis' attention. The life and words of Jesus became vitally important for Francis. Some of this is captured in the Rule for the Secular Franciscans:

> *...following the example of St Francis of Assisi, who made Christ the inspiration and center of his life with God and people.*

> *Christ, the gift of the Father's love, is the way to God, the truth into which the Holy Spirit leads us and the life which he has come to give us abundantly.*
> **Rule – Chapter 2 #4**

What does Jesus do? How does he deal with us? Jesus speaks to us through the scriptural word. Jesus forgives us when we sin. Jesus walks tenderly with us when we are weak. Jesus confronts us when we are stupid. Jesus challenges assumptions that no longer give life. Jesus desires freedom for us and seeks to bring us joy. Jesus knows that sometimes we need the desert to remember our need for him. In the desert, Jesus often speaks to our heart when we are stripped of our false-self. Waters spring up in the desert and we find a homeland in exile. Jesus wants us to be whole – to be our "real" selves. When we are stubborn and angry, he remains consistent and faithful. When we choose ways to escape growth, he draws us back to the pathway of life. In all things, Jesus remains true to himself and invites us to be true to ourselves. Jesus remains genuinely interested in us no matter what we do. Jesus continues to love us when we stop loving ourselves. For Jesus to do otherwise would be to deny his own person. How sharply he puts it in one of his conversations:

> *If you, then, bad as you are, know how to give your children what is good for them, how much more will the*

*heavenly Father give the Holy Spirit to those who ask
him.*

Luke 11: 13

In our dark moments we question such statements of scripture. It seems
that God really has abandoned us. Our sinfulness does seem more
powerful than God's forgiveness. Our weakness seems beyond even
God's ability to heal. It is easy to create a golden calf of sin and weakness
and bow down before it. Idol worship still goes on in the world – and
we practice it! Yet, God chooses to remain true to being God. God goes
so far as to become human, to walk among us through Jesus, God-
made-flesh. God has not changed. God remains as Mother/Father to
us. We discover this truth by listening to Jesus. This is a fundamental
fact of Franciscan living.

Human Helps

Much growth has taken place in the study of the human person during
this century. Like all things human, these studies have their limitations.
Many are theories that seem to fit the human person, but they are still
only theories. We need not make a god of psychology nor give obedience to every study of human nature. But we can use them wisely
and find in them help for our journey.

Though we acknowledge the uniqueness of each person, we may
practice a denial of this uniqueness in everyday life. When other people
do not fit a stereotype we have created, we try to control them even
more. Dealing with "unique" people is not always easy. We are not
always happy with friends who are too unique. People with different
ideas or lifestyles are not readily embraced. If people don't live up to
our image of them, we are irritated. When people try to put us in some
category or demand that we live up to their expectations, we become
angry. There are lots of us walking around with pent-up anger because
we were never allowed to be "ourselves." None of this changes the
basic fact – we are unique.

Another cliche tells us to "let it all hang out!" Such an attitude reflects
an insensitivity to others. Sometimes "letting it all hang out" becomes
an assault on others. "Letting it all hang out" is not always psycholo-

8

gically healthy. We have a right to privacy and others have a right to be left alone. We both have the freedom to decide what we wish to share with others. Groups or individuals who deny you these rights are suspect. Exposing yourself through forced "sharing" leaves you naked and vulnerable. Unless competent, loving people are present to help, it can be a destructive experience.

On the other hand, it can be healthy and helpful to share our brokenness with caring people. It can break through the walls of loneliness and despair that keeps us prisoner. But it needs a caring situation with people who are competent to handle such sharing. Keeping everything inside can make us a walking volcano, ready to explode at any time. Sharing our inner self with another requires trust and trustworthiness, respect for confidentiality and the presence of caring people. Respect your own and other's right to determine what is shared. Respect any sharing with loving acceptance even if you do not agree with the shared ideas.

Some of the ideas of Carl Jung are helpful tools in understanding the human person. Jung theorized that each human person possesses a masculine and feminine side (Animus and Anima). Men possess qualities we sometimes label "Feminine"... gentleness, a sense of nurturing, compassion and tenderness. Real men possess such qualities and use them well. A man can be gentle and tender without being weak. He can be nurturing and compassionate without being any less manly. Because some people in society refuse to accept these qualities in a man, many men never grow in this dimension of their person.

In the same way, qualities attributed to men are found in women. Strength, organizational ability, assertiveness, being the breadwinner and protector are some of the qualities attributed to men. A woman needs these qualities too. It is not un-feminine to be strong or assertive. A woman needs to organize things and does so in many areas of life. Today she is often a breadwinner and becomes the protector of people she loves. She fights to protect ideals that she values. Many people in society find it hard to accept such qualities in a woman. Many women may find it hard to be true to this dimension of being "woman".

Both men and women struggle in society and the church to be true to themselves. Support is not always forthcoming. It may seem easier to give up being "unique" than to engage in the hard work of being our real self. We need to examine our attitudes. It is not easy to accept people with all their differences and uniqueness. If we judge differences to be flaws or afflictions, we do them violence. When traditions of another culture annoy us, we can easily forget to allow for "uniqueness." It is easy to expect everyone to fit into our patterns, following only the traditions of the culture in which we were raised.

But if we are able to be sensitive to differences, we discover a new dimension of life. We discover a new "image" of our creative God. Our limited worldview begins to expand. A narrow view of life can be enhanced by the input of people "different" from ourselves. We need not put people into a "mold" or make them fit labels we have created. The Christian is free to allow for differences among God's people. In fact, the Christian learns to rejoice in it. It becomes an expression of the creative power of God.

The multitude of ideas on personality development in our time is a complex reality. Listen with an open mind without taking them as infallible tools. If they bring you life and light, let them help you. If they seem destructive of self or others, discard them. Being REAL is a life-long journey of discovery. It is a delightful, frightening, exhilarating and painful journey. We humans are variously strong and delicate. We tolerate a great deal of stress, yet we can fall apart in the face of simple tensions. Sometimes our masks protect us and at other times they keep us from growth. Being REAL means the ability to accept success without getting "big-headed" and to deal with failure without "falling apart." We are sinner and saint wrapped up in one package. Light and darkness are side-by-side in our lives. Jesus offers a path that leads from darkness to light, from death to life. He offers the power to walk this journey in the everyday stuff of life.

Values

Another way to approach life is to look at the values that influence our decisions. One way to define a value is this:

A VALUE IS AN ATTITUDE/IDEA/PERSPECTIVE THAT MOVES US TO ACT. When something moves us to take action, we call it a value.

10

There are obvious degrees in the world of values. To value a good pair of shoes or a friend is not the same thing. We may change values as new information or experience requires. But, if we want to critique our values, here are some signs of the presence of a value:

1. Values are chosen FREELY. We own them. If we are <u>forced</u> to act in a certain way we do not really value the decision. If we have no options to choose from, we are hardly free. Values require the ability to make a free choice.

2. Values require DELIBERATION. We don't ordinarily stumble into values. Values influence for the long haul. They require sufficient reflection and information to enable us to choose them for the foreseeable future. Once a value is embraced, it is cherished. If we choose to follow a way of life for ourselves, we value it for life. It will show itself consistently in our lifestyle.

3. Values are embraced with PRIDE. We are proud to display our values in everyday life. We show how important a value is by living it publicly.

4. Values are OPEN TO REVISION when new information or experience requires it. Since values are cherished, changes are made only with serious reflection. But as life goes on, we will find a need to change values as we change and grow.

To discover your personal values, reflect on these questions:

✛ What do you do enthusiastically? ✛ What work/hobbies absorb your time when you are free to choose what you want to do? ✛ Who do you enjoy spending time with? ✛ What kind of TV programs do you enjoy? ✛ What kind of movies/plays do you enjoy? What kind of music do you prefer? ✛ What are your dreams for the future? ✛ What are the points of conflict with other people? ✛ Is there a conflict between your value as wife/husband and as mother/father? ✛ Do values of fairness/honesty come into conflict with company policies? ✛ How do you resolve value conflicts in your life? ✛ How do you decide on priorities in your life choices? ✛ What motivates you to choose one thing over another? ✛ What attitudes do you cherish most? ✛ Look at what you "do" and you will see what you value! What we "do" and "how we act" says more about our values than fine words about values.

Only be sure that you act on the message and do not merely listen; for that would be to mislead yourselves. A man who listens to the message but never acts on it is like one who looks in a mirror at the face nature gave him. He glances at himself and goes away, and at once forgets what he looks like. But the man who looks closely into the perfect law, the law that makes us free, and who lives in its company, does not forget what he hears, but acts upon it; and that is the man who by acting will find happiness.

James 1: 22-25

Some Reflection Questions:

How do you feel about yourself? What is the balance between what you CHOOSE to do and what you do to please others? What help does psychology offer you? Do you believe you must earn God's Love? How do people perceive you? How influential are other people's opinions on the way you act? How influential is the gospel in your life? Name some of the "strange gods" you have in your life! Where did they come from? Do you believe you are lovable? Why or why not? Why did God choose to become human through Jesus? What does such a decision say about being human? List some of your most important values! Are they just words or do you act on them? Who are the people you admire the most? Why? Do you imitate them? What have you experienced as the most pretentious "idols" of our society/culture? How much time do you take to reflect on your values? What value do you give to "taking time" for reflection? What are your most unique qualities?

"Even now," says the Lord, "turn to me." – Joel 2: 12

SECULAR FRANCISCAN RULE

Franciscan Formation

The Secular Franciscan Order has a period of formation for those called to our way of life. It is a time to discover the gospel values that support our life. God calls people to this way of life. Part of the purpose of the initial formation program is to discover if there really is a call from God. The formation period offers information, prayer, scripture study and a solid look at the Rule for Secular Franciscans. One important dimension of this formation period is to discover that you and this way of life fit each other. If it does not fit you, we mutually acknowledge that fact. You are then free to seek the call of the Lord in some other path. If it becomes clear that the call "fits" you, we welcome you to join us on our Franciscan journey. Such decisions, made prayerfully and carefully, are good, imperfect decisions. We possess no infallibility, but trust the Lord to guide us in these decisions. We seek to be true to what God seems to be asking us.

The Secular Franciscan Order is not a magical way to holiness. Professing the Franciscan way of life is no guarantee of holiness any more than possessing a bible guarantees instant wisdom. Our Franciscan life is a commitment for a lifetime. It takes a faithful, long-term response to God's call to achieve wholeness. Community life is helpful, but community-life is not perfect nor do perfect people live in it. We remain human as we seek the way of the gospel. The community faces many human struggles and conflicts.

Change is not easy either as an individual or as a community. We will need faithful struggle and sharing to keep us going on this journey. Neither our personal life nor our community life can remain static in the face of God's call to conversion.

The journey toward wholeness and holiness brings times of security and times of fear. It will be exhilarating and exasperating, joyful and painful, frustrating and satisfying, exciting and boring, delightful and depressing. Franciscans struggle together, working out personal and community problems as well as dealing with anger and irritability. But we celebrate joy, enthusiasm and walk with exuberance on our common journey. It is clear that the Holy Spirit faithfully nudges us on.

> *That is why I now remind you to stir into flame the gift of God which is within you through the laying on of my hands. For the Spirit that God gave us is no craven spirit, but one to inspire strength, love and self-discipline.*
>
> **2 Timothy 1: 6-8**

The Rule

The Rule of the Secular Franciscan Order contains the foundations for the Franciscan way of life. Although the Rule alone cannot transform people, it offers an ideal that can give life to the journey to holiness. The Rule will take on life as people give flesh to what it calls for.

Beginnings

The Rule of life is preceded by the LETTER TO ALL THE FAITHFUL. There is general agreement that this letter gives Francis' reflections for his early lay followers. There is disagreement about the dating of the LETTER. Some scholars place the writing as early as 1213-1214 while others date it as late as 1222. There is a similar disagreement about the date of the founding of the Secular Franciscan Order. The variations range from 1209 to 1221.

An Order of Penitents is not unique to Francis. Many groups of penitents wandered throughout Italy in the 1100's. These groups often performed works of charity, wore special clothing and were dedicated to personal conversion. Some became extreme and heretical, losing their credibility. Others continued in a moderate style and existed for a long time. When Francis sent his first followers on preaching trips, he called them "The Penitents from Assisi." Francis added his own charism to the group and did his best to avoid any hint of heresy.

Lay people who could not join this band of wandering Friars were called to a special way of life in the world. They would be a people who trusted the Father. They would love and serve the poor in their midst. They would be peace-lovers in a society given to violence. They would willingly share material goods in a society dominated by greed. They would lay aside their own desires in order to help others in need. Where revenge, murder and senseless killing was too common, they followed the gospel way of forgiveness, reconciliation and respect for life. The followers of Francis brought the gospel message to a world lost in self-seeking and neglect of the poor.

Francis did not assume control of the Secular Franciscan Order. It seems he did not wish to be the "director" of the SFO. After his death and later in the century, the SFO came under the jurisdiction of the Friars. But initially it was an independent movement guided by the spirit of Francis. People were tired of violence and crime, greed and war. They hoped for something better. The spirit of peace and joy of Francis was attractive. Gathered together in a movement of gospel values, the SFO began to make itself felt. When Secular Franciscans refused to bear arms, it put a dent in the war-making machinery. As Secular Franciscans shared materials goods with the needy, they showed a way different than the way of greed. From its earliest history, the SFO has touched society from within and helped to change things by changing people.

Lateran Council IV (1215) began a much needed reform in the Church. St Francis attended the council which developed policies that brought changes to the Franciscan movement. Lateran IV required training for clergy and religious as well as a program of formation. It tried to give fresh direction to the many groups and movements that dotted the landscape of the Church. By 1289 Nicolas IV put the SFO under the care of the Friars of Francis. He also gave them a Rule of life. This Rule of 1289 remained basically unchanged until 1883. During its history the SFO reflects the ups and downs of Church life throughout the centuries.

The change of the SFO Rule in the 19th century was a mixed blessing. Much of what entered the Rule in 1883 reflected the political situation of the Church. In Italy various "kingdoms" were vying for power. The Church lost a great deal of property and power during these struggles. Finally the Church was confined to what we know as Vatican City. It seemed, at the time, like an awful blow. Reacting very humanly, the Church forbade Catholics to participate in any of the political parties that had reduced the Church's holdings. The Church tended to withdraw and man the battlements in a defensive stance. Social and political action became suspect. This isolationist mentality influenced many of the actions of the Church at this time.

When Leo XIII gave the SFO a new Rule in 1883, it reflected this isolationist mentality. Social action, political involvement, any form of "bad" entertainment, was forbidden to Secular Franciscans. Instead of a vibrant group of people influencing society from within, it tended to become a devotional society more concerned with prayers than with the poor. Instead of taking action to bring gospel values to society, Secular Franciscans listened to spiritual conferences. The Rule tended to encourage individual piety rather than a wider view of gospel life. It made the SFO more inner-focused than community-concerned. It was called a "School of perfection" to enable people to become holy mainly through interior changes of oneself.

But, like all things that the Spirit guides, there were many exceptions to such a stereotype of the SFO. Many local fraternities developed sound and caring outreach programs. The spirit of Francis continued to function in these groups. But despite such exceptions, the SFO was more a paper tiger than a roaring lion in society. In this it blended well with the general situation of the Church in the late 19th and early 20th century. Secular Franciscans still grew in holiness during this devotional period, but felt less certain of their role in society.

20th Century

Time does not stand still. Changes were moving within the Church. Society was changing. Wars put their stamp on people throughout the world. Biblical studies blossomed and new insights questioned old attitudes and perspectives. The Vietnamese war and the riots of the 60's influenced American society. Secular Franciscans were faced with a new world. The Rule of 1883 was obviously out of step with this new world. As the Church struggled with change through the decrees of Vatican Council II, Secular Franciscans began working on a new expression for their way of life.

Beginning with committees around the world in 1966 and continuing through 1978 Secular Franciscans struggled to write a Rule that would meet the needs of our time. Many experimental Rules were developed and tested. In a worldwide process of dialogue, consultation and lived experience, the Secular Franciscans designed a new Rule. This new Rule was approved by Paul VI on June 24, 1978. Shortly before his death Paul VI promulgated the new Rule in his letter: "Seraphicus Patriarca" (The Seraphic Father).

The New Rule

A Rule of life is important for any movement. But it is no more than words on paper. It becomes vibrant and alive as people put flesh on the words. The lifestyle called for by the SFO Rule will require struggle and pain. People who were brought up on the Rule of 1883 will think they have entered a new Order with the Rule of 1978. Gone are the restrictions. Instead, there is open encouragement to become involved in justice issues. There are clear demands for solid community life and care for the poor. There are scriptural requirements for building our life on intimacy with Jesus. There is clear direction empowering the SFO to be responsible for their Order. Rather than a host of directives, the Rule of 1978 holds up the ideals of Francis and the gospel in ringing terms. It calls for people to live the values of the gospel. The Rule expects Secular Franciscans to let the gospel touch the whole of their lives. It turns a devotional society into a movement that confronts the world with a new vision of how to live. This vision has the gospel as its primary source.

Summary

The Rule of 1978 renews an original direction of the SFO. This is apparent in the clear power given to the Secular Franciscans for the growth, formation and development of the SFO. The Rule of 1978 makes the Secular Franciscans equal partners in living the charism of St Francis. The three Orders of St Francis join together in sharing the gifts of our charism in the Church. Working together as partners offers hope not only for the SFO but for all who follow Francis. It opens the door for the kind of cooperation that will enable Franciscans to touch our world with their spirit. Even a brief glimpse at the Rule shows how responsibility is given to the SFO.

> *On various levels, each fraternity is animated and guided by a council and minister (President) who are elected by the professed … Their service is marked by a ready and willing spirit and is a duty of responsibility to each member and to the community.*
>
> **RULE – Chapter 3 #21**

> *Requests for admission to the SFO must be presented to the local fraternity, whose council decides upon the acceptance of new brothers and sisters.*

> *… Members who find themselves in particular difficulties should discuss their problem with the council in fraternal dialogue.*
>
> **RULE – Chapter 3 #23**

Working together, Franciscans will continue to touch the world and the Church with the spirit of St Francis.

FRANCISCAN FOCUS

Here are some of the more important dates in the life of St Francis of Assisi. The time between 1211/12 until 1221 is not well documented, so there are fewer events given during that period. It was the time of the Lateran IV Council (1215) and Francis' struggle with the growth of the Order as well as the period when he wrote the Rule(s) for the First Order (1221/1223)

1182 ... Francesco Giovanni Bernadone is born in Assisi. His father is Pietro Bernadone, a cloth merchant and landowner. His mother is Pica, from southern France. Francis is first named Giovanni in the absence of his father. At his Father's return from a buying trip, he names him Francesco.

1190 – 1195 ... Francis attends the Church school at St George's. He learned the fundamentals of Latin, reading, writing and numbers. His later Latin writing indicates that he was far from being a scholarly student. His father may have taught him French, for he often sang French ballads.

1202 ... Assisi and its neighboring city of Perugia engage in armed conflict. Francis joins the army of Assisi only to be defeated, captured and imprisoned in Perugia.

1204 ... Released in 1203, Francis is weak and ill for the better part of a year. His health is frail at this time.

1205 ... A new battle of warring factions draws Francis to try knight-hood again. He heads out of Assisi well groomed, but gets no farther than Spoleto. In a dream he is told to go home. This is the start of a special time of struggle for Francis. He is unsure of himself and uncertain of the meaning of his "dream" and the "message" that seems to come from the Lord.

1205 ... While praying in the Chapel of San Damiano, Francis hears a voice speaking to him from the Crucifix: "Go, repair my house ..." Accepting the literal meaning of the words, he begins to rebuild the little fallen-down chapel of San Damiano. He continues his restoration projects by restoring the little Chapel of St Mary of the Angels (The Portiuncula), his very special "home."

1209 ... Francis is living at the Portiuncula. Others are attracted by his lifestyle, so he writes a simple Rule composed of Scripture texts linked together. Innocent III gives a verbal approval of the Rule. The little band of "Penitents" lives in huts, begs for food and preaches in the towns around Assisi. Bernard of Quintavalle, Peter of Catania and Giles are his first friars. Others follow and the group of "Penitents of Assisi" grows.

1212 ... Clare of Assisi, daughter of a noble family, leaves her home and joins Francis. Clare becomes one of the most faithful followers of Francis, true to his spirit in her way of life. The "Poor Clares" begin with this faithful woman and blossom in her care. She brings the beauty of her woman's touch to the Franciscan spirit. She is the staunchest defender of his gospel "dream". Not even Popes can swerve her from the Lady Poverty that she met through Francis.

1209 – 1221 ... It seems that during this period the Secular Franciscan Order was established. It is during this period of time that Francis writes his LETTER TO ALL THE FAITHFUL. In fact, two letters to the Faithful were written by Francis.

1224 ... In September of 1224 Francis receives the Stigmata at La Verna. His health is deteriorating. He experiences much physical pain. He is blind, has stomach and intestinal problems and lives with pain day in and day out. It is during these last painful, blind years, that Francis composes his "CANTICLE OF BROTHER SUN."

1226 ... Francis dies on October 3, 1226, on a Saturday evening. Shortly before his death he adds the final verses to his Canticle of Brother Sun – "Praise to Sister death ..." Francis dies as he listens to Psalm 14 being recited by one of the Brothers. It is 20 years since the start of his conversion. He is in his 45th year of life.

1228 … Francis of Assisi is proclaimed a saint by Pope Gregory IX on July 16, 1228.

1230 … The body of St Francis is transferred to the newly built Basilica in Assisi on May 25, 1230.

ST FRANCIS OF ASSISI … Cimabue

QUESTIONS

1. It is important to be in touch with your life story. Take some solid reflective time to explore your life. Consider some of these questions in your reflection time: What is the strongest influence your parents have on you? What is the happiest moment of your life as you remember? What are your attitudes to the poor? the rich? the sick? people from others cultures? other races? How do you view people in authority? How do you feel about the way you are living right now? What do you like to do most of all? What do you hate to do? How do these things influence your life – Bible? Church? Doctrine? Feelings? Emotions? New Ideas? Sports? School? Reading? TV? Books? Social action? Gossip? Power? Control? What failure(s) have been most depressing? What successes have brought the most joy? What are your best qualities? What are your most negative qualities?

Write out your story from these questions. Get in touch with who you are. Share whatever you wish.

2. Is self-acceptance possible without the help of others? Give reasons for your answer.

3. What are the "values" that influence your life right now? Explain why they are important to you and how you act on them.

4. Why do you wish to join the Secular Franciscan Order?

5. What is the importance of the RULE in being a Secular Franciscan?

6. Describe what you believe the SFO can do for you and what you expect to contribute to the SFO.

SCRIPTURE *reading/reflection:*

✛ Psalm 139 ... God knows and loves us no matter where we are.

✛ James 2: 14-26 ... James gives us his view on the need for faith AND good works.

✛ Please share your impressions of Psalm 139 – what impact did it have as you read (prayed) it? What did the words of James say to YOU about faith and works in YOUR life?

CHAPTER 2

THE ASSISI CONVERSION

St Francis of Assisi offers a model of conversion. The process that touched his life reflects our own struggle. A look at the conversion of Francis of Assisi may resemble the story of our conversion.

Sometimes we understand better when we see the two ends of a story. In Francis' case, conversion began with a dream that brought him to San Damiano and the Portiuncula. The story continued at La Verna 18 years later. It ended in the embrace of Sister Death 20 years later. In the beginning Francis faced a radical turnabout in his life and lifestyle. At the end, he experienced a deep intimacy with Jesus that was a new surrender. In the beginning he groped for understanding. At the end he willingly plunged into the mystery of Jesus' love. The beginning was puzzling and difficult. The end was embraced with longing.

La Verna had become Francis' special place of solitude. The rugged mountain protected his privacy and prayer. It offered a respite from the quarrels and disagreements in the Order. The Order was changing, becoming different than his original dream had envisioned it. He no longer felt that he had control. The large numbers and differing inter- pretations of the way of life left him hurt and confused. On La Verna he poured out his heart to Jesus. Days and nights passed on this mountain. He sought new intimacy with Jesus and cried out:

> *"Let me experience in my heart the love you had in*
> *yours, Lord Jesus; and let me feel in my body the pain*
> *you experienced because of your love for me."*

The cry of one lover for another swirled around the mountain. Silence blossomed on this rocky crest.

Then, in the intimacy of love, Francis experienced the presence of Jesus. It seemed to fill his whole person. He felt like crying out in the wonder and pain that only lovers can understand. As he looked at his hands and feet, he saw there the signs of love – the marks of the crucified one. It was agony and ecstasy, unbelievable joy combined with new and painful intimacy with Jesus. "My God and my all!"

Francis was about 43 years old when he received the stigmata. He was in poor health, physically weak and with eyes that could not tolerate light. In two years he would be dead. This special intimacy came after 18 years of trying to live the dream of the gospel. The years had been full of struggle and deserts, of joy and delight, of satisfaction and disappointment. God had gifted this man with fresh insights into the meaning of faithful love. On La Verna he began the last years of his conversion. Now the surrender would be complete. Even his beloved Order would be surrendered into the hands of Jesus. Death alone would bring an end to this life of conversion.

The Beginning

As we trace the path of Francis' conversion, we may recognize familiar landmarks. The process is similar to our conversion. Francis' journey of conversion is an honest, imperfect search for the Lord. His human struggle resembles our own, his fears and dreams are ours.

Francis grew up in the town of Assisi, influenced by family, friends and neighbors. Pica loved him dearly. His father looked forward to the day when Francis would assume control of the business. Success and money were important to Pietro. Collecting on unpaid debts left him a lot of real estate around Assisi. The business growth showed no sign of lessening. Francis would soon learn the exhilaration of running a successful business. Riches brought power and Pietro intended to use it. Pietro could afford to indulge the merry-making of his son. He was a leader with the young people in town. That would bode well for Francis when he entered the business world. Francis would settle down soon enough. For now, it was enough to indulge his whims and youthful excesses.

Francis had dreams of his own. Knighthood was something to be sought by a young man in his prime. It opened doors to fame and glory, a springboard to the good life. Francis and his friends yearned for a battlefield to prove their mettle. Together they would conquer the world for a great cause. In their naivete, they gave little thought to the fact that glory would come through killing and conquest. In the romanticism of knighthood, such thoughts had little impact. A knight defended the weak and vanquished the guilty. A knight was forever a glorious figure in the dreams of Francis and his companions.

Society in Francis' time was a complex mixture. Emperor and Pope struggled for power. Churchmen were often more interested in power and wealth than in salvation. Many priests and monks sought prestige and power. Many of them had mistresses. The cities brewed with talk of revolt. Assisi reeked with a restless spirit of freedom-seeking. Armies fought over perceived insults. Cities engaged in violent confrontation over disputed lands and the right to rule them. New trade routes needed protection from bandits. Money could buy such protection.

Pietro Bernadone's wealth grew as he confiscated lands for unpaid debts. Both the dream of knighthood and grubby desires for wealth and power influenced Francis. He enjoyed the good times his father's money allowed him. He spent lavishly and enjoyed entertaining his friends. In the midst of this mixture of influences, God was at work.

When God spoke to Francis, it was in a language Francis could understand – the language of chivalry. The battle between Perugia and Assisi ended badly for Assisi. After his imprisonment in Perugia, Francis returns home a sick man. Pica nourishes him back to health. But the "good old days" weren't what they used to be. With no other challenges to conquer, Francis once again sets out for battle. The dream of knighthood still held him. It is on this journey that things begin to change drastically in the life of Francis of Assisi.

Leaving Assisi to join the army, Francis gets as far as Spoleto. There the fevers of the old sickness visit him again. Bedded down in Spoleto, he has a dream. He sees castles and swords and shields. He senses a vision of knighthood that has so far eluded him. A voice spoke: "Who do you think can best reward you, the master or the servant?" The answer seemed obvious: "The master!" Then the voice in the dream said: "Then why do you leave the master for the servant? The rich man for the poor man?" This was not making sense! Why such a question when Francis thought he was doing well in seeking knighthood. How do you answer such questions? But the voice went on: "Return to Assisi and there you will be told what to do."

Go back to Assisi and tell a doting father that "voices" had told him to return! Go back and share with his friends that he had heard "voices" telling him what to do! Such good news Francis could easily do without. But the words seemed real and could not be ignored. A puzzled young man rode back to Assisi.

The experience at Spoleto began a difficult time for Francis. The fury of his father was understandable. But it simply forced Francis to a deeper withdrawal from his old ways. He was uncertain about what he was to do. He worked at the cloth-business, but his heart was not in it. He and his father quarreled ceaselessly. Francis left the house to get away and found himself wandering among the poor. He hid from his father in the caves around Assisi. He prayed. But nothing seemed to help. Where was the promised message?

One day in 1205, Francis was praying in the dilapidated chapel of San Damiano. In quiet prayer he was surprised when it seemed to him that he heard a voice coming from the crucifix: "Francis, go and repair my house!" In great relief he responded quite literally. With a happy heart he began to repair the old chapel. He begged for stones and lugged them to the site of San Damiano. In response to the words he became a stone mason. When begging did not bring enough stones to meet the need, he took some cloth from his father's shop and sold it in another town. He even sold the horse to get money to fix the chapel. With the "best of intentions" he became a thief, selling what was not his to sell. But it felt good finally to be "doing" something.

About this same time, Francis writes about another experience that contributes to his conversion process. One day when he was riding his horse on the valley road, he felt great. The sunshine warmed him and the wind on his face cooled him. As he rode, a leper suddenly appeared in the road. A leper! For Francis a leper was a symbol of ugliness and evil. The stench was enough to drive one away. Loathing and fear were Francis' first reactions to the leper. He wanted to wheel his horse around and escape. But, oddly enough, something inside called him to embrace the leper! Unbelievable! Part of him wanted to run and part of him wanted to embrace this poor leper. Which would it be?

Before he could decide otherwise, he had dismounted. He ran to the leper and embraced him. Everything about the leper repulsed him. He expected to vomit and feel ill. What happened was so surprising that he never forgot it. As he put it later: "What before seemed bitter was changed into sweetness of soul and body. I tarried yet a little and forsook the world." This experience with the "dregs" of society changed Francis. He began to work with the lepers. The poor became "his people." He became one of the poor and lived among them.

His father's reaction to this "new" Francis was predictable. It was bad enough to lose a horse and cloth. But then to have his own son cavorting with lepers! That was too much! In a rage, Pietro dragged his son before the Magistrate of the town to get back the money Francis had stolen. If anger and beatings couldn't change Francis' mind, maybe jail could. Francis replied that he considered himself a servant of the Church. If Pietro wanted his money back, he would have to take him before the Bishop!

So the scene is set. Pietro and Francesco come before the Bishop of Assisi. Francis had no case. He was clearly in the wrong for taking the cloth and horse. The Bishop says as much and demands restitution from Francis. All eyes turn to Francis. Always having an intuitive sense of symbol, Francis strips off all his clothes. He lays them at the feet of his father, Pietro. Standing naked before everyone, he speaks the words of his new life: "Until now I have called you, Pietro Bernadone, my father. But now I say only: 'Our Father in heaven.'" It is an ending and a beginning. A new relationship has been embraced and acted on. Life will no longer be the same for Francis.

This event may seem dramatic, but it repeats itself in the life of Francis. Crisis and progress, blindness and seeing, helplessness and hope continue to be part of the conversion process. Dying turns into life. Endings turn into new beginnings. When hope seems fragile, Jesus brings it to new vigor in the life of Francis. It took 20 years of "daily conversion" to accomplish the goal of intimacy with Jesus. Perhaps it would be better to say it took 45 years. Francis' early life was preparation for these crucial events.

How Are We Converted?

No one just happens to have a certain personality and character. Many influences, both within and outside ourselves, have a voice in how we develop. If we were to complete the sentence: I AM THIS KIND OF PERSON BECAUSE –, all kinds of persons and events would come to mind. Family, teachers, enemies, police, pastors, friends, school, wives, husbands, writers, poets, movies, TV shows, wars, sickness, national events, presidential campaigns, jobs, joblessness, weddings, drugs, graduations, poverty, wealth, riots, accidents – these and more touch our lives. We do not live in a vacuum. We are surrounded by influences every day of our lives. When we talk about conversion, it helps to be in touch with how we got to be the way we are. Such knowledge allows us to retain things that continue to be life-giving and to discard the influences that put chains on our growth.

Then he called the people to him, as well as his disciples, and said to them:

"Anyone who wishes to be a follower of mine must leave self behind; he must take up his cross, and come with me. Whoever cares for his own safety is lost; but if a man will let himself be lost for my sake and the gospel, that man is safe. What does a man gain by winning the whole world at the cost of his true self? What can he give to buy that self back? If anyone is ashamed of me and mine in this wicked and godless age, the Son of Man will be ashamed of him when he comes in the glory of his Father and of the holy angels."

Mark 8: 34-38

The search for God often brings us to unfamiliar places. Francis is called to a very different lifestyle. From being a party-goer with rich friends, he becomes a servant of lepers and the poor. From a pampered life at home he comes to a life of begging and manual labor. Such choices would seem ridiculous unless "serving the master" is more important than "serving the servant." If Jesus is the Master, the consequences are clear. Francis will need to leave home, father and mother, money and power, for the sake of the Master. He will embrace a new vision of life, using new criteria to judge what is important. The old lifestyle no longer has meaning for Francis. The perspective that determines concrete decisions are gospel-based rather than success-based. Nothing is quite the same for Francesco Bernadone. Faced with similar issues, our lives too will change.

> "No one tears a piece from a new cloak to patch an old one; if he does, he will have made a hole in the new cloak and the patch from the new will not match the old. Nor does anyone put new wine into old wineskins; if he does, the new wine will burst the skins, the wine will be wasted and the skins ruined. Fresh skins for new wine!"
> **Luke 5: 36-38**

In my own conversion journey, I resist the new wine skins in my life. I try to discover ways to keep both the new and the old. I like some backup protection in case the Lord doesn't come through in the way I want. Sometimes I think the new wineskins are too expensive. I try to keep my scraggly old skins because they are homey and familiar. I keep discovering the quality (!?) of my faith in Jesus. It is embarrassing to realize how fragile it is. Yet, Jesus continues his faithfulness to me. Little by little I grow in reliance on that faithful love. It helps me to accept the new wineskins. It enables me to leave self-centered security for the open spaces of the security that Jesus brings.

Jesus knows when we choose other masters in our life. He knows the idols and the lifestyles that we cling to for security. With a life-giving tough love, he weans us from them and leads us to more life-giving things. Together with the Father, Jesus maintains a faithful presence in our lives, waiting for us to discover him anew. Little wonder that the Rule of the Secular Franciscans speaks of conversion as an every-day affair:

> ... let them conform their thoughts and deeds to those of Christ by means of that radical interior change which the gospel itself calls "conversion." Human frailty makes it necessary that this conversion be carried out daily!
> **RULE – Chapter 2 #7**

This is a truth for everyone. The price of daily conversion is openness to the Holy Spirit. The Spirit walks with us in our darkness and brings us to light. She celebrates with us in our joys and strengthens us when we are weak. She is faithful and loving, ready to help us overcome any obstacle to growth. She leads us to fullness of life if we surrender to her. There is no holiness without her influence.

> *Therefore I prayed, and prudence was given to me. I called for help, and there came to me a spirit of wisdom. I valued her above sceptre and throne and reckoned riches as nothing beside her; I counted no precious stones her equal, because all gold in the world compared with her is but a little sand, and silver worth no more than clay. I loved her more than health or beauty; I preferred her to the light of day; for her radiance is unsleeping. So all good things together came to me with her, and in her hands was wealth past counting; and all was mine to enjoy, for all follows where wisdom leads, and I was in ignorance before, that she is the beginning of it all.*
>
> **Wisdom 7: 7-12**

Wisdom is another way to speak of the Holy Spirit. We do not make perfect decisions. We make good decisions mixed with imperfection. The Holy Spirit continues to enhance those decisions as we act on them. As we walk in the light of the Spirit, the shadows are filled with light. We see and believe in new ways even as we see our weaknesses more clearly. We are never alone!

Ideas About Conversion

We all have ideas about what it means to "be converted." Like most things human, each of them will have something of the truth in them. Let's look at different ideas of the ways of conversion – a mix of sound and not-so-sound ideas.

1. Conversion means that we maintain all our values and attitudes as they are, but allow for an exception in particular cases. For example, we generally value making a profit no matter who gets hurt. But in

this case, it would hurt too many people, so we make an exception and call it "Conversion." We might be able to quote a suitable bible text to confirm our conversion. We haven't changed our value, only allowed for an exception.

—OR—

We may have a real hatred for power-grabbing people in government. We have clear ideas on how ruthless and uncaring they are. But then we become friends with one of them and find this one to be a really fine person. So we make an exception for this one person and marvel at our "conversion." But we still think the rest of them are power-grabbing and ruthless people. In neither of these cases do we have true conversion – only an empty shell that we call "conversion." I still believe I'm right about all these things except for _____!

2. Another way of conversion is the way of the "ball of twine" approach. In this situation, we go through life and accumulate all sorts of experiences. People influence us in a hundred different ways. Like adding to a ball of twine, we add these influences to our style of living. We don't determine to change, but life's experiences and influences change us. Crisis change us. Advertising changes us. Certain books and people change our way of looking at things. This all happens without much personal awareness or reflection. The changes may be good, bad or indifferent, but we fail to examine them. We roll down the hill like a snowball, accumulating things without reflection that could give them some direction. We may not even examine whether they are healthy or not. They simply happen to us. Such development can be called conversion, but if it remains unreflective, it is ambiguous at best.

3. Sometimes people make extreme changes in life. They move from being a hater to a lover, from being shy to being assertive, from despising Church to becoming churchy folks. People who do a 180 degree turn in their lives do not always know why they are doing it. What may happen is that the same faults that supported hatred now support love. Behavior is changed but the inner attitude changes very little. If they were aggressively hostile to the Church before they are equally hostile to the Non-Churched now. Only the object of their hostility has changed. The adulterer becomes the preacher against lust. There is no integration of old and new – only

an apparently marvelous transformation. These folks often become nuisances to family and friends as they force their "conversion" on everyone.

While the power of the Spirit can and has accomplished such conversions, it is not the ordinary path of conversion. Any true conversion requires nurturing and time for assimilation. It will be accomplished more gently and in a gradual manner. While extraordinary conversions are possible, they should be treated carefully. Conversion is not finished by such an immediate experience of change. It may be only the beginning.

4. Conversion is generally a process that opens new doors and gently closes old ones. It brings together various elements from life in a way that allows continued development. Reflection and integration are key words in this understanding of conversion. The individual experiencing such conversion knows it as one step along the way. The individual remains open to further ways of change. For mature, life-seeking people, this is the ordinary way of conversion.

It recognizes personal resistance and fear, but is not held back by it. Because the door of discovery is never closed, this form of conversion can occur regularly. We never have it "infallibly made" with nothing more to accomplish. Instead, we rejoice in the measure of truth we have discovered while we look forward to truth still to be learned.

I find myself in each of these ways at different times in my life. Several of them may be happening at the same time in different areas of life. Sometimes I have labeled people so I can control them. Then they dare to act differently than I expect. For them I make an exception. Or, I have all this experience which allows me to act infallibly in a situation. I have accumulated all this experience, so I must be right. Or I may think I have made a 180 degree turn only to discover that my basic attitudes haven't changed at all. Or, I may realize how slowly I am changing – but I AM CHANGING! I am integrating old and new – and it is exciting!

I invite you not to be surprised to find yourself in the same situations. The important point is to remain faithful to the journey. The Lord is with you!

In the Hebrew Testament there is a story about "dry bones." People felt that things were hopeless. They felt nothing could be done to change their situation. They felt like everything was dried up and they were powerless to make things different. To them (and to us) God spoke these words as Ezekiel wandered through a valley of dry bones:

> He said to me: "Man, these bones are the whole people of Israel. They say: 'Our bones are dry, our thread of life is snapped, our web is severed from the loom.' Prophesy, therefore, and say to them: 'These are the words of the Lord God; O my people, I will open your graves and bring you up from them, O my people. Then I will put my spirit into you and you shall live, and I will settle you on your own soil and you shall know that I, the Lord, have spoken and will act!' "
>
> **Ezekiel 37: 11-14**

As always, when we speak of faith-conversion, we speak of acknowledging the power of God at work in us. God brings us up from the graves of failure and despair and unleashes the power of the Spirit within us. As we grow, we recognize more and more that it is God's power at work rather than our personal accomplishment.

35

Reflection Questions

What events in my life reflect the way God worked in the life of St Francis of Assisi? How do I understand the meaning of "conversion"? Do I ever make perfect decisions? Do I ever become infallibly correct, possessing the entire truth? How would I explain God's love when darkness and pain seem to be a daily experience? How does God get my attention? Do I take solid, reflective time to integrate the new and the old in my life? What is the role of the Holy Spirit in achieving holiness? Is it possible to grow in holiness by oneself? What role does a community play on the journey to holiness? Is there such a thing as a perfect community? How can conflict contribute to holiness? What things would I like to hide from Jesus if he visited the room of my heart? Does Jesus require faithfulness or perfection from me? Support your answer i.e. give solid reasons for it! What basic experience of Christians is symbolized by the Stigmata of St Francis of Assisi?

SECULAR FRANCISCAN RULE

✛ Read the LETTER TO THE FAITHFUL
that is the prologue to the SFO Rule.
(Found on the inside cover.)

Commentary

Only someone like Francis would write a letter to everyone. Some
scholars believe that this letter is Francis' commentary on the Secular
Franciscan way of life. Through it Francis tries to convey his sense of
penance and service. Other scholars dispute this. There is evidence that
Francis wrote two LETTERS TO ALL THE FAITHFUL. Whatever the
final conclusions, the "Letter to all the Faithful" that precedes the SFO
Rule gives insight into the mind of Francis.

The LETTER says that the Christian life can go in two directions.

1) A person who responds to the Spirit of Jesus is spouse, brother and
   mother to Jesus. The focus is on relationship to Jesus. The Holy Spirit
   unites us to Jesus as a spouse, wedded in love to the Lord. We are
   Brother (Sister) to Jesus when we listen to him and fulfill the will of
   the Father. We are mother to Jesus, when we acknowledge his
   presence within us, bearing him in our bodies. We give birth to Jesus
   when we proclaim the gospel through our everyday lifestyle.

The first part of the LETTER expresses joy and wonder at such intimacy
with Jesus. Francis could only marvel at such a great gift from God. The
Spirit of Jesus unites us to himself and to one another with bonds of
love. What a cause for wonder and praise! This portion of the LETTER
stands in awe at such gracious love.

2) By contrast, the second portion of the LETTER describes the fate of
   people who refuse the love of Jesus. People who refuse to do
   penance and follow their own way will find themselves walking in

darkness, blind to God's ways. They are cursed, caught in the deceit of the Evil One. Their sinfulness offers tribulation and trial. What they acquire for themselves becomes a burden. When they face death, their relatives are angry because they have little to pass on to them. People who have been conned by the Evil One die a bitter death. They exchange true wisdom for foolishness.

The LETTER TO ALL THE FAITHFUL expresses a number of elements that Francis considered important. I see the following themes in the LETTER:

1. Praise for the person who loves God and shows the fruit of love by the way he/she lives. Such a person is truly on the journey of conversion.

2. Blessing for people who DO the works of conversion and don't just TALK about it. Francis delights in people who respond to the promptings of the Holy Spirit.

3. Francis calls for VISIBLE EVIDENCE of personal growth in holiness. He looks for a personal response to the will of the Father; a personal incarnation and birthing of the Lord through our way of life; a personal sharing of our gifts with the larger world outside ourselves. Francis extends the invitation to accept God as our "Abba", Father; to accept the Spirit as our spouse and advocate; to accept Jesus as our brother, savior and lover.

4. Francis looks at what happens when we reject the truths just listed. People who refuse real conversion and brush aside the need for penance will discover death rather than life. People like these choose attitudes and ideas that put walls in the way of the Spirit. They are blind and choose to remain so. They do not see things as God does. They follow their own "light" which is darkness indeed! Francis sees the Evil One at work in such blindness. The symbol of a body eaten by worms gives a sharp vision of the destructiveness of lives influenced by the Evil One. In refusing the light of the Lord, they lose everything.

Reflection

Franciscans of every make and model will find this letter to be strong medicine. It is not a "nice" letter, but one that challenges us to be true to God's call to conversion. We are to walk in the light of Christ. But we need to acknowledge our dark side as well. Though we are called to walk in the light of Christ, we acknowledge the presence of darkness in us. Francis keeps calling us ...

> *... to accept kindly and with divine love, the fragrant words of our Lord, Jesus Christ. ... Keep them in mind!*
> *... Carry them out!*
> **Letter to all the Faithful**

Anyone who relies on possessions or personal power as the way to joy is out of touch with Christian reality.

Franciscans ignore these words of Francis at their own risk. When God calls us to this way of life, God wants us to walk in the light of Jesus. The light not only allows us to share honestly with others, but gives clear insight into our real self. In the light of Jesus, we need not fear what the light may expose. Jesus is present to enable us to deal with the negatives inside us.

Our calling as Franciscans is not a call to a wishy-washy, merely devotional life. Neither are we called simply to hear nice sermons or be present at fuzzy-friendly fraternity meetings. The Secular Franciscan way is not a cheap way to heaven. Neither is it a serene, unencumbered journey through an enlightened world. It is a messy, dangerous journey that can bring tension and the demand to face difficult issues. It brings its share of joy and delight as we grow aware of how deeply we are loved by God. If you choose to follow the Secular Franciscan way of life, your journey will be a grab-bag of experiences. Wide open to reality, you will discover the surprising, mysterious and loving ways of God. As you re-read the LETTER TO ALL THE FAITHFUL, let it speak simply and directly to your heart.

In conjunction with the LETTER, you might read these texts from the Scriptures:

> *Romans 14: 7-12*

> *James 2: 1-9*

THE SAN DAMIANO CRUCIFIX

FRANCISCAN FOCUS

The San Damiano Crucifix

When Francis prayed in the chapel of San Damiano in 1205, the crucifix there seemed to speak to him. That crucifix is known as the San Damiano Crucifix. It holds a special spot in our Franciscan heritage.

It is called an "icon cross" because it contains images of people who have a part in the meaning of the cross. It was painted in the 12th century by an unknown artist. It was probably transported to the Assisi area by Serbian monks. It was painted on coarse cloth that was glued to a cross made of walnut. The San Damiano Crucifix is about 6 feet 10 inches high and about 4 feet 3 inches wide. It no longer hangs in the chapel of San Damiano. When the Poor Clares moved to their new monastery (Connected to the Basilica of Santa Chiara in Assisi) in 1257, the San Damiano Crucifix went with them. In September of 1958 it was permanently placed in the San Giorgio Chapel, part of the Basilica of Santa Chiara in Assisi.

The central figure of Christ dominates the painting. Christ stands upright on the cross, eyes open, looking out on the world. He is portrayed both as wounded and strong. Jesus is represented in full stature while the other figures are much smaller. Jesus is the person to be worshiped.

The next largest figures are the five witnesses of the crucifixion. Mary, the mother of Jesus, St John, the beloved disciple, Mary Magdalene, Mary the mother of James and the Centurion who expressed his belief in Christ. These figures stand beneath the arms of Jesus. In the shadow of these larger figures are three smaller figures. On the lower left is Longinus, the Roman soldier who pierced the side of Jesus. On the lower right is Stephaton, who is identified with the soldier who offered Jesus a sponge dipped in wine. Peering over the shoulder of the centurion seems to be an observer, one of the crowd around the cross.

On the crossbar are six angels. They are marveling at the crucifixion, seemingly discussing the event of the death of the Son of God. At the foot of the cross is a damaged picture of six figures. It would seem these six (two of whom are easily seen) are the patron saints of Umbria: St John, St Michael, St Rufino, St John the Baptist, St Peter and St Paul. On the right side of the picture there is a small rooster. It is a reminder of Peter's denial, as well as a reminder not to put too much reliance on our own strength.

On the top of the cross we see Jesus, fully clothed, being welcomed into heaven. He is climbing out of the tomb and carries the cross as a sceptre of triumph. Angels crowd around him. At the very top of the cross is the right hand of the Father. God blesses all that Jesus has done. The crucifix of San Damiano is like a painted theology of the passion, death and resurrection of Jesus. Little wonder that it was precious to Francis.

The San Damiano Crucifix is special for Franciscans. It connects us to our "roots" and calls us to conversion. Replicas of this crucifix are often worn by Franciscans as a sign of their commitment to the Franciscan way of life.

> *Great God, full of glory, and thou, my Lord Jesus Christ,*
> *I beseech thee to illuminate me and dissipate the dark-*
> *ness of my spirit. Give me a pure faith, firm hope and*
> *perfect charity. Grant me to know thee well and to do all*
> *things according to thy light and in conformity with thy*
> *will. Amen*
>
> **Prayer of St Francis**

QUESTIONS

1. Describe the conversion process of St Francis in your own words. Follow the sequence of events and reflect on what the Lord is doing and how Francis responded.

2. What instances in Francis' conversion most reflects your own life? What events in Francis' conversion are most meaningful to you? Why?

3. Who are the "lepers" in your life that keep you from a full living of the Gospel? Be clear on why these "lepers" hinder your personal growth in holiness. (These "lepers" can be internal or external)

4. Where is conversion most needed in your life? What changes do you feel called to make at this time? What do you need to abandon? let loose of? What things do you need to embrace? What do the events of your life say to you about moving in a new direction? – Enter this question gently ... don't force conversion if you are not ready for it!

5. What are the main issues that Francis explores in his LETTER TO ALL THE FAITHFUL? Explain why they are important?

6. Describe YOUR reaction to the LETTER TO ALL THE FAITHFUL. Were you repelled? Fearful? Attracted? Confused? Appalled? Share your feelings and explain why you feel the way you do.

SCRIPTURE reading/reflection

✝ Luke 14: 12-35
St Luke relates a number of stories about invitations and responses. Jesus uses the stories to talk about commitment. As you read and reflect on these stories, what strikes you most forcibly about Jesus' teaching? What do you feel Jesus is saying to you in these stories? Who do you identify with in these stories? Why?

I shall pass
through this world but once.
Any good therefore.
that I can do, or any kindness
that I can show to
any human being, let me do
it now. Let me not defer
or neglect it, for I shall not
pass this way again.

Henry Drummond.

CHAPTER 3

WHO'S CALLING

When God calls, God expects a response. The bible offers a variety of ways in which people respond to God's call. Moses tried to get out of the call by claiming inadequacy. Jonah disagreed with the call and headed off to Tarshish to escape. Jeremiah thought he was too young for the call. Peter and Andrew left their fishing and quickly followed Jesus – although it seems they returned to the nets later on! The rich young man couldn't handle the surrender required by the call. Mary responded with faith when God called her to accept motherhood. In short, the bible has a variety of responses to God's call.

When God calls people to a particular way of life, e.g. the Secular Franciscan Order, there are many ways that people respond. In making a decision about accepting God's call to the Franciscan way of life, a few things need to be considered.

1) Anyone who wishes to belong to the SFO must be Catholic. This does not mean that no one else can follow the spirit of Francis. Many people, Catholic or not, are attracted by the spirit of Francis of Assisi. But membership in the SFO requires people to be practicing Catholics.

2) People need to DESIRE to grow in intimacy with Jesus. Franciscan life is centered on Jesus. To follow this way of life requires a desire to make Jesus and his gospel the central focus of life. If there is no desire to know Jesus and no sense of the need to follow the gospel. the Franciscan way of life makes little sense. This does not mean that we are perfect gospel people. It does mean we desire to accept the consequences of following the gospel.

3) FAITH has close links to this desire. No one will follow Jesus unless he/she believes in him. This dimension of faith is more than head-knowledge about Jesus. Intellectual knowledge, by itself, does not always get translated into action. Phrases, memorized doctrines or scripture texts are not enough for the life-long journey of conver-

sion. There is need for a personal relationship with Jesus. It is important for people to accept Jesus and the Gospel as a vital ingredient for daily life.

Jesus was real to Francis. Jesus loved Francis and died for him. The Spirit of Jesus enabled Francis to follow the gospel. The crucifixion cries out the love Jesus has for Francis. Responding to this personal love, Francis attempted to love as Jesus loved. It takes a solid, personal relationship with Jesus to keep us steady on the Franciscan way of living. Without such living faith, our way of life makes little sense.

4) People who wish to follow Francis will need to have HOPE. This quality is not a pie-in-the-sky and Pollyanna kind of hope. Neither is it a hope founded on one's personal competence to set everything right. Hope is founded on the belief that the Holy Spirit is present in us. The power of the Spirit of Jesus is greater than any power we may face. Armed with the power of the Spirit, hope gives us courage to face life and all it offers. We believe that the Light of Christ can overcome all the darkness. We DO NOT believe that there is no darkness. We DO NOT believe that there are no evil forces in us and in the world. We are merely confident in facing problems because the Spirit of the Lord is with us.

Many Christians do not have much hope. They are pessimistic about everything. The world is falling apart! The Church is disintegrating! Governments don't care about their people! Anything new is bad! Nothing will ever change! I cannot change! Gloom and doom are spread by people who have no hope. They are not good candidates for the Franciscan Order. The SFO dare not become a "womb" in which to hide from the world!

5) Self-styled "PERFECT" people will be uncomfortable among the sinners in the Franciscan Order. We lay no claim to being perfect. Anyone who already considers him or herself to be perfect will find little help in the Franciscan Order. Perfect people are not open to growth – since the peak has already been climbed. They go around telling everyone else how to live! They would be a burden to us.

6) It may seem obvious, but people who want to follow Francis of Assisi should have SOME KNOWLEDGE of Francis. A basic awareness of what Francis stands for would be helpful. Often there

is some quality in Francis that attracts people. It helps for them to share personal ideas about what draws them to Francis' gospel lifestyle.

7) When people commit themselves to the Secular Franciscan way of life, it is not only a personal commitment. The personal commitment includes a commitment to the other people who are part of the SFO. Newcomers join a community of people trying to live this way of life. The interaction with other Franciscans will be part of their initial and continuing formation. As with any value, it will require the newcomer to give priority to community/fraternity life. Forgiveness and understanding will be needed. Isolationism, separatism, sniping and laziness will not make anyone a good candidate for the SFO. As in all relationships, a flexible and listening spirit will be good qualities to have.

8) POVERTY was important to St Francis. Francis recognized his need for God. He walked with the poor who knew their need of God. Those who were arrogant and self-sufficient were also loved by Francis. But the "Little ones" who trusted God were especially dear to him. Other Orders gift the Church with educational opportunities. Some spend their lives in silent praise of God. Still others reach out to spread the gospel in mission work. Francis' way was to be with those who knew their need of God. People who recognized the reality that they are creatures and God alone is creator. This gift is part of the "charism" of Francis. He would wander the world reminding people of their need for God. He would treat all with courtesy and respect because they were better than he. Above all, he would love the poor, and learn from them.

Profession

When people finish their initial formation in the SFO they come to the time for PROFESSION. This is a permanent commitment, basically because our whole life will now be touched by the Franciscan charism. It would normally end when we complete our journey here on earth. If anyone does not accept the consequences of profession, they should not be pushed into it. Gentle and prayerful reflection may conclude that this is NOT one's calling. It is better to withdraw than to mis-interpret

God's call. Both the Fraternity Council and the individual must approach this decision with care and prayer.

On The Other Hand

In addition to the positive qualities to look for in newcomers, there are some things that are warning signs.

1) Anyone who finds inter-personal relationships difficult will be uncomfortable in the SFO. Fraternity life calls for a great deal of inter-action between people. If the skills for such inter-action are lacking, a person might be better advised to deal with that issue before coming to the SFO. We are speaking of serious issues here, not just ordinary shyness. If the individual cannot relate to others in a healthy way, he/she needs to take further time to reflect on whether to join the SFO.

2) Sometimes people join the SFO because they are lonely. They join any group where there are people. They are professional "joiners." Beware!

3) Sometimes people join to get relief from agonizing home or family problems. These are NOT good reasons for joining the SFO. The local fraternity should be very cautious when such people apply. We cannot become a therapy club. We might choose to help such folks in other ways, but not by admitting them immediately to the fraternity.

4) Some Catholics have bizarre devotions in their lives. They follow every visionary that comes along. They indulge in odd devotions or neglect primary responsibilities because they are "doing the work of the Lord." Sometimes devotions go counter to solid church teaching. People engaging in such practices are NOT good candidates for the SFO. They often tend to be more devoted to devotions than to the gospel. Some even try to force their devotions on everyone else. Remember, we need not follow private revelations, but we are required to follow the Gospel. Solid devotions will support gospel living. Off-base devotions will be an obstacle to it. Fraternities do well to gently steer such people away from joining the SFO.

In all these situations, the people deserve to be treated respectfully but with firmness. There are many degrees in all these negative issues. Fraternity councils must deal with the people directly and with loving honesty. Combine good common sense with prayer to the Holy Spirit.

Franciscans Are...

We are ordinary people, gifted by God with a call to follow the way of St Francis of Assisi. We did not earn this gift. It is God's gift to us. We accept the responsibility of living it. We are challenged by the call to give an open response to the gospel. We join others who are seeking the same goal. Together we seek to deepen our understanding of the Gospel. We encourage one another in this pursuit.

We don't abandon the world or our families or friends. We remain plumbers and postmen, politicians and CEO's, teachers and house-wives, executives and truck drivers, bartenders and executive secretaries, mothers and fathers, sisters and brothers, workers and retired, sick and healthy. Francis' way of life puts a new light on how we perceive this world in which we live. We are unfinished people walking together to become better. We don't have all the answers, only the willingness to keep seeking answers from the Gospel. We want to make the world a fit place for all people to live in. We commit ourselves to follow the gospel-way to accomplish that goal.

The Franciscan Family

When Francis responded to God's call, he learned that direct, positive, caring actions attract people. His lifestyle drew other men of Assisi to follow him. As this group grew, he received verbal approval from Innocent III to follow a simple, bible-text Rule. This band of men grew in number and variety. It is called the "FIRST ORDER" of St Francis.

When Clare joined Francis, and other women followed her, she initiated the group called the "SECOND ORDER", viz, the Poor Clares and all who vow to follow Clare's spirit.

When lay people in the world wished to follow Francis, they became known as the "THIRD ORDER" of St Francis.

Each of the "Orders" underwent changes in the course of history. The FIRST ORDER, after the death of Francis, broke into two branches in a very short time. One group of Friars was willing to accept whatever interpretation of the First Order Rule the Church gave them. Other Friars felt this was too lenient and wished to retain the primitive spirit of Francis as expressed in his "Testament". They rejected "freeing" decrees, attempting to follow the spirit of the "Testament." As time passed, these two groups were given independence from one another by Rome. Both were considered true followers of Francis. Now there were two branches of the FIRST ORDER – the "Community or Conventuals" (Accept interpretations) and the "Spirituals or Observants" (Reject freeing interpretations). By the year 1451, after long struggles, the OBSERVANTS published their own Constitutions. In 1517 Leo X decreed total separation between Observants and Conventuals.

But the Observants were not always so "observant" of the spirit of Francis. Some Observant Friars sought to "reform" the way in which the spirit of Francis was being lived. These friars wanted a stronger sense of the contemplative and hermetical life. They saw laxity creeping into the observant living of the Rule. Once more there is a reform within a reform. In 1525 Matteo de Bascio left his friary to live the Rule more fully. Two other men joined him. They sought to live a more hermetical, contemplative life. They would leave their hermitages in order to preach and care for the sick. By April of 1529, this group had grown to 12 men. They came together and wrote the "Statutes of Albacina", describing the life they wished to live. Clement VII gave his approval to their way of life on July 3, 1528.

The children of the territory dubbed them "Capuchins" because of the Capuche on their habit. The name remains until today. By 1536 the group had over 700 members. In that year they wrote the Capuchin Constitutions. They became the third branch of the FIRST ORDER. These three branches of the FIRST ORDER today are known as: The Franciscans – The Conventuals – The Capuchins. All are legitimate and true sons of Francis. Each branch interprets the Rule of Francis in a way that fits the particular thrust of its Franciscan heritage.

The Poor Clares did not escape some of the same reforms within their Second Order. As with the FIRST ORDER, the reforms reflected the changes going on in the Church and society. The Spirit moved these women to new insights and dedication. The gifts of the Spirit continue to reshape the Orders of Francis. A number of contemplative communities of women follow Clare's Rule of life. Our own time is blessed with new tools to examine and determine the original spirit of Francis and Clare.

The THIRD ORDER of St Francis (Now called "The Secular Franciscan Order") likewise saw changes throughout the centuries. Some of the laity wished to band together and form small communities. As time went on these communities became religious communities with vows. As the Church approved these communities they became known as the "Third Order Regular" i.e. communities of the vowed life – canonically called "Regulars" or Religious. These groups form one branch of the THIRD ORDER of St Francis. The THIRD ORDER has two branches, the THIRD ORDER REGULAR and the THIRD ORDER SECULAR.

The "Seculars" are those men and women who follow the spirit of Francis in daily life, but do not join a vowed community and become "Regulars". Today the THIRD ORDER SECULAR is known as the Secular Franciscan Order. This name was given them in 1978.

Looking at our Franciscan family history, there is an obvious attempt, again and again, to return to the original spirit of Francis. Different people interpret that spirit in different ways. But with all the variety, the Spirit continues to invite us to let the gospel prompt our way of living. Vatican II invites us to return to the spirit of our founder, Francis.

The gift we offer to the world and the church is simply that charism. To know it well, to live it with integrity, is to give the Church and the world the gift that God gave through Francis. Others have differing gifts. Ours is to follow the gospel in the spirit of St Francis of Assisi. Our lives must continue to offer this gift to our age.

> *I entreat you then ... as God has called you, live up to your calling. Be humble always and gentle, and patient too. Be forbearing with one another and charitable. Spare no effort to make fast with bonds of peace the unity which the Spirit gives. There is one body and one Spirit, as there is also one hope held out in God's call to you.*

*... You must be made new in mind and spirit, and put
on the new nature of God's creating, which shows itself
in the just and devout life called for by the truth.*
Ephesians 4: 1-5 & 23-24

We belong not to ourselves, concerned only about fraternity growth, but to the Church and the world. Our task is to contribute our share to the building of the Kingdom of God. The Franciscan charism marks out the extent and limits of our contribution. The more clearly we search out our Franciscan charism, the more surely will we do our part in the building of God's kingdom on earth. God asks nothing more and nothing less. Together we try to understand and live the gospel as lived by Francis of Assisi. The Spirit of God is with us. We will BE what we are called to be.

Reflection Questions

Why has the Franciscan Order seen so many changes in its history? What quality of Francis of Assisi is especially attractive to you? Why? Why is it so important to have reasonable assurance that God is calling you to the SFO? What common sense "rule of thumb" would you use to affirm or deny that "call"? What is the role of solid devotions in our Christian life? How would you describe the special gift that Franciscans give to the Church and the world? Why is profession a lifetime commitment? What makes you feel at home with the Franciscan spirit? Why is a spirit of "give and take" in relationships important? What aspect of community life do you find most helpful? What particular contribution do you make to community life? Why is forgiveness and reconciliation important in community/fraternity life?

SECULAR FRANCISCAN RULE

The SFO is not an organization to join for its social benefits. It is a movement, a way of life built on Gospel principles. People who come to the SFO are given the opportunity to learn what it means to follow this call. This period of initial formation is important. The Rule says clearly:

> *Admission to the Order is gradually attained through a time of initiation, a period of formation of AT LEAST one year, and profession of the Rule.*
>
> *The entire community is engaged in this process of growth by its own manner of living. The age for profession and the distinctive Franciscan sign are regulated by statutes.*
>
> **RULE – Chapter 3 #23**

Formation includes study, prayer, sharing and dialogue. It includes the influence of the Secular Franciscans who have already professed this way of life. This is an important dimension of formation. Positive, human models can be very influential in developing good Franciscans. Professed members should get to know the new people. They may invite them to their homes and participate in their study program. Whatever caring thing will make people feel welcome, professed members can do.

The time of formation should include involvement in the ministry of the Fraternity. Learning without action is not a good way of formation. Involvement in ministry is an important element of a good formation program. Of special importance would be involvement with the poor.

But initial formation is only the beginning. Our formation as Franciscans never ends. The Spirit of God continues to stretch us, calling us to new insights, asking us for deeper dedication. We are always in need of renewal, open to reform in some area of life. What we do as individuals we will do as a fraternity. The Fraternity always needs reform and renewal. It is part of our life-long commitment to conversion. As St Paul says: "Let us pursue the things that make for peace and build up the common life." (Romans 14: 19)

CHAPTER 1 of the RULE:

1. The Franciscan family, as one among many spiritual families raised up by the Holy Spirit in the Church, unites all members of the People of God – laity, religious and priests – who recognize that they are called to follow Christ in the footsteps of St Francis of Assisi.

   In various ways and forms, but in life-giving union with each other, they intend to make present the charism of their common Seraphic Father in the life and mission of the Church.

2. The Secular Franciscan Order holds a special place in this family circle. It is an organic union of all Catholic fraternities scattered throughout the world and open to every group of the faithful. In these fraternities the brothers and sisters, led by the Spirit, strive for perfect charity in their own secular state. By their profession, they pledge themselves to live the gospel in the manner of St Francis by means of this Rule approved by the Church.

3. The present Rule, succeeding "Memoriale Propositi" (1221) and the Rules approved by the Supreme Pontiffs Nicolas IV and Leo XIII, adapts the Secular Franciscan Order to the needs and expectations of the Holy Church in the conditions of changing times. Its interpretation belongs to the Holy See and its application will be made by the General Constitutions and particular statutes.

RULE – Chapter 1 # 1, 2, 3

Commentary

We are a Franciscan family joined together by our common call to follow Francis. Each Franciscan develops the lifestyle that fits his/her calling to this gospel way of life. The common elements are: 1) The call by the Holy Spirit. 2) The desire to follow the gospel in the manner of

Francis of Assisi. 3) The willingness to allow our lives to be formed by the gospel and Francis' reflection of the gospel.

This may look different because of differing circumstances, but the common elements remain. Vowed religious and Secular Franciscans express this charism in their particular ways. But the source is the same.

Secular Franciscans (like all Franciscans) implement gospel values in their everyday lives. Their place for holiness will be where they eat and work, play and pray, gather in community and find the places of solitude. Our common life offers support for living the commitment we have made. In our common life we learn the skills of nurturing relationships. We will realize our need to forgive and be forgiven. We will share fears and hopes, dreams and failures – so that fears and failures do not dominate us. Underlying this common life is the binding power of the Holy Spirit. How quickly we learn our need for God and understand our poverty in the presence of our creator-God.

In Practice:

Secular Franciscans will implement the Gospel in daily life. They will:

+ Develop honest business practices and work habits

+ Support the production and sale of things that will benefit others – and may also bring a reasonable profit

+ Avoid extravagant profits that hurt people

+ Give honest work for pay received and give a just wage to workers

+ Share resources so that people throughout the world can live human lives and have dignity

+ Advertise honestly, not promising more than can be given

+ Give competent service to those who seek their help

+ Keep their priorities straight, choosing relationships over work and wealth

+ Support others when there is a need

+ Create an atmosphere in relationships that is free rather than sti-fling; open rather than dominating; forgiving rather than vengeful; flexible rather than rigid

+ Develop sound Christian devotions that support their following of the gospel

+ Contribute service and support to the groups they join

+ Treasure and affirm people and walk with them through their mountains and valleys

+ Take time to read and reflect on the Scripture. It is our way of life.

+ Support groups and policies that offer life-enhancing programs

+ Support programs, procedures and policies that work to give the "poor" human dignity and the possibility of living a human life

+ Support people in business, government or Church who promote gospel values

+ Oppose groups/policies which are destructive of life

+ Work with other groups which offer life-enhancing ideas and programs. We need not re-invent the wheel in our attempt to show love to people

+ Develop a solid life of prayer and seek the ways of contemplation. Both personal and communal prayer will be important values for us.

This inadequate list gives some idea of the vast area covered by a gospel way of life. The Rule of 1978 is not prescriptive, giving concrete direc-tions for everything. Instead, it paints a picture in large strokes, offering the "vision" of what can be if the gospel is followed. We are responsible for "giving flesh" to the gospel vision. Our common sharing and dialogue can help us find ways to make the gospel come alive in our world.

Relating To The Church

The SFO Rule urges us to make our charism available to the Church. As in any large community of people, the Church has a variety of groups for a variety of ministries. Each group is effectively "church" as it contributes its particular charism to the larger Church. We are not called to do everything that needs to be done. We are called to do the things that we are gifted to do. Again, we see how important it is to gain solid insights into our Franciscan charism. As all groups do their "charism", they contribute to the wholeness of the Kingdom of God.

> *The gifts we possess differ as they are allotted to us by God's grace, and must be exercised accordingly; the gift of inspired utterance, for example, in proportion to a man's faith; or the gift of administration, in administration. A teacher should employ his gift in teaching, and one who has the gift of stirring speech should use it to stir his hearers.*
>
> **Romans 12: 6-8**

What individuals are called to do, communities are called to do. When Franciscans are around, the poor should feel at home.

Loyalty to the Church is important to Franciscans. This does not mean an un-seeing loyalty that does nothing to make the Church more beautiful and just. It is a clear-sighted loyalty that allows us to call for change in the institutions and laws of the Church when they wander from the Gospel. Francis' critique of the Church took the simple form of calling it to live the gospel. When the gospel was ignored, Francis could not be silent. But he sought to build a more perfect Church rather than tear it down with criticism. The Church has ordinary human beings within her community. We realize that everything will not be perfect in the Church. Our love for the Church helps us to see both the glory and the weakness. If some People of God are rigid and unfeeling, we try to bring forgiveness and reconciliation. But a little education might also help. Even therapy is sometimes needed. Whenever we find brokenness or weakness, we will seek ways to mend and strengthen the Church. When we find injustice, we will work for the ways of justice. If the Church should become oppressive we will seek the ways of freedom. But in all of this, our goal is to build the Church into a more beautiful reflection of Jesus.

The more responsive we are to the Holy Spirit, the more rich will be our contribution to the Church and the world. We will collaborate in our ministries and collaborate in our searching for understanding. We will learn the price of forgiveness and offer the possibility of communion. As we learn to share our inner stories we will draw strength from our common experience with the Lord and with the world.

> *Those of us who have a robust conscience must accept*
> *as our own burden the tender scruples of weaker men,*
> *and not consider ourselves. Each of us must consider his*
> *neighbor, and think what is for his good and will build*
> *up the common life.*
>
> **Romans 15: 1-2**

Interpreting The Rule

The Rule cannot address every situation in life. Situations will arise where there are conflicting interpretations. The Rule says that the final interpretation belongs to the Holy See. The application of the Rule will be made through the General Constitutions and particular statutes. (International – National – Regional.)

The Constitutions spell out in detail things like elections, dismissal of members, accepting new members, appeals, and how to mediate conflicts. Statutes might spell out the responsibilities of officers as well as how fraternities relate to each other. Both the Constitutions and Statutes are meant to assist us in living the Rule. The Rule is more stable and permanent. Constitutions and Statutes can be changed more easily to adapt to new situations.

> *At the roadside were two blind men. When they heard*
> *it said that Jesus was passing they shouted: "Have pity*
> *on us, Son of David!" The people told them to be quiet.*

But they shouted all the more: "Sir, have pity on us; have pity on us, Son of David!". Jesus stopped and called the men. "What do you want me to do for you?" he asked. "Sir" they answered, "We want our sight." Jesus was deeply moved, and touched their eyes. At once their sight came back, and they followed him.

Matthew 20: 30-34

FRANCISCAN FOCUS

The Portiuncula (St Mary of the Angels)

In the valley below Assisi, a small chapel used to stand among some oak trees. Hermits from Palestine had built it early in the Christian era. In the 6th century the land was donated to St Benedict. It was known as "The Portiuncula" i.e. "The little portion." The chapel was a quiet place of prayer.

When Francis was told to "rebuild my church," the Portiuncula was one of the first chapels that he restored. The chapel was dedicated to St Mary of the Angels. Francis lived there and rebuilt it with his own hands. It became a special place of refuge for him. It is considered the cradle of the Franciscan Order.

At the present time this "Little Portion" stands within the large church in the valley below Assisi. The large structure protects the little church from the elements. It's paintings and simple style make it a quiet, respectful place to pray. The spirit of Francis lingers here and touches those who come to pray.

Portiuncula Pardon (Indulgence)

In July of 1216, Francis was praying in the Portiuncula. As he prayed, a bright light seemed to fill the chapel. Jesus and Mary appeared to Francis. They asked Francis to make any request he wished for the good of people. Francis replied:

> *Since it is a miserable sinner who speaks to you, O God of mercy, he asks you to have mercy on his brothers who are burdened with sin. And he asks that all those who, repentant, cross over the threshold of this place, receive from you, O Lord, who sees their torment, pardon for their evil deeds.*

He received what he asked for. Francis was told to seek the approval of the Pope. Honorius III gave his approval for this "pardon", limiting it to the anniversary of the dedication of the Portiuncula, August 2. The decree was given on August 2, 1216. Francis responded:

> I wish to send all of you to Paradise, and I announce to you the indulgence that I have obtained from the lips of the highest Pontiff. And all of you who have come today, and all who will come on this day with an open and contrite heart, shall have pardon for all your sins.

Later the Portiuncula Indulgence was extended to the whole world. Today, a single plenary indulgence can be gained by visiting a Franciscan Church (Or one designated for the indulgence) on August 2. The ordinary requirements for a plenary indulgence must be fulfilled, namely, confession, communion and prayer for the intentions of the Pope.

QUESTIONS

1. What qualities in your life affirm your call to the SFO? Are there any that indicate this may not be your call? List them. * This is an important matter. You may wish to talk it over with a competent spiritual guide.

2. What do you expect to receive from the SFO?

3. What qualities/skills/gifts enable you to relate well with other people? How does this show itself?

4. What areas of your life are most in need of change? How do you expect to meet that need?

5. Write out a short history that illustrates the development of the three branches of the First Order. Do the same for the Second and Third Orders. As you answer, imagine you are talking to someone who never heard of the Franciscans.

6. Give your own description of the SFO from what you have learned in this chapter. You might answer questions like these:

    ✛ Where does the SFO fit within the Church?

    ✛ What is the relationship between the various branches of the Franciscan Order?

    ✛ Who gives the call to follow this way of life?

    ✛ Where will the spiritual growth of SFO members take place?

    ✛ Give concrete examples of growth in your life because of the SFO.

    ✛ Why is it so important to know what our "charism" requires of us?

7. Who is the official interpreter of the Rule? What role do the Constitutions and Statutes play in the SFO?

SCRIPTURE *reading/reflection*

✝ Luke 9: 57-62

Luke addresses the issue of discipleship. Jesus asks his followers to prefer him to anything else – even to burying the dead or saying goodbye to friends. Jesus sees our relationship with him as primary. As you reflect on these words, list the things you feel Jesus expects in his disciples. Share some ideas on how you fulfill the qualities of a disciple as well as areas where you need help to grow.

CHAPTER 4

WORDS OF LIFE

> ... in sacred Scripture, without prejudice to God's truth and holiness, the marvelous "condescension" of eternal wisdom is plain to be seen "that we may come to know the ineffable loving-kindness of God and see for ourselves how far God has gone in adapting his language with thoughtful concern for our nature." (St John Chrysostom) Indeed the words of God, expressed in the words of men, are in every way like human language, just as the Word of the eternal Father, when he took on himself the flesh of human weakness, became like men.
>
> **Decree on Divine Revelation**
> **Vatican II – #13**

Scripture is a source of life for us. It is written in human language so that we can understand God's revelation. Joined to Tradition, Scripture teaches us things God wants us to know. It is done in a way that allows the meaning to touch us. There are various ways to "listen" to the Scriptural word.

1. We can use it prayerfully and reflect on the meaning that touches our personal lives.

2. We can approach it as a human work that reflects the times and personality of the writer.

3. We can see it as a "divine" work and seek the meaning that God intends through these human words.

4. We can find ourselves in the scripture stories and be confronted or affirmed by the word of God.

5. We can find in scripture the truth we need to achieve salvation.

6. We can find in scripture evidence of the beliefs that are basic to faith.

Very few scripture texts have been absolutely defined by the Church. We stand before the revelation of God with awe, aware that God wishes to speak to us. God does not wish to leave us in darkness about the way to the light. The bible is a vital source of revelation that points the way to God. When we share the word with one another, when we express our understanding with one another, we gift each other with personal insights into the meaning of scripture.

How do we discover the Truth that God reveals in scripture? The Vatican document quoted above gives a number of helps.

1. We try to determine the intention of the writer. What did the writer want to share about God? This search will lead us to a study of the writer's culture, the times in which the writer lived, as well as the particular personality of the writer.

2. We try to determine the literary form the writer is using. Sometimes writers use a story to make a point. At other times they write in an historical mode. Sometimes they use an allegory to communicate the truth. If we determine the literary form, it can help our understanding.

3. We need to look at the text in relationship to the rest of Scripture and keep it in context. Scripture and Tradition will not contradict each other, even when some things seem to be in conflict. If our interpretation goes counter to a truth already confirmed, we need to revise our interpretation.

4. The revelation of Scripture is an unfolding revelation. As the human race grows in knowledge and experience, the words of Scripture reflect that new situation. Practices that in a stone-age might seem ordinary, become repugnant as civilization grows. Scripture was not written all at one time. Knowing the dating of a book of the bible can help us understand the perspective of the writer.

Because Scripture, like Jesus, contains both divine and human elements, neither can be pushed aside if we wish to achieve good interpretation.

Fundamentalism

Some people would deny all that we have said. They see it as "messing" with the bible. For them there is only one interpretation – period! The Scriptural word is obvious and does not require interpretation. Hence, once a Fundamentalist has decided that a certain text has a certain meaning, there is nothing more to be said. From a scriptural point of view, this closes the door to fresh insights. Fundamentalism seems to give equal importance to everything in the bible.

Part of the problem with such a stance is that the "interpretation" of scripture is made from a particular cultural bias. There is a presumption that we Westerners have the real insights. It doesn't matter that the Bible was written by people from quite another culture i.e. the Middle East countries.

Fundamentalism offers a great deal of security. Once you "know" what the bible says, that is the end of any searching. There is little need for growth – only the implementation of the interpretation, which, they say, is not an interpretation! People who find the lifelong process of conversion difficult to handle will be happy with Fundamentalism. Instead of a continuing personal conversion, the Fundamentalist finds "thems" to blame for what is happening in the world. The "thems" may be the Devil, the Catholic Church, the Pope, the liberals, or whoever is handy. If they can "get" such folks, everything will be all right.

Nationalism is part of the fundamentalist ideology. For American fundamentalists, America is the promised land and what she does is right. Hence their support of power and wealth. Whatever America does is OK. Political action to support such nationalism is seen as godliness. Anyone who critiques the government is an enemy.

Fundamentalists are truly good people. But their ideas about scripture are often flawed. Their ideas on the Apocalyptic times and "End-of-the-World" scares go counter to much of the Gospel. There is a convenient forgetting of texts that would diminish apocalyptic beliefs. There is a tendency to spend a great amount of time and concern on the "end time" and very little time with social justice issues that trouble our "present time." Matthew 25: 31-46 (Last judgement scene) is often ignored. After all, God will take care of things.

Fundamentalists and their doctrines are often popular in countries with dictators. Fundamentalists tend to invite people to grin-and-bear pain and oppression quietly. Letting God take care of it means they will not create problems for the government. Dictators can easily deal with such victim types. They do not like people following a gospel that calls a government to accountability for oppressive tactics.

It is difficult to win an argument with a dyed-in-the-wool Fundamentalist. They KNOW they have the truth. Anyone else will have to come to their truth before any dialogue can happen. Hence, even if you are a Scripture scholar, you will be frustrated in trying to "convert" a dyed-in-the-wool Fundamentalist. The best thing to do is to gently love them. Let them see the love of Christ in your response. Throwing bible texts around will do little to convince the hard-core Fundamentalist. However, the uncertain Fundamentalist may be touched by a wider use and understanding of Scripture.

There are many Catholics who lean toward Fundamentalism. With these there is often the possibility of dialogue. You will need to determine how to handle each case individually.

Part of the attraction of fundamentalism is its absolutism. In a world that is changing; in a society in flux; in family life that has become complex; and in a Church that continues to call for change and renewal – a lot of stress is dealt with by simply accepting fundamentalist absolutes. Fundamentalism appears to offer a bulwark against all these changes. If absolutes can be found no where else, we can at least find them in the bible! Fundamentalism offers an apparent haven for those who are insecure, or just tired of the long-term process of conversion.

Fundamentalists, of course, do not see themselves as a problem. They are the solution! Fundamentalism invites us to drop out of society insofar as trying to change it. Only God can change anything. We will pray and let God do the work. We have no power to change things. Just be good and everything will be fine. Anything that smacks of a "process" is bad news. Take the bible the way it is – and all will turn out well.

But a fundamental question remains: How do I know whether this "one interpretation" is the right one? How can I be certain that my English translation is an accurate reflection of the language of the Bible? Who decides that this interpretation is the right one? Without some criteria for evaluation, we wind up dependent on "someone" to interpret the Bible for us. But no one has such authority for the Fundamentalist, so he/she is left hanging. It sounds like a beautiful, accepting faith. But it may go counter to much that the gospel requires.

Even IF (a big "IF") the end is near, the gospel requires us to be faithful to the ENTIRE gospel during our time of waiting. Apocalyptic fears do not release us from the call of the gospel. Parables like the Good Samaritan (Luke 9: 29-37) or the story of Lazarus and the Rich man (Luke 16: 19-31) remain operative for us. We cannot hope someone will take care of things at some FUTURE time. NOW is when the gospel calls us to be good Christians. I am certain you can understand that Fundamentalists, like any other Christian group, have a variety of reactions to the bible.

Recognize the need not to be drawn into a fundamentalist approach to the Christian life. Though it may be attractive initially, it will be unable to support a TOTAL GOSPEL life for the long haul. It is too selective and too un-scriptural to accomplish such a task. To leave everything to some vague FUTURE; to forever expect the second coming and the rapture, is to evade the responsibility of dealing with the world that now exists. Such evasion is not based on scripture.

On the other hand, love anyone who operates out of such a perspective. That is required by the gospel and is a sure way to touch them. Accept and affirm the good that they do. Share gently and with understanding your own perception of the gospel life. You may not convert the Fundamentalist, but you may offer them another way to look at Scripture. It is part of our "bottom line" as Christians to relate to all people in love.

The Bible

The Bible is inspired by God. It communicates the truth God wishes to share with us. It is written in human language by human authors. The writing reflects the various authors. It reflects their personality, their education, their ideas about the world and people, their culture and the times in which they lived. The language is not perfect even though it is inspired. It is not perfect science even thought it is inspired. It reflects the perceptions of the human author, which may be unscientific but real for that writer. The various books of the bible show a development as civilization changes. Since so many people are involved in writing the Bible, each deserves study to understand more completely the book written by that particular author.

Ordinarily, we read a translation of the Bible. Translations are fragile things. Words from one language do not always have accurate words in another language by which to translate them. Language tends to change. The meaning of words tend to change. "Gay" may have meant to "be happy" at one time only to identify a group of people at another. Hence, it is difficult to attain a totally accurate translation of both word and meaning for the Bible. The research that is required for a good translation never ends. We keep learning more about the various situations and peoples and languages of the Bible. New translations are a natural consequence of such on-going research and development.

The New American Bible is a fine translation, as is the Jerusalem Bible. I like the translation called the Revised English Bible with the Apocrypha, while others prefer the New Revised Standard Version. These are good translations. Bibles like the Good News for Modern Man and The Living Bible paraphrase the bible. They are much less accurate, but can serve as easy reading for the beginner. I suggest that you consult a knowledgeable person before you invest in a Bible.

Remember that our "hearing" of the bible may very well depend on how we are feeling on a particular day. If problems are overwhelming us, we hear differently than on days when everything is going great. Keep in touch with your own spirit, realizing it will influence your understanding of the bible. Try not to impose yourself on the Bible – let the Spirit help you listen to what the Bible is saying to you!

Structure Of The Bible

The Bible is a library of books written over a thousand-year period. Different people wrote different books. Writers came from different levels of society and approached their writing with differing perceptions. This touches the way they wrote and how they communicate God's message. Paul, with his rabbinical training, writes quite differently than Peter, with his fisherman background. Knowing this can help us listen more intelligently.

This library of books is divided into the Old (Hebrew) Testament and the New Testament. We will refer to the "old" Testament as the "Hebrew Testament."

The Hebrew Testament contains the writings of the Hebrew people before the time of Jesus.

1) *The Law* (Torah/Pentateuch) ... this includes the first five books of the Bible – Genesis, Exodus, Leviticus, Numbers and Deuteronomy.

2) *The Prophets* ... this includes books written by the prophets or in the spirit of the prophets.

3) *The (other) Writings* ... this includes the remaining books of the Hebrew Testament.

Another way of dividing the Hebrew Testament is this:

PENTATEUCH . . . . Genesis – Exodus – Leviticus – Numbers – Deuteronomy.

HISTORICAL . . . . . Joshua – Judges – 1 & 2 Samuel – 1 & 2 Kings – Chronicles – Ezra – Nehemiah – 1 & 2 Machabees.

PROPHETIC . . . . . Amos – Hosea – Micah – Isaiah – Zephaniah – Nahum – Habakkuk – Jeremiah – Ezekiel – Haggai – Lamentations – Zechariah – Obadiah – Malachi – Joel – Jonah – Baruch – Daniel

WISDOM . . . . Psalms – Proverbs – Job – Song of Songs – Ruth – Ecclesiastes – Tobit – Sirach – Judith – Esther – Wisdom

Such divisions are only helps. They need not be memorized. They offer different ways of approaching the Bible. Use them in whatever way is helpful for you.

The total listing of the inspired books of the Bible is given the technical name "Canon" of the Bible. The Council of Hippo (393 AD) and the Council of Carthage (397 AD & 419 AD) declared the "Canon" of the Bible. Any lingering doubts about the books of the Bible were alleviated by the Council of Trent in the 15th Century. Our Catholic Bible contains 46 Hebrew Testament books and 27 New Testament books/letters.

There is a difference between the Catholic Church and other churches about the Canon of Scripture. There are several books in the Hebrew Testament that are not accepted by all Churches. These are called "Apocrypha". These include Tobit, Judith, Wisdom, Sirach, Baruch and 1 & 2 Machabees. Other segments of books are also categorized by some as "apocrypha." These differences developed from the fact that there are two different Hebrew Testament texts. The Hebrew Testament that developed in the Schools located in Palestine do not have these books. The Hebrew Testament that developed in the Schools located in Alexandria, Egypt, (Septuagint) does contain them. The Septuagint text became the standard for the Catholic Church while others followed the Palestinian text. Hence the difference in the books accepted as part of the "canon."

We are blessed with many fine books on Scripture today. Contact a competent person to see what is available.

New Testament

The New Testament writings developed over a considerable period of time. The earliest writings were about 20 years (50 AD) after the death of Jesus. The writing continued until the end of the 1st century. The early preaching of the Apostles was gradually gathered into the gospels by Matthew, Mark and Luke. Many eyewitnesses shared their insights with the writers. Yet each writer had his own agenda as he developed "his" gospel. That is why it helps to know the background and person of the gospel writers. St Paul for example, used letters to communicate with his converts. He developed his theology to assist new Christians.

In some cases, his letters deal with questions and problems in early communities of faith. Peter wrote to encourage Christians who were caught in slavery and persecution. Each designed his words to meet a need of the readers.

Here is a general dating of the books of the New Testament. As you can see, many dates are uncertain and subject to change as new research develops a more accurate dating.

51 AD . . . . . 1 & 2 Thessalonians

55 AD . . . . . Philippians

57 AD . . . . . 1 Corinthians – Galatians (?) – 2 Corinthians

58 AD . . . . . Romans – James (May be as late as 61-63)

61-63 AD . . . . Colossians – Ephesians – Philemon – (Possibly – Philippians)

64 AD . . . . . Gospel of Mark – 1 Peter

65 AD . . . . . 1 Timothy – Titus – Hebrews – 2 Timothy

68-70 AD . . . . Gospel of Matthew – Gospel of Luke – Acts – Jude (?) – 2 Peter (?)

70-80 AD . . . . Jude (?) – 2 Peter (?)

90-100 AD . . . Revelations – Gospel of John – 1, 2, 3 John

This is a generalized list. The first three gospels (Matthew, Luke and Mark) are called the "Synoptic" gospels. Each gospel writer gathered and arranged material to communicate the message of Jesus as he saw it. None of the writers were particularly concerned about the proper chronological order of events. They used stories and events to communicate the truth of the message. Again, a reasonable understanding of the focus and agenda of each writer helps us listen more intelligently to his gospel.

Mark's gospel is full of movement. He is sharp and blunt in describing the disciples. There is a certain restless movement to the person of Jesus in Mark's gospel. Luke is much more forgiving of people. He finds reasons to excuse a lack of faith as well as giving more detail to some of the events of Christ's life. Matthew addresses many issues that would influence Jewish converts. He tries to bridge the gap between Jew and Gentile. John, writing much later, is interested in the message and uses events to teach theology. The gospels differ from one another and reveal the different perspectives of the writers.

Background notes at the beginning of the various books often give important material for understanding that particular book of the Bible. Take time to read these notes in your bible. Keep in mind that the Bible is both a human and divine book. Listen for both dimensions as you read. Get the full flavor of the scriptures. There is no end to the fresh insights the scripture offers. As we change and grow we hear, in new ways, the word of scripture. It is exciting to know that this happens. We will never run out of learning more about God, Jesus and ourselves as we prayerfully read the Scriptures.

St Francis & The Bible

St Francis was a wise searcher of God's communication. Even without the scriptural helps available to us, he managed to hear the God-communication in the bible. The bible was his friend, his guide, the word of his Lord and Master. He trusted the bible because Jesus spoke through it. Deeply aware of the presence of the Holy Spirit, Francis allowed the biblical word to guide his life.

St Francis had a natural and spontaneous response to the word of Scripture. For him it was the gospel-truth. He chose to put it into practice rather than merely discuss it. He accepted the consequences of the word with a loving heart. For Francis the Scripture was the revelation of the Father in human words. Francis reveled in the bible as Jesus' way of communicating. Throughout Francis' writing there is the thread of Scripture. He weaves it skillfully and realistically into his own communication with his followers.

St Paul tells us: "… the letter kills, but the Spirit gives life." (2 Cor. 3: 6) A man has been killed by the letter when he wants to know quotations only so that people will think he is very learned and he can make money to give to his relatives and friends. A servant of Jesus has been killed by the letter when he has no desire to follow the spirit of sacred Scripture, but wants to know what it says only so that he can explain it to others. On the other hand, those have received life from the spirit of Sacred Scripture who, by their words and example, refer to the most high God, to whom all good belongs, all that they know or wish to know, and do not allow their knowledge to become a source of self-complacency.

St Francis – Admonitions #7

Franciscans Today

The Franciscan way of life is based on the gospel of Jesus. Let me share some things from life that call for gospel awareness and concern.

We are influenced by many people during a lifetime. Events, both in our personal-life, neighborhood and world-life have an impact on us. It is good to be aware of HOW they influence us.

Music weaves its spell on us. The songs we hear and their lyrics touch us. Music often sets a mood. It can disturb and soothe, agitate and calm, make us raucous or pensive.

Opinions on newscasts influence us about world events. Editorials can do the same. When half-truths are presented as the whole truth, we can come to conclusions that may not be valid.

Advertising convinces us about how we should "look" and makes us worried about our "image." Education can be limited to those subjects that enable us to get a good job. It may not teach us how to be human.

Government communication can be communication of the truth or an interpretation that supports government policy. The two are not always the same.

A parish council can spend more time on Church architecture than the needs of the poor. Preachers can shout opposition to sin without finding time to share the good news. Trying to live a gospel-life in the midst of all these elements of society can be difficult and conflictual.

As gospel-people we face many decisions. What do we keep in our lives and what do we throw away? What things support a gospel life and what things are obstacles to it? Are we expected to act the same in every circumstance? Are we called to perfection or faithfulness – and what's the difference? What helps us in making our choices? Can I remain in a job that is destructive of family life? What are the important things in my life?

It would seem easier to ignore the gospel. Life would be much simpler. The gospel tends to mess things up. It requires choices everyday. Awareness is fine, but it also brings responsibility. The consequences of accepting such responsibility never ends. Gospel-people decide to accept such responsibility.

Conflict comes easily to gospel people. Society lauds the person who is dominant, who gets what he/she wants. The gospel asks us to reflect whether we want such dominance in the Kingdom. Movies tell us that to love means never having to say "I'm sorry." The gospel asks those who love to deal with conflict and say "I'm sorry" when it is needed. Society bases success on accumulation. The gospel bases success on sharing with others. Society often says that relationships are to be used for one's own benefit. The gospel says that relationships are the bedrock of community and holiness – never to be used merely for one's own benefit. Even these few contrasts make it clear how gospel-values come into conflict with society-values.

Jesus looks for strong convictions in his followers. But those firm convictions are to be used in life-giving ways. He wants strength to be tempered with gentleness. The drive for power is meant to be tempered by compassion. Power is helpful in creating breathing space within which people can grow to full potential. Sexuality is not a bad word but a beautiful gift to draw people to sound relationships. Enemies are to be forgiven, not killed. The poor are to be given dignity not only charitable help. Each of us needs to see reality as God sees it, and call God's-vision-in-Jesus "our" reality.

No matter how long the journey, the gospel calls for faithfulness to the call. No matter how many "idols" we and society may create, the gospel continues to call them "strange gods". The rush to do everything in a hurry conflicts with the human spirit's need for "catch-up" time. In short, taking the gospel seriously is pretty life-changing business! It is also called "conversion."

Reflections On The New Testament

Jesus reveals a strong relationship with his Father. It is so strong that without it, Jesus would lose his identity. As Jesus grows, the relationship grows. He glorifies the Father. He points to the power of the Father working through the marvels Jesus performs. Jesus speaks of his Father as someone who cares. The Father cares more for us than for many sparrows and all the beautiful flowers. Jesus spends time communing with his Father in prayer. When Jesus struggles in the Garden of Gethsemane, his final acceptance is a clear decision to remain united to the Father. Without that relationship, Jesus would be nothing. Such a reflection gives solid support to Jesus' message about the importance of relationships. Rules, regulations, laws and doctrines must support the growth of solid relationships.

When Jesus relates to people in the gospel, we see the same attention to relationships. Each person is given dignity. Whether lepers or tax-collectors, prostitutes or the unclean, each receives Jesus' attention. When Pharisees come to him, he is honest with them. When Nicodemus comes at night because of fear, Jesus gives him food for thought. The Samaritan woman at the well is confronted by Jesus for her marital status but in a way that invites conversion. Only the closed-minded among the religious authorities are called to task with a blistering sermon. But even there, if they could come to "see" this new vision, they would be welcome. While Jesus does not compromise his message to please folks, he is open to those who are searching. Jesus is sad when the rich young man cannot leave his riches for the Kingdom of God. Jesus weeps over Jerusalem, symbol of his people, for not letting him gather them together. He accepts the consequences of faithfulness to the Father, accepting even death to maintain intimacy with his Father.

Our living of the gospel will need the same kind of intimacy with Jesus. As our relationship with Jesus wanes we may find our gospel-living on the wane as well. When other people or things replace Jesus in our lives, the gospel becomes too demanding. If techniques or technology become our gods, they will block out the real God. If substance abuse becomes our great addiction, our desire for God will diminish. If we are so insecure as to create a god of rigidity and absolutes, we will look less and less like gospel people. If personal righteousness and opinionated dogma become our god we become judges who barely resemble gospel people. Choosing the gospel way of life is what we are called to do. Be well aware of the cost of discipleship.

"How is it," they said "that this untrained man has such learning?" Jesus replied: "The teaching that I give is not my own; it is the teaching of the one who sent me. Whoever has the will to do the will of God shall know whether my teaching comes from him or is merely my own. Anyone whose teaching is merely his own, aims at honor for himself. But if a man aims at the honor of him who sent him he is sincere, and there is nothing false in him."

John 7: 14-18

I have not yet reached perfection, but I press on, hoping to take hold of that for which Christ once took hold of me. My friends, I do not reckon myself to have got hold of it yet. All I can say is this: forgetting what is behind me, and reaching out for that which lies ahead, I press towards the goal, to win the prize which is God's call to the life above in Christ Jesus.

Philippians 3: 12-14

Reflection Questions

Are you attracted by the fundamentalist approach to scripture and life? Why? How often do you read the bible? Do you do any studying of the bible? Have you joined any groups in your parish that take time to share bible ideas? Why is the gospel dangerous to our comfort? How do you understand the meaning of "conversion"? Are your values and attitudes formed by the gospel or by something else? If something else, what? Is a Christian ever finished with growing? Why is it important to know about the writers of the bible and their times and culture? How do you think St Francis of Assisi accepted the bible? What are the different ways of approaching the meaning of the bible? How can they help for living a good life? Why is it important to share biblical insights with one another? If you make a list of what you DO in the various areas of your life, would it show that you are a gospel person? What we do tells us what we value more than the words we use.

SECULAR FRANCISCAN RULE

4. The rule and life of the Secular Franciscans is this: To observe the gospel of our Lord Jesus Christ by following the example of St Francis of Assisi, who made Christ the inspiration and the center of his life with God and people.

   Christ, the gift of the Father's love is the way to him, the truth into which the Holy Spirit leads us, and the life which he has come to give abundantly.

   Secular Franciscans should devote themselves especially to careful reading of the gospel, going from gospel to life and life to the gospel.

5. Secular Franciscans, therefore, should seek to encounter the living and active person of Christ in their brothers and sisters, in sacred Scripture, in the Church and in liturgical activity. The faith of St Francis, who often said: "I see nothing bodily of the most high Son of God in this world except his most Holy Body and Blood," should be the inspiration and pattern of their Eucharistic life.

RULE – Chapter 2 – #4 & 5

Commentary

The practicalities of life are enlivened by our vision of life. These points of the Rule offer a dream/vision for Secular Franciscans. The gospel is held up as a precious source of life. Our imagination is called upon to paint a picture of Jesus, living among us in <u>people.</u> The human Jesus is portrayed for us speaking with a human voice, touching with a human hand, physically tired in a human body, struggling with decisions in the agony of Gethsemane. The Rule calls us to follow the gospel of Jesus – period! Jesus is the center and source of all that we accomplish.

The biblical words are our way of life. The Spirit of Jesus speaks to us wherever we are – in California or Wisconsin or Maine. The Spirit can change our lives by the power of the Word of scripture. The biblical word is blessed and broken among us, nourishing our lives. We listen to the word in the silence of our hearts. We listen to the word in the sharing within the community. We listen to the word as it is proclaimed in the Liturgy. We listen to the word as it is spoken through the lives of our brothers and sisters. At the center of such revelation is Jesus Christ.

One of Francis' followers was a literal follower. Anything Francis did, he did. He thought that by doing everything Francis did he would become holy like Francis. Francis recognized the simplicity of this brother – but invited him to cease and desist:

> *When St Francis would stand in any place to meditate, whatever gestures or movements he would make, the simple John would himself repeat and copy. If Francis spat, he spat; if Francis coughed he coughed. He joined his sighs to Francis' sighs; and he accompanied Francis' weeping with his own weeping. When the saint raised his hands to heaven, John raised his too, diligently watching him as his model and copying everything he did. The Saint noticed this and once asked him why he did these things. He answered: "I have promised to do everything you do. It is dangerous for me to omit anything." The Saint rejoiced because of the Brother's simplicity, but gently forbade him to act like that in the future.*
> **II Celano – #190 (Omnibus – P. 514)**

We are not called to slavish imitation. Gospel living invites us to allow the gospel to change our lives. I am not Francis nor are you. What we hold in common is the desire to make the gospel come alive in our lives. Our way of doing this will fit our century, not the 13th century. Francis proved it can be done. We continue to prove, by our lives, that the gospel is livable.

People implement the gospel in different settings, in different cultures, through different personalities. Think of all the places and faces where the gospel is given expression. Some live the gospel in a university setting or as teachers in high schools. Some minister to the sick and in hospice work. For some the gospel is implemented in an auto assembly plant or at the local garage. Some raise children and care for a home while others live the gospel from a paralyzed body. For one person, the gospel tool is a computer, for another a calculator. Some will live the gospel by fighting for peace and others will change laws to make them more just. In short, the variety of ministries is enormous. The implementation of gospel living can happen anywhere. For Secular Franciscans, this IS their way of dealing with life and living in the world.

The Franciscan Way

1. Our observance of the gospel is meant to mirror the ready response St Francis gave to the gospel. We need not be Brother John, slavishly imitating everything Francis did. We are NOT St Francis. Each of us is called to give our unique response to the gospel in our time. We will reflect the needs of our time and be touched by the influences around us. We want to offer a gospel-alternative by our everyday manner of living. People can understand a life well-lived better than lots of sermons. If our lives reflect the gospel, people will understand what the gospel is all about.

   To do this, Jesus must be central in our lives and the gospel part of regular reflection. We go from the gospel to life and life to the gospel, each being touched by the other. It is called "reality." We share our experiences with one another to discover fresh ways to make the gospel a living influence in our lives.

2. There are a number of things the Rule offers that can help us accomplish this:

   A) Devote time and effort to careful reading of the gospel (#4) so that the Word can take root in our lives.

   B) We are to go from the gospel to life and life to the gospel (#4) in a rhythm of life. The interchange supports the process of growth and conversion. Without the interchange we might have good ideas with no action or lots of action that doesn't know where it is going. Both hearing the gospel and doing the gospel are required.

The gospel is our story. We are both Pharisee and Publican praying in the temple. We are both the woman caught in adultery and the stone throwers. Sensitive listening to the gospel will uncover stories about ourselves in the biblical word. The Rule invites us to maintain the pattern – listening to the word, doing the word. The inter-play of gospel and life changes us. Attitudes, perspectives, viewpoints and responses are touched by the formative power of Scripture.

3. Jesus is present to the whole of life. He is discovered in all kinds of people. He is found in personal prayer and liturgical celebrations. He is found in the poor and the outcast. He is present to all – and our task is to discover the mystery of his presence all around us and within us. No place or person can drive out that presence, and we discover Jesus as our intimacy with him grows.

We do not have to do this alone. Secular Franciscans are called to support each other on this journey. Together we share the struggles and celebrate the discoveries. Together we learn the ways of reconciliation and healing. We will be REAL for each other and be surprised to find Jesus in that reality. We are ordinary people, supporting one another in community life, following St Francis of Assisi. So we pray with Francis:

> *Almighty, eternal, just and merciful God, grant us in our misery that we may do for your sake alone what we know you want us to do, and always want what pleases you; so that, cleansed and enlightened interiorly and fired with the ardor of the Holy Spirit, we may be able to follow in the footsteps of your Son, our Lord Jesus Christ, and so make our way to you, most High, by your grace alone, you who live and reign in perfect trinity and simple unity, and are glorified as God all-powerful, forever and ever. Amen.*
>
> **Letter to a General Chapter**
> **Omnibus – P. 108**

These texts of St Paul might be worth reflection:

Romans 8: 18-27 / Ephesians 2: 13-22 / 1 Corinthians 1: 18-31 / Philippians 2: 1-11.

FRANCISCAN FOCUS

There are many writings by and about St Francis of Assisi. Here are some of the more basic ones.

1. **WRITINGS OF ST FRANCIS** ... Rules, prayers, reflections written by Francis himself. Among them are: The Rules of 1221 and 1223, the Testament of Francis, Letters to all the Faithful, to General Chapters, to Rulers and to Brother Leo as well as a paraphrase of the Our Father. The writings of both Francis and Clare are contained in the book: *Francis and Clare* – the complete works ... Edited by Armstrong and Brady ... Paulist Press ... 1982. Other writings of Clare are contained in the book: *Clare of Assisi – early documents* ... Edited by Regis Armstrong OFM Cap ... Paulist Press ... 1988

2. **LIFE OF ST FRANCIS** ... Thomas of Celano. Celano is the earliest biographer of St Francis. He wrote two lives of St Francis. The first is a masterpiece of theology (1228-1229). It is written in the structured manner of the 12th & 13th century biographies of saints. The second life (1247) is a more developed perspective of Francis. It offers a window into the early understanding of Francis 20 years after his death. It is structured around the virtues of St Francis.

3. **LIFE OF ST FRANCIS** ... St Bonaventure (1263) ... St Bonaventure contributes his theological and mystical interpretation of the life of Francis. The mystical spirituality is powerful. The book is meant to be prayed as well as read, meditated on as well as read for factual information.

4. **LEGEND OF THE THREE COMPANIONS** ... (cc 1246) ... There is uncertainty about the authors. Leo, Rufino and Angelo are sometimes named as the authors though this is not likely. The LEGENDA is a well ordered text with an emphasis on the early days of the friars and Francis. Begging is important as is the focus on the Portiuncula as the birthplace of the Franciscan Order.

5. **THE ANONYMOUS OF PERUGIA** ... John of Perugia (1240-1241) ... An important early biography of Francis and a primary source for the Legend of the Three Companions. It is free of much of the "editorializing" of some of the early writings. Appears to be a fairly objective historical source for the life of Francis.

6. **LEGEND OF PERUGIA** ... (1246) ... probably collected at the direction of Crescentius, Minister General of the Order. The material focuses on the later years of Francis' life. It treats especially his illnesses and hermitage experiences. It is quite polemical in taking sides in the arguments within the Order at that time.

7. **MIRROR OF PERFECTION** ... (1318) ... It describes 14th century filial piety and devotion to St Francis.

8. **LITTLE FLOWERS OF ST FRANCIS** ... (1325-1326) ... It is also called the "Fioretti". Contains charming anecdotes and stories about St Francis and his first companions.

9. **SACRUM COMMERCIUM** ... (1227) ... It is an allegorical work about Lady Poverty and Francis. It weaves a story of scripture, Lady Poverty and Francis together in a tale about the meaning and beauty of poverty.

QUESTIONS

1. What things are important to understand when you read the bible? —Or— What information can help in understanding the meaning of the bible?

2. How does a Fundamentalist and someone with a wider Christian approach differ when they read the bible? Make a list of the differences and put them side by side. Where do you stand in relation to these items?

3. Why is a Fundamentalist approach attractive to many people? Is it attractive to you? Why or why not?

4. Explain how the different books got to be part of the "canon" of the bible. When (dates) were the four gospels written? Were any New Testament books written before that? If so, which ones?

5. From your own experience, list the values / attitudes / ideals of American society. Contrast them with your understanding of the values / attitudes / ideals of the gospel. If you follow the gospel side, what changes will you have to make in your life?

6. What do you consider the most basic element of the Secular Franciscan way of life? Why?

7. From personal reflection, describe what is meant by "going from the gospel to life and from life to the gospel." Be concrete and personal in your sharing.

8. How does the local fraternity/community help your growth as a Secular Franciscan? What influence do you have in the Fraternity/Community? Do some dreaming and discuss HOW it could be better on both sides!

SCRIPTURE *reading/reflection*

✝ Isaiah 55: 10-11

Isaiah speaks of the power of the word of God. It does what it is sent to do. How would you apply this truth to the word that Jesus speaks in the gospel? Do you feel the power of the "word" in your life? How? Share any text that touched and changed you! What other things did you learn from this Isaiah text?

THEN JESUS TOOK THE LOAVES, GAVE THANKS,

AND GAVE THEM OUT TO
ALL WHO WERE SITTING
READY; HE THEN DID THE
SAME WITH THE FISH,
GIVING OUT AS MUCH AS
WAS WANTED. WHEN
THEY HAD EATEN ENOUGH
HE SAID TO HIS DISCIPLES,
'PICK UP THE PIECES LEFT
OVER, SO THAT NOTHING
GETS WASTED'!

SO THEY PICKED THEM UP,
AND FILLED TWELVE
HAMPERS WITH SCRAPS
LEFT OVER FROM THE MEAL
OF FIVE BARLEY LOAVES.

CHAPTER 5

I BELIEVE

Conversion is serious business. It requires not only a change of heart, but also an embrace of a new direction in life. Conversion puts the spotlight on areas of life that need to change. It springs from sound self-knowledge. It is nourished by a <u>desire</u> to change and the <u>vision</u> of what changes are needed. Obviously, for most of us, this will mean a struggle with ourselves. It is not easy to embrace changes. We are familiar with our "old ways" of doing things and don't appreciate a call to conversion. In fact, we may believe there is no need to change!

However, the gospel way of life does not tolerate standing still. The gospel stretches us beyond where we thought we could go. It is no simple thing to follow the path of the lifelong conversion that the gospel requires.

Faith

God is revealed to us through Jesus, the Son of God. Jesus, in turn, teaches us about the Father. In addition, Jesus gives us his own Spirit as source of wisdom and strength. These fundamentals of faith are important in our attempts at conversion. God is in the middle of things in our lives. God engages us in actions that bring us to wholeness. Our experience of God's presence is not always filled with joy. Sometimes it is painful to know what God expects. We may not always be happy to change. Our resistance brings more struggle and pain. But God does not abandon us. God sticks with us.

> *"Then what must we do," they asked him, "if we are to work as God would have us work?" Jesus replied: "This is the work that God requires – believe in the one whom he has sent!"*
>
> **John 6: 28-29**

And to all he said: "If anyone wishes to be a follower of mine, he must leave self behind; day after day he must take up his cross, and come with me. Whoever cares for his own safety is lost; but if a person will let himself be lost for my sake, that person is safe."
Luke 9: 23-24

The gospel is full of similar statements. Obviously, faith in Jesus is fundamental to real conversion. When we trust Jesus and believe in him, we stand ready to answer his call to conversion. Our lives will reflect the WORD that Jesus speaks to us.

The bible contains many ways through which God is revealed. God remains faithful to the chosen people even when they are unfaithful. The Hebrew Testament is full of stories of unfaithfulness. It is also full of stories of the faithfulness of God. God is not indifferent to unfaithfulness. God abhors it. God is angry about it. God threatens retaliation. But when the dust settles, God is still present to the chosen people. God is not put off by the foolishness and short-sightedness of the chosen people. God makes a personal decision based on faithfulness to who God is. The pattern seems to repeat itself again and again:

A) A call by God

B) An initial good response by the people

C) Doubts and failure by the people.

D) People create idols to replace God

E) A new initiative by God to call them back.

The book of JONAH, for example, shows this process. Jonah knows and hears God, but seeks to escape the call to preach to the Ninevites. He runs away – deliberately. Crisis intervenes through a storm at sea. Jonah faces himself and acknowledges what he is doing. The large fish saves him for the work of the Call. He does the work grudgingly but successfully. He is still resentful and angry about things. God dialogues with Jonah in an attempt to help him understand. God reveals the generous feelings that direct God's actions toward the Ninevites. The story stops and we are unsure of the depth of Jonah's conversion.

90

I find myself in Jonah and his story. I find God hard to understand. I do not always like what God wants me to do or what God does with other people. Thank God that the generosity and patience that Jonah received is also available to me!

Faith is strengthened and supported by the scriptural word as well as by intimacy with the word-made-flesh (Jesus). As my relationship with Jesus deepens, his words in scripture take on greater importance for me. I trust those words, even the hard sayings. I may not understand it all, but I continue to listen and try to give flesh to these words in my life. Sometimes I fight the words. Sometimes I feel that they don't make sense. Sometimes I just want to give up and forget I ever heard of the bible.

What enables me to continue on the path of conversion is the Spirit of Jesus I have received. Little by little I find myself surrendering another area of life to the word of God. My experience teaches me that Jesus is the way, the truth and the life. But I keep having to learn it again and again as conversion continues at another level. Each time Jesus calls for a stronger and deeper commitment.

Such growth makes Jesus more real. It helps me get a glimpse of the way Francis of Assisi felt about Jesus. It goes far beyond memorizing texts of scripture. This is intimacy with the Word-made-flesh and it has many consequences. Remembering scripture texts tests only our memory. Intimacy with Jesus tests the quality of our entire life. Jesus preached forgiveness and he also forgave his enemies. Jesus preached trust of his Father and showed the depth of his trust. Jesus spoke of prayer and also spent time in prayer. He called us to carry the cross and carried his own as well. He spoke of compassion and care for the little ones and showed compassion and care for the little ones of his time. This is the sort of thing that St Francis of Assisi understood very well. It is not enough to hear the word. We must live the word. Since Francis, a human being like us, has "done the Word" in his life, we cannot say it is impossible. Francis offers the hope that living the gospel is possible and brings joy.

In addition, Francis learned quickly that no one can follow the gospel without help from the Holy Spirit. The Spirit of Jesus empowers us to do what mere human power could never accomplish.

But God, rich in mercy, for the great love he bore us brought us to life with Christ even when we were dead in our sins; it is by his grace you are saved. And in union with Christ Jesus he raised us up and enthroned us with him in the heavenly realms, so that he might display in the ages to come how immense are the resources of his grace, and how great his kindness to us in Christ Jesus. For it is by his grace you are saved, through trusting him; it is not your own doing. It is God's gift, not a reward for work done. There is nothing for anyone to boast about. For we are God's handiwork, created in Christ Jesus to devote ourselves to the good deeds for which God designed us.

Ephesians 2: 4-10

Our complex age often finds such direct truth hard to accept. Society has taught us well to rely on our human knowledge and technology. It is not easy to accept the direction that comes from the bible. Sometimes we simply want others to tell us what to do. But St Francis teaches us that we are responsible for "doing" the gospel. Jesus wants us to do as he did – to follow the lead of our heavenly Father. Jesus made known the way, gave us the truth and pointed out the path to life. Our task is to follow Jesus. St Francis was so certain of the direction the Lord was giving, he convinced the Pope to approve his rag-tag group and their way of living. As one of the Cardinals put it when they discussed approving Francis' request: "If we reject this poor man's request ... would we not be declaring that the gospel cannot be practiced, and so blaspheme Christ, its author?"

Rest assured that we may feel that the gospel is too demanding. It goes counter to what we like to call common sense. It accepts the impossible because God is at work, but the impossible can be difficult to accept. We would like to be able to pick and choose bits and pieces of the gospel to follow. But Francis does not tolerate such piecemeal commitment. He asks us to follow the WHOLE gospel in all its demands. Only then can we experience the fulfillment of the gospel promises. Instead of fighting the gospel, we embrace it. Instead of backing off when it seems too demanding, we plunge in with renewed commitment. As St Francis grew in faith in Jesus, his life reflected more clearly the gospel way. The

Spirit was more free to work in Francis as he surrendered his "self" to the Lord.

> *Instruct those who are rich in this world's goods not to be proud and not to fix their hopes on so uncertain a thing as money, but upon God, who endows us richly with all things to enjoy. Tell them to do good and to grow rich in noble actions, to be ready to give away and to share, and so to acquire a treasure which will form a good foundation for the future. Thus they will grasp the life which is life indeed.*
>
> **1 Timothy 6: 17-19**

Francis had to face many disappointments in his lifetime. The Order he founded did not always fit the dream that he had for it. Physical illness made "Brother Sun" impossible to look at. Prayer was difficult and depression taunted him with its presence. The stigmata brought more pain and a greater awareness of Jesus' loving demands. Clare consistently brought him joy as did Brother Leo. In the midst of darkness, Francis could penetrate the pain and see God's love at work. No little achievement on a rigorous path of conversion. Little by little, God stripped Francis and filled the "emptiness" with the Spirit. It is the way of intimacy, handing oneself over to the beloved. The way of Jesus, cross and resurrection, became the way for Francis.

Faith for the long haul requires empowerment by God. God freely gives such power. God remains as powerful for us as God was for Francis. God has not lost the power to transform lives. As Francis expressed his love for God through the tools and times of the 13th century, we will express them in 20th/21st century ways. Our Franciscan tradition teaches us that people in every century have found ways to live the gospel. God's power has been at work in every century. What has been done by God is still being done by God in our time. What was possible for Francis and Franciscans for 800 years is possible for us today. It is very realistic for the RULE to say:

> *... motivated by the <u>dynamic power</u> of the gospel, let them conform their thoughts and deeds to those of Christ*

93

*by means of that radical interior change which the gospel
itself call "conversion."*

Rule – Chapter 2 #7

Jesus Christ

To "know" Jesus Christ means to relate to him with our entire person. Faith is not simply knowledge ABOUT Jesus. Intellectual knowledge about the life and words of Jesus is good, but not enough. Such facts do not demand that we relate to Jesus. We have such facts about lots of people whom we never meet. Establishing a personal relationship requires presence to one another. It means looking into the heart and listening with the heart. It requires taking time with the one we love. It requires sharing the deepest secrets of our heart and listening to the revelations of the loved one's heart. As relationship grows, identity with the loved one grows. Intimate relationship begins to re-shape us into the image of the beloved.

While we remain free, we find ourselves choosing the ways of the beloved. In the presence of the beloved, we are free to be our real selves. We feel as free to share brokenness as we do to share strengths. We share joy and weep in sorrow in the presence of the beloved. Building such a relationship is quite beyond mere intellectual knowing.

Faith is building such a relationship with Jesus. It is open to everyone. The personal experience of Jesus shapes our lives in new ways. Sometimes it is so exciting we can hardly contain ourselves. Sometimes it is so personally intimate that no words can describe it. It can happen in the noise of an expressway or in the quiet of reflection. Jesus can reveal himself through others or in the depths of our hearts. Whatever it takes, intimacy brings us to Jesus. Doctrines and rules can be memorized, but they may not change us. Intimacy with Jesus cries out for the response of conversion. Francis of Assisi experienced the presence of Jesus. For him nothing was ever the same again. God wishes to touch us the same way. Our faith in Jesus will grow and re-create us to new life.

> *When anyone is united to Christ, there is a new world;
> the old order has gone, and a new order has already
> begun.*

From first to last this has been the work of God. He has reconciled us to himself through Christ, and he has enlisted us in this service of reconciliation. ... Sharing in God's work, we urge this appeal upon you: You have received the grace of God; do not let it go for nothing!
2 Corinthians 5:17-18 & 6: 1

Listening – Prayerfully

Choose a place where you will be undisturbed. Get comfortable and relax. Quiet your mind and memory. Let loose of worries or anticipations of what you have to do. Simply listen to the scriptural word. Don't program things or decide what ought to happen. Don't worry about coming to pious conclusions or resolutions. Just L I S T E N!

Ask Jesus to help you to listen. If distractions come (and if you are normal, they will), simply acknowledge them and return to Jesus and his word. Choose some scriptural text. Keep it short and read it slowly. Linger with the words. If a word or phrase touches you, stay with it – repeat it to yourself. Allow the word to continue to touch you until it seems finished. Then move on slowly.

Sometimes our mind is touched with a new insight. Sometimes our memory brings special times to awareness that link to the word. Sometimes our emotions are touched and tears may come. Sometimes there seems to be nothing but a deep sense of presence. Your task is simply to allow the scriptural word to lead you. If nothing seems to happen, repeat the words again and again.

When you feel that you are finished (10-20 minutes), thank God and offer intercessory prayer if it seems right.

You might use one of these texts for your prayer.

The Spirit of the Lord is upon me because he has anointed me; he has sent me to announce good news to the poor, to proclaim release for prisoners and recovery of sight

*for the blind; to let broken victims go free, to proclaim
the year of the Lord's favor.*

Luke 4: 18-19

*Pass no judgement, and you will not be judged. For as
you judge others, so you will yourselves be judged, and
whatever measure you deal out to others will be dealt
back to you.*

Matthew 7: 1-2

*To receive you is to receive me, and to receive me is to
receive the One who sent me. Whoever receives a prophet
as a prophet will be given a prophet's reward, and
whoever receives a good man because he is a good man
will be given a good man's reward. And if anyone gives
so much as a cup of cold water to one of these little ones,
because he is a disciple of mine, I tell you this – that man
will assuredly not go unrewarded.*

Matthew 10: 40-42

*"This food the Son of Man will give you, for he it is upon
whom God the Father has set the seal of his authority."
"Then what must we do," they asked him, "if we are to
work as God would have us work?" Jesus replied: "This
is the work that God requires; believe in the one whom
he has sent!"*

John 6: 27-29

*… Jesus, aware that power had gone out of him, turned
round in the crowd and asked: "Who touched my
clothes?" His disciples said to him: "You see the crowd
pressing upon you and yet you ask 'Who touched me?"'
Meanwhile he was looking around to see who had done
it. And the woman, trembling with fear when she
grasped what had happened to her, came and fell at his
feet and told him the whole truth. He said to her: "My
daughter, your faith has cured you. Go in peace, free
forever from this trouble."*

Mark 5: 30-34

Theology – Christology

Theology is the study of God. Literally theology means "a word about God." It is that portion of our faith that seeks deeper understanding of scripture and revelation. Throughout the centuries men and women have explored the meaning of God and our faith. Through research and insight they have deepened our understanding of the truths of faith. They do not create faith, but help us to understand it.

Theologians from many centuries engage in the process of dialogue and discussion before arriving at a consensus. Some teachings are left behind to be replaced by fresher insights. Other teachings are developed over the centuries by theologians building on one another's ideas. Such dialogue, discussion and even disagreement allows the truth to be gradually uncovered. Augustine, Cyprian, Anselm, Bernard, Bonaventure, Duns Scotus, Catherine of Siena, Theresa of Avila and a host of others have contributed to our understanding of the faith. Theologians offer opinions for consideration rather than dogmas for belief. Their work is vital in the Church.

It can happen that "opinions" are sometimes taken as "dogma." Not a little confusion has been caused in this way. The idea of "Limbo", for example, is a theological opinion. But many people think it is church dogma. Some opinions are more sound then others because of the reasons supporting the opinion. The danger is accepting a theological opinion as dogma and closing the mind to any other opinion.

Theological opinions are many and diverse. When tradition and common acceptance support a particular opinion, it is presumptuous to reject it. Theologians, like all human beings are human. They make mistakes. Sometimes they use theology to support a comfortable lifestyle. They are not immune to using theology to escape personal conversion. Like all of us, they can be out of touch with the reality of everyday life. They can create a theology that bears little relationship to the everyday needs of ordinary people. They can be opinionated and obstinate in clinging to "their" theology. They too live in a particular culture and are influenced by it. They may find themselves supporting non-gospel values or rationalizing injustice. They are NOT infallible.

But despite this, they continue to offer important insights to the Church. Theologians and scripture scholars play an important role in the Church. Their contributions push out the horizons of our understanding of the faith. The Holy Spirit is always at work, deepening our understanding. She often highlights truths that a particular time badly needs.

CHRISTOLOGY is the study of Christ. It looks at who he is and explores his life and words for deeper understanding. It is a part of theological exploration. This aspect of theological study looks at the role of Christ and his person. It theologizes about the meaning of salvation and redemption. It looks at various ways of explaining how Christ saves us. Again, there will be a variety of opinions. The value of an opinion is based on the reasons that support it. In many areas, the Church has not declared any opinion as THEE dogma. She leaves us free to choose the opinion that best supports our journey of faith.

We will respond differently to life depending on how we perceive Jesus and how he saves us. One opinion may see the shedding of blood as the way of salvation. Another may contend that the faithful love of Jesus saves us. Still another may present Jesus' death as the ransom that bought us back. Each opinion has its supporters. Each opinion creates a particular way of viewing our understanding of Jesus and how we are saved. It is important to know the theological ideas that support our lifestyle and beliefs.

St Francis saw God as a loving Father, not an angry judge. Francis tried to imitate that love. His theology moved him to love the outcasts and little ones of his time. His theology opened the door to the demands that love can make. Francis recognized his weakness and sinfulness as God's love enlightened his heart. But rather than becoming depressed, such a reality moved him to work harder to reflect God's love. We too will find that our theology can make a difference in our response to God, Church and people. It will make a difference in how we see ourselves.

> *We ask God that you may receive from him all wisdom*
> *and spiritual understanding for full insight into his will,*
> *so that your manner of life may be worthy of the Lord*
> *and entirely pleasing to him. We pray that you may bear*

fruit in active goodness of every kind and grow in the knowledge of God. May he strengthen you, in his glorious might, with ample power to meet whatever comes with fortitude, patience and joy; and to give thanks to the Father who has made you fit to share the heritage of God's people in the realm of light.

Colossians 1: 9-12

Fear – Doubt

Faith encounters many stages in its growth. One of those stages is doubt. Many people think that doubt means they have lost their faith. The opposite is true. Doubt offers the opportunity for a fresh look at faith. It often invites us to question our past beliefs and move to a new way of understanding our faith. Doubt pushes us to new searching and seeks new understanding of faith. It can be healthy to leave behind childish ideas of faith for more mature insights of faith. Doubt invites us to face the problem of incomplete belief and open ourselves to the Spirit leading to new insights.

Such an experience can be fearful. God seems to have disappeared. A crisis, a tragedy or depression can bring us to doubt that there is a God. It is frightening to face such a situation. The bottom seems to drop out of life. We feel guilty for doubting. We no longer know what we believe in. It is important to acknowledge these feelings without giving them control of our lives. Most often it does not mean we are losing our faith. More likely God is calling us to a new and deeper dependence on the Holy Spirit. It is a call to surrender and an invitation to walk in the dark with trust. Not very attractive, perhaps, but most healthy.

God is a mystery. We should not be surprised that our meager knowledge of God is inadequate. God seeks our trust. God seeks our surrender to the revelations of the Holy Spirit. St Thomas doubted the resurrection of Jesus (John 20: 24-29). He even demanded certain signs before he would believe. Jesus gave him what he needed. He will do the same for us. Lots of folks thought Jesus and his teachings were too much to swallow. They listened and left. Jesus asked his disciples about their doubts: "Do you also want to leave me?" Simon Peter answered

him: "Lord to whom shall we go? Your words are words of eternal life."
(John 6: 67-68).

Doubts help us to lose some of our righteousness and recognize our limitations. Without doubt, I might never have the courage to question and I could remain stagnant in my faith.

Like doubt, fear is common to us. Sometimes the price of following Jesus seems too high. I am afraid of what it will demand. My prayer gives me "too much answer." Most of us feel comfortable with what we know and do. We are not anxious for the discomfort the gospel may require of us. We are afraid to take a chance on God. I may fear being responsible for my own life, loving to have people tell me what to do. I am afraid to trust my own insights. I fear that I will not be able to live a gospel lifestyle when it demands too much of me. Fear can invite me to deal with it, explore its sources within me, and MOVE ON! Both fear and doubt can be good gifts that invite me to new growth.

> *All which I took from thee I did but take,*
> *Not for thy harms,*
> *But just that thou might'st seek it in my arms.*
> *All which thy child's mistake fancies as lost,*
> *I have stored for thee at home.*
> *"Rise, clasp my hand, and come."*
> **Hound of heaven – Francis Thompson**

Reflection Questions

Why is conversion sometimes frightening? How long does a
conversion take? What are some of the elements that might
keep me from pursuing a call to conversion? What role do
theologians play in the Church? What theology of salvation
do you believe in? Is God a judge for you? A loving Father?
A distant power? What? What fears most often dictate your
behavior? What do you do about these fears? Are you
satisfied with the way you handle fear? How might you
improve your way of handling fear? What doubts most often
influence you? Why do doubts come into our lives? Why is
faith in Jesus important in the conversion process? Is God's
love for you or God's power over you the dominant force in
your faith? What do we mean when we speak of "Christology"? What role can a good community play in our faith-
growth? Is it possible for anyone to maintain a good faith life
alone? What is the role of the Holy Spirit in our faith-growth?
Why is prayerfulness an important element in conversion?
How did you experience the scriptural prayer that was suggested in this chapter? How does dialogue with other search-
ers help in the conversion process? How willing are you to
continue the conversion process when nothing seems to be
happening? What is it you would need to maintain your
desire to change? What scriptural word or phrase is most
supportive to you when things are rough?

SECULAR FRANCISCAN RULE

6. They have been made living members of the Church by being buried and raised with Christ in baptism; they have been united more intimately with the Church by profession. Therefore, they should go forth as witnesses and instruments of her mission among all people, proclaiming Christ by their life and words.

   Called like St Francis to rebuild the Church and inspired by his example, let them devote themselves energetically to living in full communion with the Pope, Bishops and Priests, fostering an open and trusting dialogue of apostolic effectiveness and creativity.

7. United by their vocation as "brothers and sisters of penance" and motivated by the dynamic power of the gospel, let them conform their thoughts and deeds to those of Christ by means of that radical interior change which the gospel itself calls "conversion." Human frailty makes it necessary that this conversion be carried out daily.

   On this road to renewal the Sacrament of Penance is the privileged sign of the Father's mercy and the source of grace.

Rule – Chapter 2 #6-7

Commentary

The word "Church" occurs frequently in the Rule. It is a word with many meanings and bears exploration.

The Rule does not seem to be using the word "Church" to indicate a physical building. The Church can exist with or without a church building. Neither does the Rule use the term to describe the organizational structure of the Church. Structures and administrative procedures are helpful in guiding such a large group of people. But the church exists even if administrative structures disappear. We are invited to be in communion with leaders in the Church, but that is not the heart of the meaning of "Church."

The Church is "a people brought into unity from the unity of the Father, the Son and the Holy Spirit." (Lumen Gentium #4) These people believe in Jesus Christ. They work to proclaim the gospel in word and life. They work in union of mind and heart with pope, bishops and priests. This people proclaims that Jesus is Lord. The presence of these people in the world reminds others that God is with us. They are a "sacrament" proclaiming the love of Jesus. They are most clearly "church" as they fulfill the gospel and imitate Jesus. Jesus in turn, is the primary sign (sacrament) of God's love for us.

Faith in Jesus is a relational and personal thing. Faith focuses on the person of Jesus and our relationship to him. I choose to believe Jesus because of my personal relationship with him. The Church can exist without buildings or efficient structures. She cannot exist without Jesus and people who believe in Jesus.

The Rule invites us to "rebuild the church." That means we will bring people to know Jesus and follow his gospel. It means we support those who know Jesus so that they might grow in intimacy with him. It means that we give a clear example of what happens when people follow the gospel. It means we encourage intimacy with Jesus. It means we offer the gospel as an alternative way of life, with values that reflect the person of Jesus. It means we have hope and bring hope to others. It means we work to develop communion among people. It means that we create a Church known for its imitation of the words and life of Jesus. We rebuild the Church as we rebuild our own lives through daily conversion. We rebuild the church as we share life and possessions with all people. We rebuild the Church by removing any false ideas of church or actions that diminish the power of the gospel. We rebuild the church through actions of reconciliation and forgiveness of enemies. We rebuild the church through sharing gospel values with young people while we invite adults to be faithful to the gospel. Since human frailty makes our own conversion a daily affair, it shouldn't he surprising that rebuilding the Church will be a daily affair.

Such work of rebuilding is done everywhere. It happens in parishes and in parish groups. It happens in Franciscan fraternities and the halls of the Knights of Columbus. We will rebuild as we come to understand that relationships are more important than furnaces. We will be good stewards of material things, but never at the cost of good relationships in our community of faith. We will seek the truth that frees rather than gossip that binds people. We will acknowledge our own weakness and not be surprised to find it in others. We learn to listen rather than judge and to accept people rather than reject them. If you think this "rebuilding" is easy or ever finished, then you have not learned much about people, even those called the People of God.

Franciscan fraternities should support such rebuilding. We need to be the kind of community that deals realistically with the hard work of rebuilding the Church. Though we begin with ourselves, we can never limit ourselves to that. In fraternity life we will learn what it means to be hurt and how to forgive. We will learn how to deal with annoying people and still remain in communion with one another. We do not live some heavenly existence remote from human frailty. But the atmosphere of the fraternity should help us deal with reality realistically. Dialogue is not a way to dominate, but a way to listen and even disagree about issues. Many issues have various valid sides and opinions. We learn to respect different ideas about issues.

Conversion has two sides to it. It requires that we are aware of our weakness, sin and limitations. We need to see the obstacles in our lives that keep us from Jesus. If we are iron-fisted and rigid, we need to develop flexibility and openness. If we feed our minds with trash and are undisciplined, we need to cut out the trash and develop habits of discipline. When we see our faults, we need to invest the time, energy and reflection (alone and with others) that will help us change things.

Conversion also moves us TOWARD Jesus. We need to have a good sense of what a Christian looks like. We need the positive vision that stretches to new life. We will move from enmity to friendship; from non-involvement to real concern; from workaholism to playfulness; from a purely intellectual faith to a more total response to the Spirit. The process of conversion brings us to new places. We are not always comfortable there. We may be clumsy trying to change things in our lives. Virtue does not come magically with profession in the SFO.

The <u>desire</u> to change is important. It adds the power of strong motivation when the process of change is tough. As we move from personal slaveries to the promised land of responsiveness, we cross our own deserts. We need help on the way. If we are actually going to have a radical interior change, we need Jesus' help. People enter our lives to help us. Jesus helps us through our experiences. He touches us with the insight of his word. He allows both cross and resurrection to bring us to himself. This journey is a faith-in-Jesus journey. We are unable to persist without Jesus' gift of the Holy Spirit. It is impossible to go it alone!

The Sacrament of Reconciliation expresses God's desire to offer us forgiving love. The focus of the sacrament is God's love, not our sins. If we believe that our sins are bigger than God's forgiving love, we are heretics. God's interest in our sins is only to get rid of them so we can be free to be gospel people. God is not happy with our sin and unfaithfulness. But God wishes us life – and sin has no part with that.

> *Or do you think lightly of his wealth of kindness, of tolerance, and of patience, without recognizing that God's kindness is meant to lead you to a change of heart?*
> **Romans 2: 4**

Be well aware that responding to the call to conversion will reveal the darkness in us. Letting in the light of God's love disperses the shadows that hide sin and weakness. It is a good sign of growth to become more aware of our need for forgiveness. It means the light is growing stronger and things cannot be hidden from it. There are hundreds of ways in which we deceive ourselves and try to deceive others. God's love brings such deception to the light. Then we have a fair chance to deal with it and undergo the radical interior change known as conversion.

These scriptural texts may offer insights for you on this journey of conversion. Use them prayerfully.

Jonah	*Jeremiah 18: 1-6*	*Isaiah 43: 1-4*
Hosea 11: 1-9	*Isaiah 55: 1-13*	*2 Cor 5: 16-21*

FRANCISCAN FOCUS

The Christmas crib – Greccio

In 1223, St Francis contacted his good friend John who lived in Greccio. "I wish to do something that will recall the memory of the little child who was born in Bethlehem and set before our eyes, in some way, the inconveniences of his infant needs; how he lay in a manger; how with an ox and an ass standing by, he lay upon the hay where he had been placed." Francis gave John specific directions. John carried out his assignment to the letter.

On Christmas eve people came to the place with candles and torches. The night was lit with twinkling light. Francis was delighted with the surprise he had prepared. Simplicity and poverty were in evidence. The people sang as they came, filling the night with melody. Mass was celebrated and Francis served as deacon. He sang the gospel with delight. Then he preached about God's great love in becoming human and living on earth among us.

During the Mass, a man had a vision. He saw the child laying in the manger, lifeless. He saw Francis go to the manger and arouse the child. Then he took it in his arms and held it. The child was alive! The vision reflected reality. Francis gave the people a new sense of the reality of the presence of the living Christ.

What Francis and John created at Greccio has become a part of Christmas. Artists have designed beautiful statues for cribs around the world. Poets have written words of wonder while musicians sang songs about this silent night. What Francis wanted us to remember was the simplicity and poverty of God coming to us in a stable. God chose to accept our human limitations and give dignity to our human nature. Such unlimited love found expression in Francis' simple crib. We hope that our lives become the resting place of Jesus and make his presence felt.

QUESTIONS

1. Give your personal definition of FAITH. Reflect on what it means to you as well as what you want it to mean. Share your reflections.

2. The gospel is our way of life. What changes are happening in your life because you are responding to the gospel? Get in touch with the things that are different because you are taking the gospel seriously. If you can find nothing, reflect on the reasons for that.

3. What is most difficult/confusing for you as you try to apply the gospel to daily life? What problems does it cause? HOW do you show love in particular situations of everyday life? How are your business ethics? How do you deal with conflicts between justice and mercy, discipline and gentleness; sharing and privacy? Sharing these struggles can help to deal with them.

4. Who is Jesus for you? "Who do you say that I am?" is the question Jesus asked his disciples. Share your present relationship with and knowledge of Jesus.

5. Share some of the impressions you had as you spent time in prayer with the bible texts. Any new insights? feelings? experiences?

6. Define your understanding of "Church." Give a definition that makes sense to you.

7. What connection is there between "conversion" and the "Sacrament of reconciliation"? Address the issue from personal experience rather than intellectual explanations.

8. What happens when we bring our sinfulness and brokenness to the Lord in the sacrament of Reconciliation? Punishment? Instant conversion? Guilt? Nothing? Strength for the journey? Forgiveness? Experience of God's love? Try to give an answer from your experience of the Sacrament.

SCRIPTURE *reading/reflection:*

✝ Jonah – read the whole book

This book was written about 500 BC. The story is meant to teach us about ourselves and about God. Identify and share the events in Jonah's story that most resembles your story. Share what God reveals about God in this story. Share what God reveals about you in this story.

CHAPTER 6

FAITHFUL RESPONSE

We live in an age filled with problems. Crisis pop up with frightening regularity. Violence, drugs, crime, terrorist activity seem to be the common fare of everyday life. As violence escalates, the call for swift punishment sweeps across the land. Law and order become the battle cry of the day. An "eye for an eye" becomes the approach to justice. We use force as the key to control.

Sometimes it is the force of weapons of violence. At other times it is the more subtle force of economic pressures. In such an atmosphere of fear, we begin to rely on the power of force to create a livable world. But such dependence is bringing us to bankruptcy both economically and as human beings.

Franciscans cannot ignore this fear-filled world. Neither can we be drawn into believing that force alone can make this world a humane place to live. Francis of Assisi began his adult life as a soldier. But he wound up as someone who preached and lived the way of peace. The "force" that changed him was the force of God's love. He found it to be a power stronger than military weapons. He found it to be more powerful than economic progress. It was a power that countered much of what society preached. It seeks to share with others rather than accumulate for oneself. It looks to affirm people rather than take advantage of them. It looks for ways to create structures of cooperation rather than building individualistic empires to control others. The power of love seeks way to achieve reconciliation rather than create situations of confrontation.

But the power of love is not naive. It recognizes that destructive forces are at work in individuals and society. It understands that governments can use power to destroy and rob and oppress people. It realizes that individuals can use people for personal advantage. The power of love does not live in a pollyanna world that is out of touch with reality. Quite the contrary. Its clear-sightedness recognizes evil and its power.

But the power of love will not act like its enemies. In the face of violence, oppression and life-killing actions, the power of love stands firm for an alternate way of acting. It will be true to its conviction that the power of love is stronger than all the violent and death-dealing weapons that are brought against it. It believes that the human spirit, touched by the power of the Holy Spirit, can ultimately overcome the power of evil. The words of the gospel remain a source of power:

> To you who are my friends I say: Do not fear those who kill the body and after that have nothing more they can do. I will warn you who to fear; fear him who, after he has killed, has authority to cast into hell. Believe me, he is the one to fear.
>
> ... When you are brought before synagogues and state authorities, do not begin worrying about how you will conduct your defense or what you will say. For when the time comes the Holy Spirit will instruct you what to say.
> **Luke 12: 4-5 & 11-12**

The spirit of Gandhi, the non-violent prophet of India, is captured in his words. These words offer a sense of a Franciscan approach to dealing with the threat of force and violence.

> I will not coerce you. Neither will I be coerced by you. If you behave unjustly, I will not oppose you by violence but by the force of truth – the integrity of my beliefs. My integrity is evident in my willingness to suffer, to endanger myself, to go to prison, to die if necessary. But I will not cooperate with injustice. Seeing my intention, sensing my compassion and my openness to your needs, you will respond in ways I could never manage by threat, bargaining or body force. Together we can solve the problem. IT is our opponent, not each other!
> **Mahatma Gandhi**

When we reflect on the life of Jesus, we see him relying on the power of love. His consistent rhythm of prayer and action gave him the freedom to confront hypocrisy and human violence in all its forms. Convinced that his Father's way was the way to follow, he faithfully implemented it and accepted the consequences. His words, his actions, his attitudes flowed from his deep inner identity with the way of his Father. From that inner source of intimate relationship came the power of personal integrity. His words and actions matched each other. His convictions and his way of life reflected one another. Jesus was real, allowing the vision of his heart to find expression in the flesh of his life.

> *And so you are not to set your mind on food and drink; you are not to worry. For all these are things for the heathen to run after. But you have a Father who knows that you need them. No, set your mind upon his kingdom, and all the rest will come to you as well.*
> **Luke 12: 29-31**

Authority – Obedience

In the bible obedience and authority are connected. When God calls, obedience is our response. The foundation of obedience is our love of God. Love is at the heart of authority and obedience. For people who do not believe in the power of love, obedience and authority are used quite differently. Authority becomes a power to enforce obedience. Authority is used as a way to achieve one's own way without regard for the good of others. The Pharisees hypocritically presumed their own wisdom. They looked down on others. They used the authority of their office and their presumed wisdom as a battering ram to impose human laws as though they were God's laws. In family life, in communities, people can follow the same sort of pattern – using power to get their own way. Abandon the power of love and all sort of oppression develops.

Jesus did not see his Father's law as a problem. He saw the Pharisaical interpretation – laying burdens on people – as the problem. He saw the substitution of human rules for God's law as the problem. He saw it as blasphemous that such human law should be identified as God's law as the problem. He saw people subjected to law instead of being served by law as the problem. In such a situation, Jesus was blunt in his condemnation.

Alas, alas for you, lawyers and Pharisees, hypocrites that you are! You shut the door of the kingdom of heaven in men's faces; you do not enter yourselves, and when others are entering, you stop them!

Alas for you, lawyers and Pharisees, hypocrites! You clean the outside of cup and dish, which you have filled inside by robbery and self-indulgence! Blind Pharisee! Clean the inside of the cup first; then the outside will be clean also.

Alas for you lawyers and Pharisees, hypocrites! You are like tombs covered with whitewash; they look well from outside, but inside they are full of dead men's bones and all kinds of filth. So it is with you; outside you look like honest men, but inside you are brimful of hypocrisy and crime.

Matthew 23: 13 & 25-28

Jesus clearly confronts the hypocrisy of mis-used authority. Read in isolation, this condemnation is a frightening side of Jesus' love. In another place in Matthew we find these words that reveal another side of the heart of Jesus:

O Jerusalem, Jerusalem, the city that murders the prophets and stones the messengers sent to her. HOW OFTEN HAVE I LONGED TO GATHER YOUR CHILDREN, as a hen gathers her brood under her wings; BUT YOU WOULD NOT LET ME.

Matthew 12: 37

The sadness of rejected love speaks loudly in these words. Yet Jesus would not condemn without holding out hope that he still loves these hypocrites. Despite their actions, Jesus longs to draw them to himself. The power of such love brings much pain when it is resisted. "How often have I longed to gather your children ..." The example of Jesus offers a model for those in authority. The self-styled authority of the Pharisees offers a use of authority that Jesus condemns. For Jesus, authority calls for service of all. The Rule for Secular Franciscans puts it well:

*Their service ... is marked by a ready and willing spirit
and is a duty of responsibility to each member and to the
community.*

Rule – Chapter 3 #21

What is difficult for those in authority is not the general understanding of service. What is difficult is to know HOW to serve in a particular situation. We are faced again with the vital need of the wisdom of the Holy Spirit. For example: What is the best way for parents to treat children who are on drugs? What is the best way for spouses to deal with infidelity? What is the best way to deal with fraternity members who always disrupt community life? What is the best way to confront the mis-use of authority? How can I confront a parish that is prejudiced? How can I deal with an employer who allows unsafe working conditions? How can I love myself when I have acted in destructive ways? How can I confront a government that is oppressive? How can I deal with a clinic that performs abortions?

None of us live in a nice world filled with saints who do everything right. Instead we live in a very imperfect world and we are trying to follow the gospel there. We need not seek the cross. Our attempt to be gospel-people in a very imperfect world, among very imperfect people (including ourselves), offers plenty of room for suffering.

Jesus' relationship with his Father is the source of his power to love. As Jesus grew, this relationship gave vitality and strength to his humanity. He cultivated the relationship – with prayer in deserts, on mountains, before miracles, in a quiet garden. Jesus "listened to" (Obedience) his Father and identified with the Father. Jesus' identity was linked to that relationship. Separated from the Father he would be nothing, no one, a nobody.

In the garden of Gethsemane, Jesus struggled with obedience to this Father. His enemies were gathering for the kill. He recognized the signs and could imagine the outcome. It was frightening! His whole person rejected the notion of pain and death at the hands of the Romans. Yet, he sensed that this way may be part of his Father's will. To reject it would be to destroy a relationship that gave him identity. Both sides of his heart had a legitimate call on his decision. He struggled with it, bled with it, agonized with it, prayed with it. But in the end, remaining intimate with his Father tipped the scales. To refuse the Father would be to lose his very self. So the choice is made – "Not my will, but yours be done." The struggle finished, Jesus is calm. For the rest of the passion, notice his peacefulness. There was still pain. He still experienced loneliness on the cross, feeling abandoned by the Father – yet "Into your hands I commend my spirit."

> For the divine nature was his from the first; yet he did not think to snatch at equality with God, but made himself nothing, assuming the nature of a slave. Bearing the human likeness, revealed in human shape, he humbled himself, and in obedience accepted even death – death on a cross. Therefore God raised him to the heights and bestowed on him the name above all names, that at the name of Jesus every knee should bow – in heaven, on earth and in the depths – and every tongue confess: "Jesus Christ is Lord," to the glory of God the Father.
>
> **Philippians 2: 6-11**

St Francis understood God's "bottom line". It is obedience to the authority of the Father made known through Jesus. This is the source of the power of obedience. It can withstand oppression and domination because it is given freely. It overcomes fear because it offers the guidance of a God who loves us. It springs from a sense of identity with the Father. From such intimacy we grow in a sense of trust that the Father will ask only for things that bring life. Even when we don't understand, we trust the call of this Father.

> So Jesus cried aloud: "When a man believes in me he believes in him who sent me rather than in me; seeing me, he sees him who sent me. I have come into the world as light, so that no one who has faith in me should remain in darkness. But if anyone hears my words and pays no regard to them, I am not his judge; I have not come to judge the world. There is a judge for the man who rejects me and does not accept my words; the word that I spoke will be his judge on the last day. I do not speak on my own authority, but the Father who sent me has himself commanded me what to say and how to speak. I know

114

If we accept such ideas of authority and obedience, we face the task of
DOING something about it. Our world often uses force to get what it
wants. Countries use torture to get information from people. Authority
is used to punish people. We even use the power of silence to punish
people who hurt us. Guilt puts people in a straitjacket and can be used
as a way of control. Fear and threats can be used by those in power to
keep people in line. False information can prolong injustice. Authority
can be used as an excuse to avoid change – "I'm the boss and my way
is right!" The stories of the misuse of authority or irresponsible obedience only prove the reality of human foibles and imperfection.

Responsible freedom will use authority wisely – requiring the things
that are life-giving. Responsible freedom will obey wisely – recognizing
the call to embrace life. Coercion and freedom cannot sleep together.
When authority springs from love, even confrontation becomes a tool
for growth rather than a "gotcha" attitude.

We will struggle to implement such ideas of authority and obedience.
Pat answers are not often at hand. We learn as we go. Sometimes our
insecurity makes us dogmatic. We are afraid we'll lose control if we
allow for freedom. Sometimes our desire for power and control makes
us indifferent to the needs of others. We become little gods who always
know best. These and many other struggles will be part of everyday
life. As always, conversion will require change in many of our attitudes.
It might seem easier to withdraw from life and the struggle. But
Franciscans do not accept such an option.

> *After washing their feet and taking his garments again,
> he sat down. "Do you understand what I have done for
> you?" he asked. "You call me 'Master' and 'Lord', and
> rightly so, for that is what I am. Then if I, your Lord and
> Master, have washed your feet, you also ought to wash
> one another's feet. I have set you an example; you are to
> do as I have done for you. In very truth I tell you, a
> servant is not greater than his master, nor a messenger*

than the one who sent him. IF YOU KNOW THIS,
HAPPY ARE YOU IF YOU ACT UPON IT!"
John 13: 12-17

The final "bottom line" of love is surrender. Life itself is handed over to God. That free decision (made frequently), gives God free reign in our lives. Such an action is difficult to take. So we do it a piece at a time. It is not easy to always believe. It is not easy to always follow the gospel when we are being mocked as naive and stupid. It is not easy when our own heart is uncertain of the way to go. It is not easy when we get deserts instead of promised lands. What kind of God is this anyway?

Jesus, on the cross, reminds us that this is not some cheap way to happiness. The struggle is not the end of the story nor is dying to self the finish of living. As we choose again to surrender to God we experience the cost involved. We also experience the reward that God gives to faithful people.

> *"Anyone who loves me will heed what I say; then my*
> *Father will love him, and we will come to him and make*
> *our dwelling with him. ... but your Advocate, the Holy*
> *Spirit whom the Father will send in my name, will teach*
> *you everything and will call to mind all that I have told*
> *you."*
> **John 14: 23 & 26**

St Paul experienced both the price of faithfulness and the fulfillment of faithful love. His life-experience brought him to rely on Jesus and the God who sent him:

> *But, in the words of Scripture: "Things beyond our*
> *seeing, things beyond our hearing, things beyond our*
> *imagining, all prepared by God for those who love him",*
> *these it is that God has revealed to us through the Spirit.*
> **1 Corinthians 2: 9-10**

When true love is linked to authority it creates a climate for growth. When authority is used in a loving way, it allows lives to blossom. Loving authority is a servant, intent on creating the atmosphere for life and light. Loving authority dialogues with opponents to discover the truth. Loving obedience supports such authority and enables it to fulfill its role. Loving obedience is respectful of responsible authority, for authority and obedience become partners to give life to one another. St Paul's description of love might well be understood as a description both of authority and obedience.

> *Love is patient; love is kind and envies no one. Love is*
> *never boastful, nor conceited, nor rude; never selfish, not*
> *quick to take offense. Love keeps no score of wrongs; does*
> *not gloat over other men's sins, but delights in the truth.*
> *There is nothing love cannot face; there is no limit to its*
> *faith, its hope and its endurance.*
> **1 Corinthians 13: 4-7**

As those in authority and those who are called to obey listen to one another the presence of Jesus is manifest. If authority calls for something contrary to the gospel, obedience will require questioning such decisions. If authorities and obeyers work together, living the gospel can be enhanced. No one person has total wisdom. Having authority does not invest anyone with instant perfection and perception. But neither do the people on the street receive instant perfection or perception. Working together much can be accomplished. Being antagonistic to one another creates a stalemate that limits growth in gospel living. Gospel use of authority and gospel response of obedience demands surrender. Surrender does not come easily to any of us.

Franciscan Authority – Obedience

Within the Franciscan Order we face the need to deal with the roles of authority and obedience. Structures in any organization are meant to nurture and nourish the organization. Since times and needs change, structure will need regular evaluation. When some element of structure hinders growth and development, change is called for. In the SFO the structures must be treated in like manner. They are meant to serve the nurturing and nourishing of Franciscan life. When they cease to accomplish that task they need to be adjusted and/or changed.

At the local level of SFO life is the LOCAL FRATERNITY. It is the grass-roots structure of the SFO. It is composed of the Secular Franciscans from a particular area who come together regularly for support, prayer, socializing, sharing and ministry. The RULE puts it this way:

> *The local fraternity is to be established canonically. It becomes the basic unit of the whole Order and a visible sign of the Church, the community of love. This should be the privileged place for developing a sense of Church and the Franciscan vocation and for enlivening the apostolic life of its members.*
>
> **Rule – Chapter 3 #22**

A number of things are required of the local fraternity:

1. It is established canonically – i.e. in accord with the applicable canons of Canon Law.

2. It is meant to make present the community of love known as "Church".

3. It should help people develop a good sense of what it means to "be Church".

4. It should nourish and nurture the Franciscan vocation of its members.

5. It should help people develop solid apostolic ministry and outreach to others.

The Secular Franciscans who govern the local fraternity are known as the COUNCIL. Elected by the professed members, they are to create the atmosphere that allows the fraternity to grow. The Council handles administrative details of fraternity life. A number of points in the Rule and the Constitutions spell out these responsibilities. The Council is accountable to the fraternity for its administration.

The Rule provides for similar COUNCILS on a regional, provincial, national and international level. In each case SFO members are elected to work together at the various levels. At each level the SFO is joined with members of the other branches of the Franciscan Order. The role of these various Councils is described in their Rule:

To promote fidelity to the charism as well as observance
of the Rule, and to receive greater support in the life of
the fraternity, the minister or president, with the con-
sent of the council, should take care to ask for a regular
pastoral visit by competent religious superiors as well
as for a fraternal visit from higher fraternities (Coun-
cils), according to the norm of the Constitutions.
Rule – Chapter 3 #26

An open interchange between the Councils at various levels allows for clear communication. It provides a place to share ideas from the wider Franciscan community, regionally and worldwide. In addition, these councils offer a channel of communication with authorities in the Church.

The "fraternal visit" (Visitation) of local fraternities provides an opportunity for helping the growth of the local fraternity. It gives assurance that the charism of Francis is being taught and lived. The Visitor can also help clarify issues and assist in dealing with problems. Clearly, both Visitor and local Council have one goal – to strengthen and enliven Franciscan life. The wise use of the Visitation can help a local fraternity bear clearer witness to the gospel life.

Reflection

Council members are servants of the fraternity. They have the authority and responsibility for the functioning of the fraternity. Responsible use of such authority requires that they involve fraternity members in the work of fraternity life. They should invite participation and keep everyone informed. A good use of committees will help the council deal with particular issues and ministries.

Formation is important and council members need to be involved. Good meetings are important and Council members need to involve the membership. Programs for ministry are important and the Council needs the input of the membership. A good Council will work WITH all the members to strengthen fraternity life.

It is important to know both the gifts and limitations of people in the SFO. Opportunities for learning should be provided. Opportunity for ministry should be available. Sharing faith experiences strengthens the bond between members. It also offers a variety of ways to practice the faith. Sharing ministry experiences or discussing common problems can help fraternity growth. Special care of the sick and homebound is a Franciscan trait. Encouraging participation in parish and diocesan programs is part of our Franciscan calling. Wherever we are, we find the ways to "rebuild the church" in that place.

> *You must live at peace among yourselves. And we would urge you, brothers (sisters), to admonish the careless, encourage the faint-hearted, support the weak, and to be vary patient with them all.*
>
> *Be always joyful; pray continually; give thanks whatever happens; for this is what God in Christ wills for you.*
> **1 Thessalonians 5: 14 & 16-18**

Reflection Questions

How do you use your authority? How do you feel when you are treated without respect? What attitudes of yours strangle your sense of fairness? What role do you think authority has in society? In home life? In the Church? In organizations? What contribution does loving obedience make in your life? Does obedience remove personal responsibility for decisions? Explain! What do you think is the source of Jesus' willingness to obey his Father? What has intimacy to do with obedience? In your opinion, when must authority be challenged? Why? In your opinion, what role does love play in authority and obedience? How firm is your belief in the power of Jesus? When you see the power of evil and violence in our world, how firm is your belief in the power of Jesus? In your daily life, how much do you rely on the power of the Holy Spirit to guide you? How would you explain Jesus' willingness to accept death? What changes of attitude or ideas will you make after reading this chapter? Why?

SECULAR FRANCISCAN RULE

2. As Jesus was the true worshiper of the Father, so let prayer and contemplation be the soul of all they are and do.

Let them participate in the sacramental life of the Church, above all the Eucharist. Let them join in liturgical prayer in one of the forms proposed by the Church, reliving the mysteries of the life of Christ.

Rule – Chapter 2: #2

Jesus prayed. He spent nights in prayer with his Father. He prayed before he healed people. Sometimes he praised the Father. At other times he pleaded with his Father to take the cup of pain away. Prayer was as much a part of the rhythm of Jesus' life as was his preaching and healing. Real love seeks time with the beloved.

Faith in Jesus means a relationship leading to intimacy. As faith grows, our desire to "be with" the Beloved (Jesus) will grow. Intimate moments with Jesus change us because real faith has consequences. We struggle to love our neighbor and our enemy, because we believe. We struggle for justice for all people, because we believe. We try to show compassion and forgiveness to others, because we believe. We design ways of proclaiming the gospel, because we believe. We acknowledge brokenness and trust the healing power of the Holy Spirit, because we believe. We believe in Jesus Christ and recognize our need for him.

Francis was impressed by God's willingness to become human. Jesus reveals a passionate God, willing to take flesh and live among us. Jesus reveals everything he received from the Father. Jesus embraced the cross and took love to its extreme to convince us of God's love. The more Francis read the gospel, the more amazed he was at God's love made visible in Jesus. When he prayed and came close to Jesus, it brought consequences that Francis willingly embraced. It was like a contest of lovers. If God, through Jesus, does so much for me, I want to do everything I can to respond. One of the "things" is to "let prayer and contemplation be the soul of all they do and are!" (Rule #2)

Gospel living is a call from God. Jesus is the source of that call, planting the desire in the heart of Francis. Prayer is the teacher that affirms the call and desire. Prayer calls us to compassion as God shows compassion. Prayer brings intimacy with Jesus and moves us to intimacy with neighbor. Prayer gives the insight that recognizes our need for God. Contemplative prayer brings us to the surrender that gives God perfect freedom during our prayer. Communing with Jesus faithfully and consistently, brings us to be a new creation.

> *Rise up, my Darling; my fairest, come away. For now the winter is past, the rains are over and gone; the flowers appear in the countryside; the time is coming when the birds will sing, and the turtle-dove's cooing will be heard in our land; when the green figs will ripen on the fig-trees and the vine give forth their fragrance. Rise up, my Darling; my fairest, come away.*
> **Song of Songs 2: 10-13**

Eucharist

The Eucharist is a sign that Jesus is with us. We are not alone or abandoned. Jesus is here – signed with the symbols of life and celebration – bread and wine, the staples of life and joy. The symbols are not simply memory helps. Jesus is present. Eucharist shouts that we are meant to be one people, in communion with one another through Jesus. Jesus remains with us because we have not yet achieved the vision. Jesus is present because we need him. Jesus reminds us again and again that we need him to achieve communion with one another. Jesus cannot let us forget his promises and his desire for unity with us.

> *"... May they all be one; As you Father, are in me, and I in you, so also may they be in us, that the world may believe that you sent me. The glory which you gave me*

I have given to them, that they may be one, as we are
one; I in them and you in me, may they be perfectly one."
John 17: 21-22

Eucharist is not simply a ritual from 2000 years ago. It is not simply a connection with a long gone past. Eucharist is a "today" presence for us. It proclaims the same call for unity and communion it always has. What Jesus prays for is still God's will for his people. The Spirit is present not only to transform bread and wine but to transform people as well. The Holy Spirit seeks unity among all people. Such a vision is not yet real, so that dimension of Eucharist is always incomplete. It is like a constant proclamation of the work we still have to do. We are not one. We are not united. We still reject some people. Tax collectors and lepers of our time are still unwelcome. We do not always forgive our enemies nor bless those who curse us. The scriptural word needs to be heard again and again and again – because many of us have still not heard it and done it. The Eucharist, from this perspective, struggles for completion among us. Until the kiss of peace embraces all people, we are not what we are called to be. Eucharist both reminds us and enables us to do more.

Some people say that our attendance at Eucharist is hypocritical if we are not really united. Lots of sinners, big and small, come to Eucharist. The dishonest and unforgiving come to Eucharist. The sex offenders and robbers come to Eucharist. The oppressors and violent come to Eucharist. The child-beaters and spouse abusers come to Eucharist. The liars and gossips come to Eucharist. The drug addicts and drunks come to Eucharist. The strugglers and incompetent come to Eucharist. Good people and honest people come to Eucharist. Loving families and faithful spouses come to Eucharist. Dedicated justice-seekers and pro- claimers of the Word come to Eucharist. Compassionate people and forgiving people come to Eucharist. In short, it is a motley array of folks who gather around the altar. Not all of them love each other. Some are there under duress. Some come because of guilt. Some come to praise God. Some come because they want to avoid hell. Some come because they need nourishment for the journey.

I suppose such people are a bit hypocritical. That seems to me to be part of the human condition. But Eucharist, if they let it, will challenge their hypocrisy. Perhaps it is precisely because we are hypocritical and know it that we come. We need help – and we won't get it by staying away. Instead, we discover how much we need conversion in order to come to unity with all these folks. It's hard to stay on the "bus" with all of "them" sitting there. Such a challenge is common to our Eucharistic experience. If we listen to the Word-proclaimed, we can't stay in disarray. The scripture will regularly call us to change.

Consider our human reality in the light of the Eucharist. We hear the gospel call to reconciliation and we escalate the arms race. The gospel calls for forgiveness and we seek revenge. The gospel calls for stewardship and care for the earth, and we pollute our environment. The gospel calls us to peace and we refuse to drop our weapons. The gospel calls us to gather in unity and prejudice keeps us apart. Our fear of crime and violence and change keep us paralyzed even as the gospel calls for the development of the tools of trust.

Eucharist is a dangerous place. God's word speaks loudly and confronts us with God's vision for living. It is attractive. But it is not easy to stick with a vision that is opposed by such powerful forces.

The Eucharist keeps reminding us of the constancy of God's love for us. Throughout history people have tried to block out the memory of Jesus. Throughout history they have failed. The words and actions of Jesus remain. The Eucharist offers the challenge of the presence of Jesus among us. The liturgy of word and sacrament blend to convince us that God's power is at work in our world. The implications for our world and our lives are unending. The Eucharist says that even life itself must be given up to create the kingdom of God. The call to commitment is total. Our response is not – and we will return again and again to improve the quality of our response.

We cannot do it alone. Eucharist tells us that. We NEED Jesus and the power of his Spirit. In no way can we face the power of evil by ourselves. We are unable even to deal with the evil in ourselves by ourselves. We need Jesus. That is a fact of life. Eucharist, Jesus' presence, reminds us of our need to learn (from the word) and be nourished (by the person of Jesus).

> *I am the real vine, and my Father is the gardener. Every*
> *barren branch of mine he cuts away; and every fruiting*

branch he cleans, to make it more fruitful still. You have
already been cleansed by the word that I spoke to you.
Dwell in me, as I in you. No branch can bear fruit by
itself, but only if it remains united with the vine; no more
can you bear fruit, unless you remain united with me!

I am the vine, and you are the branches. He who dwells
in me, as I dwell in him, bears much fruit; for apart from
me you can do nothing.
John 15: 1-5

Looking at Eucharist from another perspective, we see it as a celebration of our vision of faith. We come together as a community to remember that Jesus is risen. God is present in this community through the Holy Spirit. The Holy Spirit unites us to one another. Little by little we discover the unity that is already given. In Eucharist we celebrate the wonder of this belief. God's gracious gift brings us together as one people. Our common fellowship with Jesus draws us into fellowship with one another. The consequences of that belief are very demanding.

God gives us the gifts of the Holy Spirit:

But the harvest of the Spirit is love, joy, peace, patience,
kindness, goodness, fidelity, gentleness, and self-con-
trol. There is no law dealing with such things as these.
... If the Spirit is the source of our life, let the Spirit also
direct our course.
Galatians 5: 22-23 & 25

These gifts are to be used in daily life. If they go unused, we make a mockery of Eucharist and God's gifts. If they are not used, our Eucharistic celebrations become dry and dull, untouched by joy. If they are not used, many people remain in a state of self-hatred, unaffirmed by a loving community. If they are not used, self-indulgence goes unchecked and brings death because the self-control that brings life is un-developed. While the Eucharist cries "Unity", if we have no patience, gentleness or kindness, we remain separate and isolated from one another. Eucharist is a powerful and dangerous action for people who wish to remain uncommitted.

But Eucharist remains for us. Jesus is not driven to abandon us by our stupidity and stubbornness. Quite the opposite. He continues to draw us hypocrites to himself to empower us to change. He never gives up hope for our conversion. He chooses not to leave us to our own devices. He speaks his word again and again until we hear and do it. He nourishes us with his presence so that we feel strong enough to tackle our personal and community problems. The Eucharist tells us that God is faithful. The gathering of the community says that God is present among us. Little by little we come to understand that the cornerstone for building God's temple is Jesus. Little by little we realize that the presence and power of Jesus is what enables us to build the kingdom of God. Little by little we discover that, in the long run, the power of Love cannot be defeated. Building our own lives on the solid rock that is Jesus, we CAN build the Kingdom of God in our world.

How great is the need for the Eucharistic community! The world longs for such unconditional love that confronts only in order to enliven. It (and we) need a love that forgives rather than condemns. We and the world need a love that looks beyond color and race and sex and nationality to the heart of a human person. We and the world need a love that will not give up on us. The Eucharist says that such a love exists and dwells among us. The Eucharist says that the community gathered around the table will try to live such love. That is an exciting vision. Giving it flesh in our lives, it will create a better world for all people.

Personal Prayer

In a later chapter I want to share ideas on prayer. For the purposes of the Rule's call to prayer, allow me a few words.

Prayer and contemplation are vital ingredients in the life of a Franciscan. Nothing can replace them. They support and demand the actions of love. Prayer is our means of communicating with Jesus. Communication can take place in many ways.

We communicate through words, so common vocal prayer can communicate with Jesus. We communicate with gestures and bodily expressions, so dance and bodily movements can communicate with

Jesus. We communicate through presence to one another in the silence of togetherness. So silence can be a way of communicating with Jesus. We communicate through the ministry of music and song. So songs and music can be our prayer. We communicate by knowing how to listen to the heart of another. Prayer will find us listening to Jesus. We communicate through the expression of our feelings, negative and positive. We will communicate with Jesus by sharing our feelings, negative and positive. Quite frankly, the ways of communication are limited only by our imagination's limitations. So too, with prayer. Each of us will find the way that fits life on any given day.

As friendships deepen, we find that words become clumsy in expressing what our heart feels. We write poetry or music to express what sentences cannot say. A hug can communicate more than a paragraph of words. As intimacy grows presence is enough without the need of words. Being with a friend brings a deep communication that is hard to describe. Our sensitivity to the friend helps us understand and respond to the friend even without words. Contemplative presence draws such friends to a unity that reflects the oneness of God. To lose such a beloved friend would be to lose oneself. Whatever would separate such friends must be surrendered. Taken into such friendship we can only babble when we try to describe it. It is beyond words – it is union. I believe this is the real goal of prayer – union with the beloved.

Experience tells me that we move up and down through the levels of prayer. Sometimes the quiet glimpse of union is followed by the need to recite the psalms in vocal prayer. Tragedy can move us to mournful intercession and anger only to be followed by a quiet peace of acceptance. God is forever faithful in seeking us. God initiates in us the desire for prayerful union. God walks with us through all our struggles with prayer. We will need to be as patient with ourselves as God is with us. Gentle, persistent and faithful attempts at prayer will bring us to union with Jesus.

> *Then put on the garments that suit God's chosen people, his own, his beloved; compassion, kindness, humility, gentleness, patience. Be forbearing with one another and forgiving, where any of you has cause for complaint; you must forgive as the Lord forgave you. To crown all, there must be love, to bind all together and complete the whole.*

Let Christ's peace be arbiter in your hearts; to this peace you were called as members of a single body. And be filled with gratitude. Let the message of Christ dwell among you in all its richness. Instruct and admonish each other with utmost wisdom. Sing thankfully in your hearts to God, with psalms and hymns and spiritual songs. Whatever you are doing, whether you speak or act, do everything in the name of the Lord Jesus, giving thanks to God the Father through him.

Colossians 3: 12-17

FRANCISCAN FOCUS

St Francis and the wolf of Gubbio

The Little Flowers of St Francis contain many legends about Francis. Among them is the story of the wolf of Gubbio. This story may be just a story. But it is a story with a message. Some writers believe that the wolf in the story was actually a rather "terrorist" robber known as "Lupo" (wolf). He had terrorized the town of Gubbio. Francis converted "Lupo" by challenging him to change. On La Verna there is a rock outcropping where the converted Lupo is supposed to have spent much time in penance and prayer. This story can speak to the "wolfs" in our lives. Our stories of fear and timidity find an echo in this story of the Wolf of Gubbio.

✛ ✛ ✛ ✛ ✛ ✛ ✛ ✛

Once upon a time a large wolf terrorized the town of Gubbio. It was so hungry that it killed not only animals but little children as well. Those who tried to kill or capture the wolf were themselves killed by him. People feared to venture outside the walls out of fear for the wolf.

When Francis came to Gubbio, the people told him about the wolf. Francis decided to go out and meet "brother" wolf. Some townspeople went part way with him. They turned back when they saw the wolf. From the safety of the city walls they watched to see what would happen.

The wolf bounded toward Francis, eager for a good meal. Francis was unimpressed. He simply made a sign of the cross in the direction of the wolf. The wolf slowed down, closed his mouth, and looked puzzled. Then Francis called out: "Brother Wolf, come to me! In the name of Christ I order you not to hurt me or anyone else." At these words the wolf approached Francis and lay quietly at his feet.

St Francis proceeded to lecture the wolf for his misdeeds, especially for killing people. "But now you can make peace so that both you and they can live decent lives." The wolf nodded his assent. Francis persuaded the people to furnish the wolf with food. The wolf, in turn, promised not to hurt anyone. To confirm the pact the wolf followed Francis into town where a crowd had gathered.

St Francis used the occasion to preach to the people. Though this one animal had terrorized them, they should fear the greater evil of sin and listen to the words of the Lord. "Dear people, come back to the Lord and do fitting penance. Then God will free you from the wolf in this world and from the devouring fire of hell in the next world."

The wolf lived two years after this incident. Both the people and the wolf kept the pact they had made. When the wolf died, the people were sorry because its presence reminded them of the kindness and goodness of St Francis.

Reflection

The power of God is able to deal with our fears. In the name of Jesus we can overcome fear and establish new relationships. This simple story illustrates the power that faith has. The presence of faith can turn fearful situations around and bring peace.

QUESTIONS

1. What do YOU consider to be the most powerful force in this world? Give reasons to support your answer.

2. Share reasons/scripture texts that show how Jesus felt about his Father. What does this illustrate for you as you develop a relationship with Jesus?

3. What is the biggest obstacle to loving obedience? Try to avoid abstractions, share YOUR biggest obstacle to loving obedience!

4. Write a paragraph describing your ideas on the role of authority and obedience in the SFO. E.g. Why is it important? What does it accomplish? What atmosphere does it create? How does it help spiritual growth? What does it require of you and me? What would the SFO look like without it?

5. What is the goal/purpose of the local fraternity? Do a critique of the your fraternity: Is this purpose being fulfilled in your fraternity? What are the pluses and minuses of your fraternity in fulfilling its role? How could it be improved? What can you do to help improve it? What is the atmosphere like at fraternity meetings?

6. Who is responsible for the growth and development of the fraternity? What are the duties of individual fraternity members in relation to the fraternity and its life?

7. Compare your ideas on Eucharist with those expressed in the commentary on the Rule. What new things have you learned about Eucharist from this chapter? Why do you think the Eucharist is important for our gospel life?

8. Please give your definition of prayer. Using that definition, evaluate your own prayer life. How well does your prayer accomplish the goal of union with Jesus? Reflect on how it might be improved.

9. What forms of prayer are most comfortable for you? Why do you feel good about that form(s)? Do you ever sense a call to another form of prayer? If so, what do you do about it?

10. How consistent are you at taking time to pray? Do you pray regularly? Sporadically? Not at all? Only during crisis? With others? How could you improve your prayerfulness?

SCRIPTURE reading/reflection

+ Philippians 2: 1-11
  St Paul's words spring from his heart. The Spirit of Jesus prompts us to come "alive" to one another. Jesus calls us to serve one another in love. This is the way Jesus acted. WRITE OUT the impressions this text makes on your heart. Did it call for conversion? Were you aware of a call to service of neighbor? Other? Share the feelings you had as you prayerfully read this text.

Graphic by Michael Gaffney, Capuchin

CHAPTER 7

MAMA MIA!

People talk a great deal about "The Church". Since Vatican II our ideas of church have grown. As a good beginning for this chapter, I invite you to take some reflective time to examine your "church" ideas. Some may be solid. Others may be inadequate or even inaccurate in defining "church". Here is a suggested process for your reflection:

1. Through reflection and writing, be aware of your present definition(s) of church and where you got them.

2. Open yourself to additional or new ideas you have heard about "church" and see how they might expand your vision.

3. Write out your present ideas before reading this chapter.

4. After reading the chapter, see if you wish to change any of your ideas.

Our goal in this chapter is to look at various ideas of Church.

Vatican II

The DOGMATIC CONSTITUTION ON THE CHURCH (Lumen Gentium) is the document on the Church from Vatican II.

Scripturally, this document speaks of biblical images of Church. The Church is a flock – with Jesus as shepherd. The Church is a tract of land to be cultivated – with roots in the prophets and patriarchs. The Church is the temple of God built by Jesus. Jesus is the cornerstone of the Church on which "living stones" are built. The Church is the "Jerusalem which is above" and is also described as "our mother". The Church is the "body of Christ" present in the world. The Church is the new people of God, covenanted to the Father by Jesus through the work of the Holy Spirit. The Church is the "sacrament" of the presence of Jesus in our world.

Just as Christ carried out the work of redemption in poverty and oppression, so the Church is called to follow the same path if she is to communicate the fruits of salvation to men. Christ Jesus, "though he was by nature God ... emptied himself, taking the nature of a slave" (Phil 2:6-7), and "being rich, became poor" (2 Cor 8: 9) for our sake. Likewise, the Church, although she needs human resources to carry out her mission, is not set up to seek earthly glory, but to proclaim, and this by her own example, humility and self-denial. Christ was sent by the Father "to bring good news to the poor ... to heal the contrite of heart" (Luke 4: 18), "to seek and to save what was lost" (Luke 19: 10). Similarly the Church encompasses with her love all those who are afflicted by human misery and she recognizes, in those who are poor and who suffer, the image of her poor and suffering founder. She does all in her power to relieve their need and in them she strives to serve Christ. Christ, "holy, innocent and undefiled" (Heb 7:26) knew nothing of sin (2 Cor 5:21) but came only to expiate the sins of the people (Heb 2: 17). The Church, however, clasping sinners to her bosom, at once holy and always in need of purification, follows constantly the path of penance and renewal.

Lumen Gentium – #8

Looking Back

Our understanding of "Church" has many sources and our experience of Church is not a monolithic one. We have been influenced by a variety of people, books, experiences and attitudes. Some people taught us that the church is like a pyramid. The Pope is at the high point of the pyramid, supported by bishops and priests. At the base of the pyramid are the laity whose task is to listen and follow the instructions given by those above them. The authority of the Pope was unassailable. He is infallible and through him God filtered the truth to the rest of us.

The consequences of this understanding of church were many. It was dangerous to question anything the Pope said. Infallibility seemed to extend to any words he spoke. It was presumptuous to study too much doctrine lest we start to act like we knew better than the Pope. Bishops and priests were simply to implement directives from Rome. Any tampering was considered next to heresy. Our role was to listen and obey. In many ways, we were discouraged from thinking for ourselves or taking responsibility for what we believed. That was all taken care of by listening to the Pope.

Such simple, accepting faith has a certain beauty to it. Many truly holy people lived with such direct, simple faith and did marvelous things for others. Perhaps the pioneer days of our own country did not allow for more than this. The struggle for survival, for building home and family, was enough to fill peoples' time. There was little time for the pursuit of theological ideas or to question the implications of Church teachings. Simple acceptance was the rule. No one thought there was anything wrong with it.

Perhaps the disservice in this kind of atmosphere was accepting this one perspective as the ONLY perspective of faith. The pyramidal idea is not wrong, only incomplete. It is not the ONLY way of defining the role of authority. Other ideas, equally valid, are also taught by the Church. A look at some other ideas might offer a fresh look at "Church".

The Church is a SERVANT. Jesus spoke often of this quality. He suggested to his followers that they were not to act like lords, but rather be servants to others.

> But he said: "In the world, kings lord it over their subjects; and those in authority are called their country's 'Benefactors.' Not so with you. On the contrary, the highest among you must bear himself like the youngest, the chief of you like a servant."
> **Luke 22: 25-26**

A servant-church is present to the poor when they cry for help. She goes where the sick need to be cared for. She is the one who demands justice in the face of oppression. The servant-church will wander the streets of the world bringing the hopeful message of Jesus. She will meet the educational needs of children and adults. She will serve the newly-married as well as those who are separated and divorced. She will seek to serve single people and those who are lonely. As servant-church she will serve the needs of priests and religious.

Anything that keeps people from being able to live a human life will be addressed by the servant-Church. She will work for a just system of economics as well as just prison and correctional institutions. She will walk among gangs and neighborhoods filled with fear. She will strive to make authority work for the benefit of all people, especially those who have no voice in the halls of power. Such a role of servant brings persecution and resistance. It has always done so. But the Church IS servant and she will accept the consequences thereof.

The Church serves people in many ways. She has built hospitals and orphanages, developed large educational systems as well as hospices for the dying and homes for AIDS patients. Our history proclaims that we understand what it means to be servant to people in the name of Jesus.

The Church is INSTITUTION. The large number of people who belong to "church" need an organizational dimension. Without solid organization, much confusion and chaos would result in this worldwide organization. There is need for direction for relationships within the Church. There is need for law and people to interpret the law. There is need for people to change the law(s) to meet changing situations. There is need for someone to speak to the world on behalf of the Church.

Organization and structure are human needs in the church. It is naive to try to function without some structures and institutionalization. But structure and institution are meant to SERVE THE SPIRIT. They are to support and encourage the promptings of the Holy Spirit. They offer a perspective that helps us discern the ways of the Spirit. So long as structures help God's people to achieve such ends they are healthy and good. When the institution becomes an obstacle to such growth, it will need to change. But that is normal for any institution.

In its humanness, the institutional Church is capable of injustice and inhumanity. It may be done for the best of motives. But the Church, like all of us, can lose sight of its role as servant when it gains political power. The people in the Church are tempted like all people are. When that happens, the people of the Church are responsible for returning to the role of servant once again. Misuse of power and authority in the Church needs to be challenged. This is not to do away with authority, but to affirm again that authority is to be used as Jesus used it – for LIFE and LIGHT! In these areas, respectful dialogue is vital to the institutional Church. Critique of the Church in these situations shows a deep love for her. Critics must avoid the danger of becoming "infallible" or "self-righteous" as they work to love the Church to new life.

> *"Simon, Simon, take heed. Satan has been given leave to sift all of you like wheat. But for you I have prayed that your faith may not fail; and when you come to yourself, you must lend strength to your brothers." "Lord" he replied: "I am ready to go with you to prison and death." Jesus said: "I tell you, Peter, the cock will not crow tonight until you have three times over denied that you know me."*
>
> **Luke 22: 31-34**

The Church is HERALD. It is our task, as Church, to proclaim the gospel of Jesus. The word "Evangelization" comes to mind. It means that the values, the ideas and ideals, the focus and direction of the gospel is shared with others. We are called by Jesus to share all of this with people. There are many ways in which this is done. We do it by the lifestyle we live. We do it with speeches and homilies. We do it through bible study groups and getting together for prayer. We do it over a beer at the local tavern or at the coffee break in an office. We do it when we take action to promote greater justice for people.

It means sharing things that identify us as followers of Jesus. Sometimes it is direct talk about the gospel. At other times it is the way we express opinions or question policies of companies or legislatures. Our ideas and opinions, attitudes and convictions flow from our commitment to the gospel. We may not always hang a label on it, but we know the source.

Spreading the gospel is done anywhere we go – from football games to charity banquets. It happens on vacations and it happens at work. It shows itself as we deal with opposition as well as how we love our families. It can happen at a bargaining table that deals with disarmament or at a tupperware party in our living room. It happens when someone is dying and when a child is born. To be a herald of the gospel has no known limits. But it does require solid knowledge and practical implementation of the gospel.

> *"Go forth to every part of the world, and proclaim the Good News to the whole creation. Those who believe it and receive baptism will find salvation. Those who do not believe will be condemned. Faith will bring with it these miracles: believers will cast out devils in my name and speak in strange tongues; if they handle snakes or drink any deadly poison, they will come to no harm; and the sick on whom they lay their hands will recover."*
>
> **Mark 16: 15-18**

The Church is COMMUNITY. Theologically the Church is the union of people with Jesus and one another. This dimension of Church will be filled with human and divine elements. Our union with Jesus is accomplished by the Holy Spirit. The foundation of any solid community is the Holy Spirit. The bonding is already being done by the Spirit. Our task is to uncover a unity that already exists. Intimacy and communion with Jesus is the work of the Spirit. This is part of the divine dimension of the "Mystical Communion" of the Church.

On the human side, the Church will always work to develop a community of relationships. The "People of God" are asked to develop an atmosphere of welcome and warmth, courtesy and compassion. Since no community is ready-made, creating such a community requires a lot of consistent work. This is a human community called to act "divinely". It would be unrealistic to expect magic-community to happen because we develop a good theology of community. The needs we have are many. The gifts in the community are many. Bringing need and gift together is part of what community does.

A solid community will help nourish personal growth. It will provide reflection time and acceptance of persons. It will provide the ways for people to interact with one another. It will develop strategies that touch the wider world with the gospel vision of justice. A good community will fulfill the words of the prophet Micah:

God has told you what is good; and what is it that the Lord asks of you? Only to act justly, to love loyalty, to walk humbly with your God.

Micah 6: 8

A good community will use the tools of the natural sciences that can help with community-building. Understanding the process of human growth and group development can be helpful in community building. Discovering the ways of inner healing and reconciliation with God, self and others is important. A Christian community will need to deal with the human side of its members. The size of an individual community within the Church Community will make a difference. A smaller group may be able to offer more personal attention. On the other hand, a larger group might be able to have a bigger impact when injustice or needs overwhelm a smaller group. In short, the Church as community will require a commitment that is lifelong, joined to a willingness to share self and wealth with others.

There are always stumbling blocks within community living. Small intimate groups can withdraw into splendid isolation. Enamored of the cozy, warm feelings, they may ignore the call of justice and peace, of compassion and unselfish love. Large groups may become over-organized, more concerned with efficiency than empathy. The structures in a large group may get more attention than servanthood. It is clear that our experience of Church as community will be varied and both delightful and disappointing. That is when we try to bring the reality of the gospel-light to the situation. A brief reading of Paul's letters to the Corinthians or the Galatians will give a clear idea that communities always need renewal and reform.

... I did not want, I said, to come and be made miserable by the very people who ought to have made me happy; and I had sufficient confidence in you all to know that for me to be happy is for all of you to be happy. That letter I sent you came out of great distress and anxiety; how many tears I shed as I wrote it! But I never meant to cause you pain; I wanted you, rather, to know the love, the more than ordinary love, that I have for you.

141

*Any injury that has been done has not been done to me;
to some extent, not to labor the point, it has been done
to you all. The penalty on which the general meeting has
agreed has met the offense well enough. Something very
different is called for now; You must forgive the offender
and put heart into him; the man's sorrow must not be
made so severe as to overwhelm him. I urge you therefore
to assure him of your love for him by a formal act.*

2 Corinthians 2: 3-8

Personal experience reveals the presence of sin and brokenness both in ourselves and in the community. No one should be surprised at this. What keeps us from being hopeless is the presence of the Spirit of Jesus within the community and within our own hearts. As the human and divine were joined in Jesus, so are they joined in the Church community.

No single community reflects the WHOLE CHURCH. The mystical communion known as Church has many expressions. Charismatic prayer groups, Secular Franciscan groups, Cursillo groups, Marriage encounter groups, Singles groups and Separated and divorced groups, parish groups and many other groups within the Church give witness to community life. But they belong to something bigger than themselves. They belong to a larger community known as CHURCH. Their role is to support the Church in building the Kingdom of God among all people. St Francis of Assisi sensed the value of loyalty to the Church – a church most genuine when it most clearly reflects Jesus. Francis' gift to "being Church" was to reflect Jesus to the best of his ability.

*By the power of the risen Lord, it (the Church) is given
strength that it might, in patience and love overcome its
sorrows and its challenges, both within itself and from
without, and that it might reveal to the world, faithfully
though darkly, the mystery of the Lord until, in the end,
it will be manifested in full light.*

Constitution on the Church #8

The Church is SACRAMENT. A sacrament offers a sign that reveals the presence of another reality. The Church exists in the world as a sign of the saving presence of Jesus. She is a sign of all that Jesus revealed.

The Church is also the sacrament FOR all men and women, Christian and non-Christian alike. This seems to be borne out by the Vatican Constitution on the Church, LUMEN GENTIUM in which the light of the entire world is Jesus, and the Church, when it truly acts as Church, reflects the light of Jesus to all men and women.
Sacramental Theology – Osborne
Paulist Press – Page 46

Jesus' humanity reflects God and is the primary sacrament. Jesus is the reason why anything else can be called sacrament. The Church, reflecting the presence of Jesus in the world, is a basic sacrament, signing Jesus' presence among us. The individual sacraments are expressions of particular aspects of Jesus' presence in the action of the Church. The "communities" within the Church form a sign of people coming together. Whatever reflects unity in these communities reflects the presence of Jesus. Elements that illustrate disunity hide the Church as a sacrament.

One reason why the Church is always in need of reform is a simple human fact. The human side of the Church is not perfect. It has the same problems and difficulties of other human groups. What keeps the Church alive and vibrant is the presence of the Holy Spirit. St Francis was aware that he was the moon, not the sun. So the Church, in her human side, is the moon reflecting the light of Christ (her divine side). The more clearly she reflects Jesus, the more she is "Church" as sacrament.

Just as Jesus used human words and stories, imagination and parables to reveal his Father, so the People of God reveal the presence of Jesus by what they say, what they do and who they are for others. The more clearly the People of God reflect the ideals of the gospel, the more clearly are they a "sacrament".

And in union with Christ Jesus he raised us up and enthroned us with him in the heavenly realms, so that he might display in the ages to come how immense are the resources of his grace, and how great his kindness to us in Christ Jesus. ... For we are God's handiwork,

created in Christ Jesus to devote ourselves to the good
deeds for which God has designed us.
Ephesians 2: 6-7 & 10

To Summarize

The Church is institution, servant, herald, community, sacrament and more. She is a gathering of people who believe in Jesus Christ. She is the gathering of imperfect people around the table of the Lord in Eucharist. She is forever seeking greater perfection and in need of reform. In her earthly journey she seeks to follow the way of the Spirit of Jesus. She struggles and sometimes fails.

But she also stretches the human spirit, opens the door to alternatives that only a gospel could require. She seeks reconciliation rather than revenge, unity rather than separation, communion rather than isolation. Like St Paul, the Church prods and pushes people to new heights and new insights. She does not shrink from the suffering of her beloved poor nor deny compassion to the rich. In all things she continues to seek to make present the message and person of Jesus. On her pilgrimage, she is willing to walk with saints and sinners, thieves and honest folk. She welcomes to conversion the arrogant as well as the humble and tries to show the way by her own example. What is said of her is said of us, for WE ARE CHURCH – the People of God.

Ministry

The seeds of faith need nourishment and nurturing. Our ability to address human and world issues from a gospel perspective is an important ingredient of faith. Ministry is our "doing" the gospel in everyday life. It is most often influenced by an attitude of support, concern and compassion for others. It includes the awareness of our need to receive the ministry of others. Sometimes we are the "others" who are supported and shown compassion. Ministry is a mutual quality of faith-life. It is a giving and a receiving, a letting loose and an embrace, a buying and a selling. Ministry enables us to reveal Jesus' presence among us (sacrament).

Ministry calls us to accept and embrace the mind and spirit of Jesus. Jesus lived among the people he served. He spoke in a language they could understand. He was clear in his use of authority and ready with compassion. He listened to the needs of people and quietly communed with his Father. He could be frustrated with slow learners and angry with the arrogant who listened to no one but themselves. He understood the politics and power plays and could confront and conciliate both. His identity with his Father was an intimate one and part of who he was. He recognized the dynamic, wise power of love and the price and consequences of love. Putting on the mind and spirit of Jesus means dealing with these issues in our ordinary world.

Our personal ministry is meant to reflect the ministry of Jesus for our time and space. Ministry forms us as well as giving us opportunity to "gospelize" (Evangelize). Ministry teaches us the need for the support of community. Such support encourages us in ministry. Ministry is our response to human need and divine call. It is imperfect and always in need of development. In ministry, there are times when we fish all night, like Peter, and catch nothing. At other times the fields are rich for the harvest. Sometimes our ministry is the solitude of communion with God, at other times the confusing cacophony of neighborhood sounds. We need to dream and have a sense of vision for good ministry. We also need to plan and organize for good ministry. The heart of ministry is the Spirit of Jesus prompting us and sending us to proclaim the good news of Jesus. The deeper we plunge into the mind and heart of Jesus, the richer will be our ministry.

We always thank God for you all, and mention you in our prayers continually. We call to mind, before our God and Father, how your faith has shown itself in action, your love in labor, and your hope of our Lord Jesus Christ in fortitude. We are certain ... that he has chosen you and that when we brought you the gospel, we brought it not in mere words but in the power of the Holy Spirit, and with strong conviction ...
1 Thessalonians 1: 2-5

> *The local fraternity ... becomes the basic unit of the whole Order and a VISIBLE SIGN of the Church, the community of love.*
>
> **Rule – Chapter 3 #22**

The local fraternity is called to reflect the qualities of Church. Take time to re-read the above words on the Church with your fraternity in mind. Let me add some of my own reflections.

The fraternity is an institution. It has organizational elements that are important. The local FRATERNITY COUNCIL is empowered to conduct the business and see to the growth and development of the fraternity. It decides on the admittance of new members. Not everyone who applies is automatically accepted. The call needs testing and deliberation. The Council has the responsibility to carefully and prayerfully decide about admitting new members.

There is a mutual responsibility for fraternity members to see to the growth and development of the fraternity. Hence, regular communication between Council and members is vital. Engaging the membership in the ministries and work of the fraternity is important. This will require some knowledge of the gifts and skills of members. As in many organizations, Councils may ask members to do things at which they are not competent. This usually is debilitating for both the individual and the fraternity. Good structures are assessed by their fruit.

As a community, the local fraternity gathers very human people and works to create a vibrant, loving, reconciling and evangelizing community. It will take time to accomplish such a task. In fact, it will always be in process as some members pass on and new members enter. Each change of membership calls for change in the fraternity. It is God's way of molding and re-molding all of us. It is called "conversion". It is a lifetime task. Human problems and opportunities must be dealt with in a gospel-way – for we are gospel people. To be gospel-people requires creativity and humility, visioning and reflection, compassion and leadership. The Spirit of Jesus will prompt us and a solid fraternity will respond with courage and joy.

The Fraternity is servant, herald, sacrament and the place of union. Our role is to serve one another in the love of Jesus. Loving action is a way of being a herald of the gospel, making visible (sacrament) the gospel in today's world. Words, discussion, dialogue and study are combined with action to touch peoples' lives.

Solitude and contemplative prayer keep us in touch with our Savior and moves us to serve the "little ones" of society. Our lives point in the direction of the gospel vision. As Franciscans, as Christians, we "image" Jesus in our world. As we do this, Jesus continues to transform us through those we serve.

For a Franciscan fraternity to accomplish such a task, all the members must co-operate. Commitment to Franciscan living requires accepting the consequences of following the gospel. "Knowing about" the Church will need to be translated into "building the church" into a true community, gospel-style. Research and study will need to be translated into actions that promote human ways of life for all people. Celebrations will be as normal for fraternity life as mourning with those who weep. Tears of joy will be mingled with tears of sorrow and pain. Temporary frustration and disappointment will be replaced by hope and opportunity. Weak as we are, wounded as we may be, we will bring to fraternity the healing of Jesus. In our bonded pilgrimage, we will join love and justice and discover mercy. With God all of this is possible. Without God it becomes a fruitless search.

> *Therefore take up God's armor; then you will be able to stand your ground when things are at their worst; to complete every task and still to stand firm. Stand firm I say. Fasten on the belt of truth; for coat of mail put on integrity; let the shoes on your feet be the gospel of peace, to give you firm footing; and, with all these, take up the great shield of faith, with which you will be able to quench all the flaming arrows of the evil one. Take salvation for a helmet; for sword, take that which the Spirit gives you – the words that come from God. Give yourselves wholly to prayer and entreaty; pray on every occasion in the power of the Spirit.*
> **Ephesians 6: 13-18**

Groups, like individuals, can become dominating – forcing people into their "one way" of doing things. It is dangerous when this happens. It is one of the problems with cults. People stop being responsible for themselves and/or the group and hand over responsibility to one or more leaders. When any group or leader is disrespectful of people there is need to change that situation. When people are "broken down" to make them conform, something is wrong. When guilt-imposition is used as a manipulative way of control, something is not right in the group.

A good fraternity will have problems. But it will face them honestly and deal with them openly. Our humanness will quickly make it clear that a fraternity is not paradise. But there are healthy and positive ways to help one another. Domination and manipulation, power plays and "my-wayism" is not healthy. The Franciscan fraternity must always struggle to reflect Jesus and his message. Our need to deal with the joys and frustrations of fraternity life will also be one way that we learn to grow as a community. Change and conversion will be a constant companion for us.

> My children, love must not be a matter of words or talk; it must be genuine and show itself in action. This is how we may know that we belong to the realm of truth and convince ourselves in his sight that even if our conscience condemns us, God is greater than our conscience and knows all.
>
> ... This is his command: to give our allegiance to his son Jesus Christ and love one another as he commanded.
> **1 John 3: 18-20 & 23**

Reflection Questions

We learn from people and we learn from God and gospel. Think about the people who have influenced you. What did they do that impressed you? How were they "sacrament" for you? Why did you admire them? What promptings in prayer have moved you to change? Do you trust the working of the Spirit within your own heart? What is the biggest obstacle for you to be a gospel person? What things in the Church cause you difficulty? How are you dealing with them? Do you think there is a better way to deal with them? If so, what is it? How regularly do you act on what you learn from the gospel? What makes it most difficult for you to follow the gospel? What problems exist in your fraternity that make it less than a real community? What are you doing about it? Are you part of the problem or are you helping toward a solution? Does the fraternity allow freedom of action and response, or do you feel confined and programmed? If freedom is absent, what needs to be done? Do you feel pressured by a "power group" so that you sense there is little respect for you? Is such a situation healthy? What are you doing about it? Does the group seem too dependent on one person who controls everything? If so, what can be done to improve the situation?

SECULAR FRANCISCAN RULE

9. The Virgin Mary, humble servant of the Lord, was open to his every word and call. She was embraced by Francis with indescribable love and declared the protectress and advocate of his family. The Secular Franciscans should express their ardent love for Her by imitating her complete self-giving and by praying earnestly and confidently.

RULE – Chapter 2 #9

The Rule does not ask us to say the rosary or recite litanies to Mary. Neither does it require us to pray novenas or belong to Marian organizations. It does not ask us to make pilgrimages to Lourdes or Fatima. There is nothing in the Rule requiring us to read books about Mary. The Rule does not dis-approve such things but simply gives us a sound basis for Marian devotion.

Mary is "open to his every word and call". We know Mary to he someone who gave a "yes" to the call of God. Her yes brought consequences beyond her initial understanding. Her question at the Annunciation receives an answer only faith could accept. She becomes involved in the salvation story and her life is changed. She became pregnant without "knowing man" and had to deal with Joseph's confusion. She was told she would be the "mother of the most high" and had to try to understand what that might mean. She carried her child to full term, only to have him born in poverty away from home. His early years brought her fear and travel to a foreign land to protect his life. She watched his growth and wondered what he would be like. She heard his words about "his Father's business" and did not understand them. She wanted to be part of his life, but another (the Father) took over the direction of his life. To be open "to his every word and call" was no little thing for Mary.

"Self-giving" was part of who Mary was. She went to aid her cousin, Elizabeth, who was pregnant in her old age. She stayed with her for several months. She accepted her role as mother of the most High with faith. Only in the way of faith did it make any sense. Humanly she was not certain of the path her life would take. Confusion often touched her. Wonder was a constant companion. All she could do in so many situations was to reflect on what was happening. Even when she did not understand the ways of her son, she chose to walk with him. A woman of love is Mary, following the love in her heart even as she feared for her son. The rumors and stories about his actions worried her at times. But she tried to understand and she remained faithful to his "every word and call."

All of this happened in her ordinary life. There were no angels to take care of the house or make the meals. There was nothing "different" about the way Mary was mother and wife. The differences were within this woman. The quality of her faith allows her to walk into a new ministry without overwhelming fear. She learned to accept God's way, mysterious as it was. She learned what sorrow meant when she lost her son to death, and on a cross. She maintained hope when things seemed uncontrollable. She wept and grew tired. She celebrated and prayed in the synagogue. She remembered the Exodus experience of her people in the Passover celebrations. She taught her son to pray and reach out to Yahweh from the heart. She continued faithful when the son of her womb was killed. Joy and pain ran through her life because of her son.

What is her response to the puzzling ways of God?

> Tell out, my soul the greatness of the Lord, rejoice
> rejoice, my spirit, in God my savior; so tenderly has he
> looked upon his servant humble as she is. For, from this
> day forth, all generations will count me blessed, so
> wonderfully has he dealt with me, the Lord, the Mighty
> One!
>
> **Luke 1: 46-49**

This is the Lady we are asked to imitate. To imitate her listening to the word. To imitate her self-giving. To imitate her prayerfulness. These are the qualities that Marian devotion will strengthen in us. It goes far beyond saying a rosary or making a pilgrimage. It is connected directly to our "radical conversion". It is not our devotions that will bring us to intimacy with Jesus. It is the quality of our lives that change because of the example of Mary. One realistic way to assess how true is our devotion to Mary is to see how closely we resemble her son.

Mary gave flesh to Jesus in the womb of her body. We are called to give flesh to Jesus in the womb of our lives. Mary brought the world a presence that saves. We are called to do the same. Mary listened to his word and call and was faithful to it. We are called to listen to the "gospel-word" and be faithful to it. Mary was consistently responsive to her need for prayer. We are called to be prayerful in our daily lives. Mary is a loving, feminine, life-giving and self-giving woman. We are called to be true to our real "self" and learn the ways of love.

> *Let the faithful remember that the true devotion (to Mary) consists neither in sterile or transitory affection, nor in certain vain credulity, but proceeds from true faith, by which we are led to know the excellence of the Mother of God, and we are moved by filial love toward our Mother and to the imitation of her virtues.*
> **Constitution on the Church – #67**

Franciscan Tradition

The Franciscan Order has always shown a deep devotion to Mary. She is a special person for us. Among the traditions in our Franciscan heritage is the story of the FRANCISCAN CROWN ROSARY. As with all devotions to our Lady, this one invites us to celebrate God's power at work in the life of Mary.

In the 1400's, a young man with an enthusiastic devotion to Mary joined the Franciscan Order. One day, while he was praying, our Lady spoke to him. She invited him to reflect on her joys, reciting our Fathers and Hail Marys as he did so. He shared this devotion with others. Thus the Franciscan Crown Rosary had it origin around 1422. It is recited in this manner:

> *Begin at the first decade with one Our Father and ten Hail Marys. Follow this pattern for seven decades. At*

*the end of the seventh decade say two Hail Marys in
honor of our Lady's life on earth. Follow this with an
Our Father, Hail Mary and Glory Be for the intentions
of the Holy Father. Amen.*

The joys of our Lady are used for the decades.
1) *The Annunciation – Mary's call to trust God*
2) *The Visitation – Mary ministers to Elizabeth*
3) *The Nativity – Mary gives birth to Jesus*
4) *The Visit of the Magi – the Gentiles come to Jesus*
5) *Finding Jesus in the Temple – fear and concern that
    end in discovery*
6) *The Resurrection – death gives way to new life*
7) *The Assumption/Coronation – consequences of a
    life of service.*

St Francis loved Mary. The Franciscan Order began in the little chapel
consecrated to St Mary of the Angels. His followers have written
top-notch books on Mary. They have helped develop the theology of
Mary. Duns Scotus helped develop the theology of her Immaculate
Conception. St Lawrence of Brindisi (Capuchin) is known as the Marian
Doctor for his many writings on Mary. Her "littleness" is a quality dear
to Franciscans. She is the advocate of our Franciscan Family. Her
human example of faithfulness calls us to be faithful.

*The Secular Franciscans should express their ardent
love for her by imitating her complete self-giving and by
praying earnestly and confidently.*
Rule #9

FRANCISCAN FOCUS

The "TAU CROSS" is an ancient Christian symbol. Some writers trace it back to the Prophet Ezekiel. Ezekiel spoke of people being marked with an "X" or "T" to indicate that they belonged to God.

> *"Go through the city, through Jerusalem," said the Lord,*
> *"and put a mark (T) on the foreheads of those who groan*
> *and lament over the abominations practiced there."*
> *Then I heard him say to the others: "Follow him through*
> *the city and kill without pity; spare no one ... but touch*
> *no one who bears the mark!"*
>
> **Ezekiel 9: 4-6**

Other research connects the TAU with the cross of Jesus. It is a sign that links the wearer to Jesus. In the book of Revelations the TAU signifies God the Father and is related to the name of the Lord. In the "Didache" (An early Christian writing), the "TAU" means the word of God. In a number of ways then, the "TAU" is connected to the crucifixion and is a symbol of Jesus' willingness to die for us.

St Francis often used the TAU to sign his name. Dedicated to the crucified Lord, Francis uses the TAU to identify with Jesus. Throughout Franciscan history the TAU has been a sign of commitment for us. It reminds us of the love that Jesus has for us.

Pope Innocent III reflected the spirit of Francis when he wrote:

> *The TAU has exactly the same form as the cross on*
> *which our Lord was crucified on Calvary (T). Only those*
> *will be marked with this sign and will obtain mercy who*
> *have mortified their flesh and conformed their lives to*
> *that of the crucified savior.*

QUESTIONS

1. At the beginning of this chapter, you were asked to reflect on your ideas of "Church". Please compare these ideas with any new ones you have learned. Indicate any areas in which you notice some change.

2. Describe, in your own words what is: Church as herald – Church as servant – Church as community – Church as sacrament – Church as institution.

3. Which of the elements in question 2 most influences your life right now? What new awareness did this chapter give you?

4. Write out your definition/description of "ministry"?

5. The local fraternity is called a "little Church". Evaluate your fraternity in the light of what you have written about "church". In what ways does your fraternity best fulfill the role of "little church"? In what ways does your fraternity fail to fulfill that role? What could be done to improve your fraternity in this regard?

6. What role does Mary have in the life of a Franciscan?

7. What criteria would you use to judge that devotions to Mary are on the right track?

8. What qualities of Mary are Franciscans expected to imitate? Describe how you imitate them in your life!

9. What are some of the qualities needed in the local fraternity to provide for community and personal growth? Explain why you believe they are necessary.

SCRIPTURE reading\reflection

✛ Colossians 1: 15-29
St Paul shares some powerful feelings in this text. Jesus is the focal
point of Paul's words. Jesus is clearly the source and end of all
things. Our response to Jesus is to live the gospel and to share it
with others.

Prayerfully reflect on Paul's words. What qualities of "Church" do you
discover in this text? Why do you believe they are important for the
"Church"? What role does Jesus play in the Church?

CHAPTER 8

ORDINARY PEOPLE

Biblical spirituality is important to Franciscans. The gospel is our way of life. The insights offered by the bible are endless. In this chapter, I want to offer a few ideas on biblical spirituality.

The people of the bible are ordinary people. Even when we try to put them on pedestals, they quickly reveal their humanness. What becomes clear as we explore their lives is God's power at work in the lives of these people.

Abraham is one of the ordinary people of the bible. St Paul calls him the father of faith, a man who hoped when there was little reason for hope. Paul gives him high marks for his response to God. But behind this marvelous faith is the human person of Abraham.

Abraham lived in Ur. He enjoyed his life there and was at a point where he was ready for social security. At this contented point in his life, God invites him to leave and head to a place "I will show you." (Genesis 12: 2) God does not even tell him which direction to take. Abraham is given very little information. He had no map nicely marked by a travel agency. There is simply the invitation to go!

> *TIP #1 – The Lord has a mind of his own and reveals it in his own good time.*

Abraham went. He picked up what he owned and left Ur. Not having any directions, he simply went, presuming God would offer directions as he went. He trusted the Lord to make things clear as he traveled. Since he was following God's call, he figured God would let him know if he got lost or took the wrong route.

> *TIP # 2 – Good spirituality requires us to trust God even when God is vague.*

As Abraham moved into new territory, he met lots of new people. He had to interact with them, sometimes negotiate with them. Had he stayed in Ur, he could have avoided all these new people and new experiences.

TIP # 3 – God expands our horizons and relationships when we follow God's call.

In the course of his journey, Abraham enters the country of a king known for his eye for beautiful women. Abraham's wife was such a beauty. Often Kings would simply kill husbands so they might have the wife. So Abraham tells Sarah to say she is his sister. Abraham was afraid he might be killed otherwise. A little lie would protect him. But God made it clear to the King that Sarah was wife to Abraham. Slightly upset, he still gives Sarah back without hurting Abraham.

TIP # 4 – So-called "holy" people make mistakes and have to deal with fear.

Abraham continues his journey, but God is still silent. Sarah and Abraham grow older. Child-bearing is no longer a possibility for Sarah. Then God presents them with a rather astounding promise. They are going to have a child! Sarah laughs and Abraham wonders. But the messenger is quite clear in saying that they will have a child within a year. Nothing is impossible to God! (Genesis 18: 9-15) So it happens. Next year they have a child whom they name Isaac. (Genesis 21: 1-3)

TIP # 5 – "Is anything too marvelous for the Lord to do?" (Genesis 18: 14)

Isaac brings great joy to Sarah and Abraham. The child is a sign of God's faithfulness to the promise made to an old couple. Isaac is the light of Abraham's life. Through Isaac he would be the father of a great nation. What he considered impossible is happening through the power of God. But then God speaks again to Abraham: "Take your son Isaac, your only son, whom you love ... offer him as a sacrifice on one of the hills I will show you." (Genesis 22: 2) What a strange request! But Abraham sets out in obedience to the call.

What a long, sad journey for this old man. The questions must have rolled around in his old head. How can the promise be kept now? Why is this being asked of me? What kind of God is this anyway? But despite all the questions, Abraham goes. When Isaac asks his father (and how it must have hurt Abraham): "Here are the fire and the wood, but where is the young beast for the sacrifice?" How can he tell his son that he is the sacrifice? "God will provide himself with a young beast for a sacrifice, my son". (Genesis 22: 8) Abraham ties up his son and puts him on the altar of sacrifice. He is willing to trust God even now. But as Abraham raises his knife to kill the boy, God intervenes. "Do not raise your hand against the boy; do not touch him." (Genesis 22: 12) The test is over. God expresses his deep love for Abraham.

TIP # 6 – God chooses life for us, not death.

Abraham, an ordinary man, shows what trust in God means. He must have doubted and wondered, questioned and struggled with the call of God. What strange ways God has. When he left Ur the directions were vague. When he is asked to sacrifice his son, the directions are very clear. In some situations Abraham lies to save his own skin. Yet he is still willing to struggle with his faithfulness to God. This man is someone not unlike myself as I struggle to understand God and God's ways.

Jonah is a reluctant prophet. He gets a clear message from God to preach to the Ninevites. The communication is clear. But Jonah does not want to preach to the Ninevites. He hates them and refuses to think about being in their presence. So, quite deliberately, he buys a ticket to Tarshish. He wants to get as far away from Nineveh as he can. Jonah consciously invests in an attempt to escape from the ministry to which God calls him.

TIP # 7 – God has a long history of experience with reluctant and resistant human beings.

Jonah boards the ship and heads into the hold to catch some sleep. He figures he has safely circumvented God's call. But a great storm comes up and the ship is in grave danger of sinking. Fear grasps everyone on board. And Jonah sleeps on. Finally the Captain finds him and wakes him up. At least Jonah could pray to his God for help. The confusion and fear on the ship is a palpable presence. It is a grave crisis for all of them – but Jonah recognizes it as especially crucial for himself. He faces the reality of what he is doing and acknowledges that he is running from God. The crisis forces him to face reality.

TIP # 8 – Sometimes a crisis forces us to face reality rather than run from it.

Jonah is thrown overboard in order to placate his God and save the ship. Jonah figures it will be the end of life for him. The power of the sea and the distance from land make it impossible for him to survive. But God sends a large fish who swallows Jonah. After three days of retreat to consider what he has done, Jonah is spewed back on shore.

TIP # 9 – God patiently seeks us out no matter how far we try to run from God.

Jonah is given a second chance to go to Nineveh. He goes! He may not go with great desire, but he goes. He preaches to the Ninevites and waits to see them destroyed. He still thinks God is making a mistake by bothering with them. But he is successful in his preaching and the Ninevites repent. Then Jonah is angry because things are turning out differently than he anticipated. Though he preached grudgingly he figured God would at least give him the satisfaction of seeing Nineveh destroyed. But no such luck! They are saved and Jonah feels like a fool. Full of self-pity he upbraids God for making a fool of him.

TIP # 10 – Check your reasons for sulking – you may discover some uncomfortable truth(s) about yourself.

Jonah continues to bicker with God. He thought that God might be merciful and he wanted no part of it. That is why he ran away to Tarshish. What marvelous foresight Jonah has – and he is clearly peeved at God. The story ends with God telling Jonah that he always listens to the needs of people who need help. Jonah remains unconvinced and angry.

TIP # 11 – God is not distracted by our sulking. God remains generous even when we are angry.

There might be a little of Jonah in all of us. I easily makes judgments about who deserves help and who doesn't. I can refuse to allow God's generosity to touch my heart when I'm dealing with an enemy. When I look foolish because of my attitudes it's easy to blame God for making me look dumb before my friends. I even resent it when God does good things for people I don't like. How dare God love them! I am not certain I like the way God acts.

TIP # 12 – God loves being God and is true to Godliness. God is not looking for a replacement.

TIP # 13 – My stubbornness is often the cause of my frustration and suffering.

Esther is another special, ordinary person. She and Mordecai were caught in a "Holocaust" situation. Haman, a confidante of the king, hated the Jews because Mordecai refused to bow to him. So he set about getting the king to decree the death of all the Jews. No little revenge – Haman hates big! Esther is herself a Jew as well as being Queen. Mordecai appeals to her as the only one who can save the Jews. She must appeal to the king on their behalf. But there is a problem. No one is allowed to approach the King unless called by the King. Anyone daring to do so was liable to death. Esther is in a difficult situation. So Mordecai calls on all the Jews to pray and fast for three days. Esther does the same. At the end of her prayer, she dresses in all her beauty and walks through the palace to see her husband the king – even though she has not been called. Scripture tells us that while she looked radiant on the outside, her heart was in the grip of fear.

TIP # 14 – The presence of fear need not keep us from making good choices.

TIP # 15 – Prayer and fasting and community support does not mean we lose our fear – only that it does not control us.

When she comes into the presence of the king, "he glanced at her in towering anger". Esther fainted. At that moment God changed the heart of the King. He came to her, held her in his arms and asked what she wanted. Her plea saves her people.

Hosea receives an unwelcome call from God: "Go, take a wanton (Prostitute) for your wife and get children of her wantonness." (Hosea 1: 2) So Hosea took Gomer for his wife. They had three children, two boys and a girl. But Gomer continued her profession and was repeatedly unfaithful to Hosea. Money and jewelry came to her and she flaunted them before Hosea. But he chose to remain faithful to her and love her. Gradually this faithful love reached the heart of Gomer. She began to see how other men used and discarded her. But Hosea remained faithful. Little by little Hosea's faithful love changes Gomer and she too becomes a faithful spouse. During all the days and months when it looked hopeless, Hosea was faithful in his love.

TIP # 17 – God trusts the power of faithful love.

TIP # 18 – God loves people with a faithful love and brings them to wholeness through such a love.

But God also used Hosea's struggle to prepare him for ministry among the Israelites. Hosea would preach to his people about their unfaithfulness to God. He would speak from a heart that had experienced the pain of unfaithfulness. His words would reflect the pain of God when God's people were unfaithful. How well Hosea could speak about the peoples' "prostitution" of God's faithful love.

TIP # 19 – Personal experiences often prepare us for ministry and the ability to reach out to help others.

Jonah, Esther, Abraham and Hosea are but a few examples of ordinary people responding to God. Involvement with God changed their lives. They found new meaning for life in their experiences. Other scriptural figures did the same. Moses, stutterer, murderer, and reluctant leader led his people out of slavery in Egypt. The desert-experience of the people brought out the worst and the best in them. Yet it was here that they came to rely on God. Moses never entered the promised land – but he was content with the role he had played. Though he did not enter the promised land, he was content to look across the river to see the land of promise.

TIP # 20 – God's ways are not our ways.

Reflection

Notice that these ordinary people responded to God in a variety of ways. Sometimes their inner heart was changed by their experience of God. Sometimes they were called to a new relationship with others. Sometimes they called people to a sense of justice and concern for others. True spirituality will touch each of these dimensions. It will call us to an interior, radical change of heart. It will call us to deepen and strengthen inter-personal relationships. We learn to serve the cause of justice, creating a just, non-oppressive society. Wholeness in spirituality will reflect these elements.

We are like people building a house. As we look around at the material, we wonder how the finished building will look. Some supplies are not yet delivered. We know that they will look different when they are part of the house. We realize that we have materials in our spiritual lives that are not yet put into our spiritual building. The scripture offers much more material for our structure. We put them together gradually to form the building of our life. Constructing our biblical spirituality is a life-time job. Take time to reflect on the tips we have discovered so far.

+ The Lord has a mind of his own and reveals it in his own good time.

+ Good spirituality requires us to trust God even when God is vague.

+ God expands our horizons and relationships when we follow God's call.

+ So-called "holy" people make mistakes and have to deal with fear.

+ "Is anything too marvelous for the Lord to do?" (Genesis 18: 14)

+ God chooses life for us, not death.

+ God has a long history of experience with reluctant and resistant human beings.

+ Sometimes a crisis forces us to face reality rather than run from it.

+ God patiently seeks us out no matter how far we try to run from God.

+ Check your reasons for sulking. You may discover some uncomfortable truth(s) about yourself.

+ God is not distracted by our sulking. God remains generous even when we are angry.

+ God loves being God and is true to Godliness. God is not looking for a replacement.

+ My stubbornness is often the cause of my frustration and suffering.

+ The presence of fear need not keep us from making good choices.

+ Prayer and fasting and community support does not mean we lose our fear – only that it does not control us.

+ God helps us precisely when it is needed and not before.

+ God trusts the power of faithful love.

+ God loves people with a faithful love and brings them to wholeness through such a love.

+ Personal experiences often prepare us for ministry and the ability to reach out to help others.

+ God's ways are not our ways.

Life keeps teaching us about the ways of God. God is unique and follows the promptings of love. God's creative abilities constantly find ways of reaching into our lives. One of our problems is the narrowness of our vision. We are limited and often have a vested interest in having things go a certain way. God wants us to be less concerned about how it turns out for us and more concerned to be one with God. When we sulk or get impatient or get angry with God, God remains a faithful lover. God knows how difficult it is for us to change ingrained attitudes and ideas. So God waits patiently for our conversion. God's gentle persistence breaks through our hard hearts.

But we have yet to explore the New Testament. Jesus offers us still more insights into the ways of biblical spirituality.

The New Testament

The writers of the New Testament give us a variety of insights into the spirit of Jesus. A sound biblical spirituality will reflect these insights. We will try to find ways of absorbing Jesus' ideas about life and living in this world. Being human, Jesus shows the beauty of our humanity. God embraced humanity and the Incarnation reveals something about the worth and dignity of being human. Jesus' willingness to be a servant to all reveals an attitude he wants us to have. A solid biblical spirituality will become familiar with the words, actions and attitudes of Jesus.

> *Your world was a world without hope and without God. But now in union with Christ Jesus, you who were once far off have been brought near through the shedding of Christ's blood. For he himself is our peace.*
>
> *... So he came and proclaimed the good news: peace to you who were far off, and peace to those who were near by; for through him we both alike have access to the Father in the one Spirit. Thus you are no longer aliens in a foreign land, but fellow-citizens with God's people, members of God's household. ... In him you too are being built with all the rest into a spiritual dwelling for God.*
> **Ephesians 2: 13-14 & 17-19 & 22**

> *It is now my happiness to suffer for you. This is my way of helping to complete, in my poor human flesh, the full tale of Christ's afflictions still to be endured, for the sake of his body which is the church. I became its servant by virtue of the task assigned to me by God for your benefit; to deliver his message in full; to announce the secret hidden for long ages and through many generations, but now disclosed to God's people, to whom it was his will*

to make it known – to make known how rich and glorious
it is among all nations. The secret is this: Christ in you,
the hope of glory to come.
Colossians 1: 24-27

Jesus' presence on earth reveals the quality of God's love for us. Our
biblical spirituality is built on the foundation of God's love.

What we have seen and heard we declare to you, so that
you and we together may share in a common life, that
life which we share with the Father and his Son Jesus
Christ. And we write this in order that the joy of us all
may be complete.
1 John 1: 3-4

But to those who did receive him, to those who yielded
him their allegiance, he gave the right to become children
of God … Out of his full store we have all received grace
upon grace.
John 1: 12 & 16-17

TIP # 1 – "All life, all holiness comes from you through your
Son, Jesus Christ, by the working of the Holy Spirit."
(Eucharistic prayer #3)

God has taken the initiative in the battle against evil. Jesus inaugurates
a new era in the battle of good and evil. God's people had begun to feel
abandoned. Law and structure had replaced faith and hope in God.
With the coming of Jesus, God's power was obviously at work again in
the world. Jesus faces the devil in the desert – and defeats his wiley
temptations. Again and again Jesus shows a power greater than the evil
one. A new creation is happening – God is creating new life through
Jesus.

The desert testing ground for Jesus resembles temptations we all face.
We are tempted to take shortcuts to holiness. Gurus give us simplistic
ways to achieve holiness, quickly and without much work. The Devil
invited Jesus to fling himself from the temple and let angels save him.
One big sensational event and you'll have the world eating out of your
hand!

TIP # 2 – Temptations come to Christians – don't be surprised at this.

Jesus makes it clear that "You are not to put the Lord, your God to the test." (MT 4: 7) Rejecting the easy way, Jesus chooses to remain faithful to his Father. That is more important to him than the quick-fix of the devil.

TIP # 3 – Intimacy with Jesus is more important than trying to shortcut our way to holiness.

Power is a common temptation for people. The attempt to control events and other people is a real temptation. Jesus is tempted by the devil to bow down before the Devil's power. If Jesus will do so, he will get power over all nations. Just a little bowing to a superior (sic) power and Jesus will have great control. No doubt we all face various sizes of this temptation. A little more money will give me control of a business. A little more education will give me control over the ignorant. A little more muscle will give me control over weaklings. A little more beauty will give me control over emotions. A little more authority will give me power to direct others with my commands. The temptation of power is a pervasive one for human beings. It happens within the family as well as among nations. It can be economic power or physical power. It may be psychological or emotional. The temptation is there. Jesus' answer to the temptation was clear: "Begone Satan! Scripture says you shall do homage to the Lord your God, and worship him alone!" (MT 4: 10)

TIP # 4 – It is important to maintain faithfulness to our God even when we are tempted to take God's place and usurp power that belongs to God alone.

Hunger became a temptation for Jesus. His long fast in the desert left him vulnerable to such a temptation. So the devil chooses to tempt him to use power on his own behalf. "Change these stones into bread!" To prey on weakness is a natural and devilish temptation. We all find ourselves taking advantage of weaknesses in others. You name it, we can be tempted to do it. It can be emotional blackmail that takes advantage of mental disease. It can be economic blackmail that keeps someone in "control." Public officials can be threatened unfairly, but

167

with power. The big lie technique can diminish another's reputation. Whatever our hunger may be, the devil can tempt us to use it to get things for ourselves rather than have concern for others. Jesus once again called on Scripture to answer the temptation: "Scripture says: 'Man cannot live on bread alone; he lives on every word that God utters!' " (MT 4: 4)

> *TIP # 5 – The scripture and God's word gives life. Do not allow*
> *yourself to be led away from the words of life.*

Jesus is clear about his mission on earth. He came to call sinners to repentance and new life. Self-righteous and pompous people felt no need to change. They rejected Jesus and his message. They already knew all they needed to know. Little people, poor people – they who trusted God even in dire circumstances – listened to Jesus. Tax collectors, lepers, prostitutes, the "unclean", fishermen, shepherds, sick and suffering people, they listened. Jesus was concerned about them and was friend to them. Such friendships angered the elite and self-righteous people. They relied on laws and interpretations of the "LAW" that kept people yoked "in their place." But Jesus refused to bind people with new laws. Instead, he looked for ways to free people of oppression whether from within or from without.

> *TIP # 6 – Jesus cares for sinners and the poor. A good biblical*
> *spirituality will lead us to do the same.*

To read the scriptures is to discover the contrast between the attitudes of Jesus and our own society. Jesus chose to remain faithful to his Father even when it meant the suffering of the cross. He did not underestimate the cost of love. Neither was he willing to evade the consequences of a faithful love. Because of his faithful love, even to a death on the cross, God raised him up to new life.

> *TIP # 7 – Faithful love is demanding. To practice such faithful*
> *love, with all its consequences, is part of the path to holiness.*

Jesus was not naive. He recognized the weakness of people and how easily they succumb to temptation. Despite his awareness, he proclaimed the worth of all people, even those despised by society. Jesus believed that real change begins in the heart and spreads out to touch society. People could develop a passion for loving one another. They might face fear and failure on the way, but he would simply say: "Fear not. – Do not be afraid. – Why are you fearful little flock? – I am with you!" Presence makes all the difference. Imitating his Father, he trusted the power of love.

> *TIP # 8 – The power of love is ultimately more powerful than fear. Jesus calls us to be faithful lovers!*

Anyone who has lived knows the consequences of such ideas. How can I love people who murder others, torture prisoners, abuse children, abuse the elderly, rape one another, destroy reputations, give others the "silent treatment", induce physical and psychological fears in others? What power will enable me to endure the arrogance of some of the powerful or the ingratitude of some of the poor. How can I work among the awful smells of shanty towns or in the opulent luxuries of the rich? How can I bring forgiveness and healing to years of anger and hatred, resentment and frustration? Can I believe in a loving God when I see the pain and misery of the innocent? How can I be faithful to love in all of these situations?

> *TIP # 9 – "For men this is impossible; but everything is possible for God." (MT 19: 26)*

> *... Let us exalt in the hope of the divine splendor that is to be ours. More than this: let us even exult in our present sufferings, because we know that suffering trains us to endure and endurance brings proof that we have stood the test, and this proof is the ground of hope. Such a hope is no mockery, because God's love has flooded our inmost heart through the Holy Spirit he has given us.*
>
> **Romans 5: 3-5**

> *... whenever you have to face trials of many kinds count yourselves supremely happy, in the knowledge that such testing of your faith breeds fortitude, and if you give fortitude full play you will go on to complete a balanced character that will fall short in nothing. If any of you falls short in wisdom, he should ask God for it and it will*

be given him, for God is a generous giver who neither refuses nor reproaches anyone. But he must ask in faith, without a doubt in his mind; for the doubter is like a heaving sea ruffled by the wind. A man of that kind must not expect the Lord to give him anything; he is double-minded, and never can keep a steady course.

... All good giving, every perfect gift comes from above from the Father of the lights of heaven. With him there is no variation, no play of passing shadows. Of his set purpose, by declaring the truth, he gave us birth to be a kind of firstfruits of his creatures.
James 1: 2-8 & 16-18

TIP # 10 – Our hope is based on the faithful love and power of God. With God's help, we can endure all things.

When we look around at the values and attitudes of society and compare them with the gospel, we see many contrasts. It also becomes obvious that the Christian who follows the gospel needs to be alert to the differences. We have already chosen the gospel. We now face the daily decisions that will reflect our choice.

Society

1. Get all you can in whatever way you can – take care of #1 first of all!

2. Make certain everyone knows the "boss".

3. If someone hurts you, return the favor.

4. Peace is achieved by having strong, powerful weapons. Be strong and flex your muscles!

Gospel

1. Think of others before yourself.

2. A person in authority is to be servant to all.

3. Love your enemies and do good to those who hurt you.

4. Peace comes when justice is done and we trust other people, finding creative ways to love people.

170

5. Success means CONTROL-LING people & events. Dominate and avoid failure by any means.

5. Success is linked to intimacy with Jesus – vital to real wholeness. Relationships are our priority.

6. We are only human. The gospel is pious phrases. Be realistic! Do your own thing and forget this "love" stuff!

6. Love is the only way to a realistic life. Even death cannot overcome real love. Intimacy with God & neighbor brings real joy.

7. Play it safe! Go to church "just in case!" Keep up appearances – but don't get too involved!

7. Giving God worship is a natural consequence of our love for God. It is a privilege to praise God.

8. Don't bother with justice and mercy – they get in the way of profits! Give as little as possible and take as much as you can get!

8. Justice and mercy are natural qualities of the followers of Jesus.

9. We own this earth and we can do whatever we want with it.

9. The earth is God's and we are only stewards. God will hold us accountable for our stewardship.

10. Go to court with any case – sue for all you get. Fight for every penny!

10. Settle your differences before they come to court. Settle things without trying to get revenge.

11. If you don't get caught it is all right. Don't worry about the truth of the matter.

11. The truth will set you free. Deceit destroys trust and breeds suspicion.

Such a list could be extended. But even this short list illustrates the values of a society that go counter to the Gospel. There is tension and stress connected to being a Christian in such a world. No one should expect our life as Christians to be easy. But with the support of a solid

Christian community we will find help. We need God and we need one another.

TIP # 11 – There is a natural tension for the Christian as he/she tries to be faithful to God in everyday situations.

As we try to implement the gospel it becomes clear that it is not easy to make clear decisions. If, for example, we oppose nuclear weapons production, what action do we take? Do we march in protest? Withhold a portion of our income tax? Spill blood on weapons? Design an educational packet on such weapons? If we are concerned about race relations and a WE-THEM polarization in our neighborhood what do we do about it? Take sides? Try to mediate? Accept the underdog as our rallying cry? Label people in order to avoid facing the real issue? Get people to know one another? What do we do when people gripe about religious and priests not wearing their religious ID? Add to the fight? Accept any and all opinions as equally valid? Try to understand both sides? Talk about our cultural expectations? Offer to bring in a speaker to address the issue? How do we accept a foreign family in our neighborhood when our neighbors don't want them there? How do we avoid polarizing the situation?

Such situations call for creative responses. Caught in these tensions, we want to follow the gospel values. But the practical decision is not easy. Any decision we make does not have automatic success built into it. Yet, we will try to make a decision based on gospel values and attitudes. As we struggle with such decisions, we quickly realize that we are not Solomon. We still make good, but imperfect decisions. As we walk with our decisions and their consequences we are alert for facts that call us to change or adjust our decisions.

But the harvest of the Spirit is love, joy, peace, patience, kindness, goodness, fidelity, gentleness and self-control. There is no law dealing with such things as these. And those who belong to Christ Jesus have crucified the lower nature with its passions and desires. If the Spirit is the source of our life, let the Spirit also direct our course.

We must not be conceited, challenging one another to rivalry, jealous of one another. If a man should do

172

something wrong, my brothers, on a sudden impulse, you who are endowed with the Spirit must set him right again very gently. Look to yourself, each one of you; you may be tempted too. Help one another to carry these heavy loads and in this way you will fulfill the law of Christ.

Galatians 5:22 – 6:2

TIP # 12 – "… the Holy Spirit whom the Father will send in my name, will teach you everything, and will call to mind all that I have told you." (John 14: 26)

Jesus recognized human weakness and sin. He saw it in his followers and warned them about it. Peter was told that a rooster would reveal his weakness. When the rooster crowed, Peter knew – and Jesus forgave him. I suppose we need to be aware of the roosters in our life who remind us of our weakness or unfaithfulness. When he faced the issue of the woman caught in adultery, Jesus asked the crowd to be honest with themselves. Any non-sinner could throw the first stone. When they all left he had brought a new reality both to them and to the woman. When Jesus chose his friends, he chose people with little or no power or sophistication. Fishermen, tax-collectors, zealots – a radical political group, "sons of thunder", a greedy man and a young, untried youth became his "cabinet." Not much of a selection from a political point of view. But Jesus sought dedication rather than sophistication, the possibility of open hearts rather than closed minds.

Jesus sought to deal with intellectual arrogance among some of the Pharisees. When they questioned him, he answered wisely and questioned them in return. When some of them refused to accept any fresh perspectives, he called them hypocrites and white-washed tombs! But when a lawyer came to him, sincerely seeking God, he offered a special invitation to surrender as he looked on him with love. When Lazarus died, Jesus wept. But his delay in going to Bethany was mis-read as lack of love. Yet Jesus saw the situation as a place where his Father would receive glory. He was not deterred by peoples' interpretations of his actions. When he raised the 12 year old girl to life, he was very practical. "Give her something to eat." Jesus responded with integrity to all these situations.

*TIP # 13 – Jesus made his human decisions in the light of his
trust in his Father – and remained faithful to the Father. We are
called to trust Jesus and remain faithful to his gospel.*

Franciscans accept the gospel as their way of life. The more consistently
we reflect on the gospel, the greater will be its impact on our decisions.
We will be flexible in responding to life. We will realize that there can
be many creative responses to life situations. We will have hope even
when failure or depression touches our lives. Such hope is founded on
Jesus, the faithful one. Without Jesus it is impossible to follow the
gospel. As Jesus gained his strength and direction from the Father, we
will gain our strength and direction from Jesus and his gospel. Jesus
calls us to com-union with him and each other. Such unity will enable
us to be GOSPEL PEOPLE, for Jesus gives us his own Spirit.

Always and everywhere, we are brought back to Jesus. Any biblical
spirituality will be centered on Jesus and a personal relationship with
him. Jesus shares his own Spirit with us. We are brothers and sisters
with a common Father … the Father of Jesus. We are called to be
FAITHFUL to Jesus and the message of his gospel.

*TIP # 14 – A personal relationship with Jesus is the foundation
of a solid biblical spirituality.*

*TIP # 15 – Jesus' gift of his Spirit enables us to follow the gospel
as our way of life.*

And Then...

There is no conclusion to gospel growth until we are taken home to
God. Perhaps even heaven will offer the excitement of discovery and
celebration without hindrance. On earth, each new day brings the
possibility of change and growth. Experience teaches us that our faithfulness is still incomplete. Jesus came into our world to bring light to
the world. We continue that task today. Jesus came into our world to
reveal the Father to us. We continue that task today. Jesus came into
the world to forgive sinners and to find those who were lost. We
continue that ministry today. Jesus came to heal the sick, give hope to
the depressed and bring justice to the oppressed. We continue that

ministry today in the name of Jesus. The only sensible reason for following such a course of action is love. St Francis was a Spirit-filled lover for the 1200's. We are to be Spirit-filled lovers for our century. God continues to gift us with his Holy Spirit – and all things are possible for us!

> *But when the kindness and generosity of God our Savior dawned upon the world, then, not for any good deeds of our own, but because he was merciful, he saved us through the water of rebirth and the renewing power of the Holy Spirit. For he sent down the Spirit upon us plentifully through Jesus Christ our savior, so that, justified by his grace, we might in hope become heirs to eternal life. These are words you may trust.*
>
> **Titus 3: 4-8**

Our patient God knows the power of love. God trusts in the power of love to transform people. Gently, persistently, God faithfully reforms us with a love that can be tough or gentle. It is a love that seeks life for us, calling us out of the tombs that poor choices may have created.

> *TIP # 16 – God's love cannot be diminished by our actions, for God's love reflects the very nature of God.*

> *Here is the proof that we dwell in him and he dwells in us: he has imparted his Spirit to us. Moreover, we have seen for ourselves, and we attest, that the Father sent the Son to be the savior of the world, and if a man acknowledges that Jesus is the Son of God, God dwells in him and he dwells in God. Thus we have come to know and believe the love which God has for us.*
>
> *God is love; he who dwells in love is dwelling in God, and God in him.*
>
> **1 John 4: 13-17**

> *TIP # 17 – "Come, Lord Jesus."*

Summary

✛ "All life, all holiness comes from you through your Son, Jesus Christ, by the working of the Holy Spirit." (Eucharistic Prayer #3)

✛ Temptations come to Christians – don't be surprised at this.

✛ Intimacy with Jesus is more important than trying to shortcut our way to holiness.

✛ It is important to maintain faithfulness to our God even when we are tempted to take God's place and usurp power that belongs to God alone.

✛ The Scripture and God's word gives life. Do not allow yourself to be led away from the words of life.

✛ Jesus cares for sinners and the poor. A good biblical spirituality will lead us to do the same.

✛ Faithful love is demanding. To practice such faithful love, with all its consequences, is part of the path to holiness.

✛ The power of love is ultimately more powerful than fear. Jesus calls us to be faithful lovers.

✛ "For men this is impossible, but everything is possible for God." (Mt 19: 26)

✛ Our hope is based on the faithful love and power of God. With God's help we can endure all things.

✛ There is a natural tension for the Christian as he/she tries to be faithful to God in everyday situations.

✛ "... the Holy Spirit whom the Father will send in my name, will teach you everything, and will call to mind all that I have told you." (JN 14: 26)

+ Jesus made his human decisions in the light of his trust in his Father and remained faithful to the Father. We are to trust Jesus and remain faithful to his gospel.

+ A personal relationship with Jesus is the foundation of a solid biblical spirituality.

+ Jesus' gift of his Spirit enables us to follow the gospel as our way of life.

+ God's love cannot be diminished by our actions, for God's love reflects the very nature of God.

+ "Come, Lord Jesus."

Reflection Questions

What elements in this chapter are most demanding for you? How would you define/describe the trust Abraham's example asks of us? If we love one another, what action is needed to create a society where justice is practiced? Is it possible to be a gospel person and ignore evil and its consequences? What IS required of the Christian in such situations? Reflect with others on the various "tips" of this chapter. Let the dialogue call you to deeper change of heart. Gain support for gospel life from each other!

SECULAR FRANCISCAN RULE

10. United themselves to the redemptive obedience of Jesus, who placed his will into the Father's hands, let them faithfully fulfill the duties proper to their various circumstances of life. Let them also follow the poor and crucified Christ, witness to him even in difficulties and persecutions.

11. Trusting in the Father, Christ chose for himself and his mother a poor and humble life, even though he valued created things attentively and lovingly. Let the Secular Franciscans seek a proper spirit of detachment from temporal goods by simplifying their own material needs. Let them be mindful that according to the gospel they are stewards of the goods received for the benefit of God's children.

    Thus, in the spirit of "the Beatitudes", and as pilgrims and strangers on their way to the home of the Father, they should strive to purify their hearts from every tendency and yearning for possession and power.

12. Witnessing to the good yet to come and obliged to acquire purity of heart because of the vocation they have embraced, they should set themselves free to love God and their brothers and sisters.

RULE – Chapter 2 # 10, 11 12

These points of the Rule bear directly on the lifestyle of a Franciscan. Gospel values are held up for imitation and implementation.

Reflections

1. The Franciscan's growth in the Lord is everyday stuff. It is not a once-a-month program. It doesn't happen simply because people faithfully attend meetings or bible-study groups. Daily living is the field of

growth in gospel values. People, events, disease, jobs, unemployment, death, parties, birthdays, weddings and anything else that happens has an influence on us. Here is where we "faithfully fulfill the duties proper to the various circumstances of life." (Rule #10) This covers a variety of situations.

Single people face different realities than married couples. Each of us perceives life from our individual perspective. Each style of life offers both possibilities and limitations. Married, single, divorced, student, sick, healthy, widowed, unemployed, employed, worker, manager and other personal data touches the way we live. Our environment makes a difference. Rural settings differ from urban settings. Poverty stricken areas differ from luxury apartments. Neighborhood atmosphere has its influence on us. All of these things touch the way we can love people on any given day. It will touch the way we are able to surrender to the Lord and/or practice our faith. There are enough differences to make our responses unique.

The Rule offers a two-pronged approach to daily life. On the one hand it calls for the imitation of the poor and crucified Christ. Somehow, on this day of life, we will find ways to reflect our dependence on Jesus. We will find ways to show concern for the "little people" in our lives. We will be less self-centered and more concerned about others today. We share our gifts so everybody "wins". This sort of approach to life will counter some of the "me-first" approach that often happens in society.

On the other hand, the Rule calls for willingness to witness to Jesus even if it is tough. Simple living is not easy in a society geared to consumerism. Advertisers are not paid to help us live simply. They create needs out of our desires. We need to sort out the difference between what we actually need and what we want. Simple lifestyle tries to acquire what is needed, not necessarily what is wanted. In some countries of the world, the decisions are bigger. Showing concern for the poor or protesting oppression can bring death-squads to the door. The world of power is not eager to hear the gospel call to freedom among the poor and dispossessed. Life as a Christian can be life-threatening in some places.

We might evade the gospel call because we can label people and rationalize ourselves out of offering help. Calling people communists or lazy or stupid foreigners or immature allows us to evade dialogue with them. If a governmental structure mis-uses and abuses its service to the homeless and helpless, we are called to critique it in a way that brings about positive changes. But such action is neither easy nor readily accepted by bureaucrats. Following a gospel-lifestyle is not always popular.

2. Simplifying our needs and being good stewards is another element of gospel living. Things have a way of becoming important to us. The acquisition of things can be a dominating desire. The ability to accumulate things is often used as a yardstick of our worth. Things are used as a criteria of success. Possessing many things means you are successful. Being without them makes you a failure.

Our society builds itself on the gross national product and economic profits. In itself this is neither good nor bad. It is simply our economic reality. It is human and imperfect. It can show concern for people or become their oppressor. Goods and profits can become gods to be worshiped. They can replace the real God in our lives. This "god" of material things promises happiness and the good life. Having more things will bring more happiness. It is a tempting lie and Franciscans will struggle with it like everyone else.

In its extreme form, the god of material possessiveness can lead to slavery. Life revolves around things. I need to defend my "things." I need to accumulate more "things." Work and life focus on getting things I want. I work two jobs and increase my stress. Relationships suffer. I find myself feeling alone. Cuddling up to a cash register or computer chip leaves me untouched by human warmth and love. Many lives become bankrupt from this disease.

There is no disease-control center for greed and selfishness. But gospel people are asked to seek a different way to happiness. We want to offer an alternative way of living. People trapped in greed or selfishness need concern rather than condemnation. Only if we show a lifestyle that reflects a joy for life can we attract their attention. As we simplify our needs and wants we have more time for one another. Yet, if ordinary needs are not met, our struggle for survival may become an obstacle. Both the unreflective rich and the destitute find little richness in everyday living.

The Rule invites us to be good stewards of creation. We will find ways and means to share and distribute the gifts of creation so that all people can live human lives. We will care for the earth, treating it lovingly and attentively. We will protect the things people need for life. We will try to develop attitudes that protect our environment both for present and future generations. We do this because we are responsible to God for the way we use our earth. To mis-use and abuse the earth is to go counter to our Franciscan way of life. Reflection, both personal and communal, will help us find practical ways to implement this point of the Rule.

We are called to be free. So we will try to avoid being possessed by the desire for possessions. We will try to avoid using all our energy to protect our possessions. We will try to be sensitive to the needs of others as we share our possessions. If we own a business, we will treat people with respect, both workers and customers. Profit is not evil, but a desire for excessive profits can be evil. Whenever people are hurt or diminished by our drive for profits, Franciscans will work to change such attitudes. Technology can make business and service into an impersonal matter. We don't destroy technology to solve the problem. Instead we become more creative to make certain technology serves people rather than dictating to them. Whenever we find oppression of any sort, we cry out against it. We are not judge and jury, condemning others. But neither can we stand by when actions and policies destroy peoples' lives. When people are forced into inhuman living conditions by economic injustice, we will confront such injustice. We will try to work together to change things.

Our ways and ideas will be good but imperfect. So the Rule is wise in asking us to purify our hearts from the yearning for possessions and power. Even in doing good we can succumb to such yearnings. How easily we can become righteous and condemnatory as we oppose injustice. Once again we will need personal and communal reflection on the gospel to walk wisely in these areas of life. This is no easy task – but it is the way of life we have chosen.

3. The Rule invites us to a sense of wonder as well as a simplified lifestyle. As possessions, fears, and selfishness diminish in us, intimacy needs to grow. As we grow more intimate with Jesus and one another, we gain a new sense of wonder. God's love, made visible in Jesus, seems far beyond what we deserve. The people who care for us and walk with us in joy and/or suffering are special gifts. It is with wonder that we grow in respect for the earth and the people who live there. Wonder opens the door for fresh and creative ways to create a climate of freedom for all people. So we avoid the subtle tools of control that may have slipped into our family life. We try to change our desire to decide issues for everyone we know. Instead, we attempt to learn together through open dialogue, affirmation of the good, confrontation of the destructive – but always in a way that reveals our caring love.

To be free to love our brothers and sisters, we will let loose of our own self and surrender to Jesus. Strange as it seems, this surrender brings freedom. We are free of entrapment by things. We are free of the need to control people and events to get what we want. We are free to see the good around us in people and creation. We are free to praise God for such goodness. We are free to identify with other Christians without a fear of losing ourselves. Such freedom moves us from self-centered concern to a rich caring for others. Such freedom is the work of a lifetime. But it is cluttered with the ways of joy and intimacy promised by the gospel.

> *I thank my God always when I mention you in my prayers, for I hear of your love and faith towards the Lord Jesus and all God's people. My prayer is that your fellowship with us in our common faith may deepen the understanding of all the blessings that our union with Christ brings us. For I am delighted and encouraged by your love; through you, my brother, God's people have been much refreshed.*
>
> **Philemon 1: 4-7**

FRANCISCAN FOCUS

The Stations Of The Cross

The stations of the cross are reflections on the passion and death of Jesus. Early in Christian history pilgrims would walk the Via Dolorosa in the Holy Land. It recalled Jesus' journey to his crucifixion.

The first "Stations of the cross" outside the Holy Land were erected in the Church of San Stefano in Bologna, Italy in the 5th century. From the 5th to the 15th century shrines recalling the "Stations" were common. The number of stations varied. Crusaders returning from the Holy Land in the 12th and 13th centuries popularized the devotion in Europe.

In 1342 the Franciscans were given charge of some of the Holy Places in Palestine. They began to spread the devotion of the "Stations" in their churches and chapels. In the 18th century St Leonard of Port Maurice, a Franciscan, promoted this devotion with great fervor and much success. He became known as the preacher of the way of the cross. Between 1731 and 1751 he erected more than 570 sets of stations of the cross in various parts of Europe.

The present number of stations (14) was stabilized by Clement XII in 1731. Earlier, in the 5th century, there were five stations in Bologna, seven stations in Antwerp and as many as twenty or thirty in other places. The list of the 14 stations developed in the 16th century. The number of stations depended mainly on the choice of devotional writers. The Church simply gave approval to a popular devotion.

Good theology goes beyond the 14 stations of the cross. The death of Jesus is followed by his resurrection from the dead. The burial of Jesus is not the end of the story. Many contemporary stations of the cross contain a 15th station – the Resurrection of Jesus. It is sound theology and makes good sense for this devotion. Like all good devotions, the stations are meant to draw us to Jesus. The stations help us walk with Jesus in this time of his life. Stations of the Cross that focus only on the gruesome elements of the passion should be avoided. Rather than imposing guilt or creating fear, the stations bring us hope in a Jesus who dies for us. It can also help us to genuine sorrow for our sinfulness.

Franciscans delight in the stations as another reminder of the humanness of Jesus. Jesus persists in loving us even unto death. The Father's love for Jesus shows itself as Jesus is raised from the dead. The Stations of the Cross reflect our own struggles with the death brought by sin and the resurrection brought by reconciliation.

QUESTIONS

1. Which "ordinary persons" in this chapter impressed you the most? Give reasons for your choice.

2. What qualities of these ordinary people helped you most in your journey to wholeness? Pinpoint your answer – explain what insight you gained and what it means to you.

3. Give yourself a good period of time with this question. Write an essay describing/explaining what "biblical spirituality" means (in your own words). You might reflect on questions like: A) What qualities belong to a good biblical spirituality? B) What attitudes does a biblical spirituality require? C) How does your "image" of God affect your ideas of biblical spirituality? D) How does a biblical spirituality affect your everyday life? E) What are some concrete consequences of a biblical spirituality in YOUR life? F) What element of biblical spirituality is most important?

4. Re-read the LETTER TO ALL THE FAITHFUL (on the inside cover). What elements of a biblical spirituality do you find in this Letter? Compare this answer with your answer to question #3 (above). How do the two answers parallel one another?

5. How do the points of the Rule in this chapter relate to biblical spirituality i.e. what help/direction do they give to a solid biblical spirituality?

6. Give some concrete examples of your personal implementation of WONDER and a SIMPLIFIED LIFESTYLE. How do you value created things ATTENTIVELY AND LOVINGLY? How are you striving to purify your heart from every TENDENCY AND YEARNING FOR POSSESSIONS AND POWER? (Sharing personal experience(s) is helpful to all of us – be as honest and concrete as you can.)

+ Luke 17: 1-10

   Luke gathers a number of sayings of Jesus into this one text. They reflect one facet of Jesus' teaching. Jesus is strongly aware of sin and weakness and calls for some strong responses. The "sayings" paint a partial portrait of a Christian.

   After reflection and prayer, make a list of the things today's society might expect of people in situations similar to the "sayings" of Jesus. Then list the things Jesus requires in these situations and COMPARE the two. Share your conclusions.

CHAPTER 9

WHAT A WOMAN!

Mary, the mother of Jesus, plays an important role in our Franciscan life. Francis loved Mary as a woman of faith. St Bonaventure writes:

> *After this, under the guidance of heavenly grace, the shepherd Francis led the little flock of twelve friars to St Mary of the Portiuncula, so that there, where the Order of Friars Minor had its beginning, by means of the merits of the Mother of God, it might also begin to grow with her assistance.*
>
> **Bonaventure – Spiritual Classics – Paulist Press Page 210**

From its inception the Franciscan Order has honored Mary. Francis spoke of her with deep reverence. Francis' love for her was "inexpressible" for "it was she who made the Lord of majesty our brother." (Celano's 2nd Life – #198). Listen to Francis' own words:

> *Hail, O Lady, holy Queen,*
> *Mary, holy mother of God*
> *You are the virgin made church*
> *and the one chosen by the most holy Father*
> *in heaven*
> *whom he consecrated with his*
> *most holy beloved Son and with the Holy Spirit,*
> *the Paraclete,*
> *in whom there was and is*
> *all the fullness of grace and every good.*
>
> *Hail, his palace! Hail, his tabernacle!*
> *Hail, his home! Hail, his robe!*
> *Hail, his servant! Hail, his mother!*
> *And Hail all you holy virtues which,*

through the grace and light of the Holy Spirit
are poured into the hearts of the faithful
so that from their faithless state
you may make them faithful to God.
Francis & Clare – Paulist
Press – Page 149-150

Francis perceived Mary as the one closest to Jesus. She is praised because of her relationship to Jesus. She is the Mother of God. From that privilege springs the reasons for honoring Mary.

For all the salvific influence of the Blessed Virgin on men originates, not from some inner necessity, but from the divine pleasure. It flows from the superabundance of the merits of Christ, rests on his mediation, depends entirely upon it and draws all its power from it. In no way does it impede but rather does it foster the immediate union of the Faithful with Christ.
Constitution on the Church
#60

Women And Spirituality

God is the fullness of gender. From the beginning women have been a part of the history of God's people. Having a common source in the creative power of God, men and women are partners on the journey of gospel living. Our religious history offers examples of women who were instrumental in the growth of God's people. Judith and Esther, Hanna and Sarah, Ruth and Naomi are among the names that come to mind. Adam and Eve, Sarah and Abraham, Esther and Mordecai, Benedict and Scholastica, Francis and Clare all show a consistent partnership of men and women throughout history. There are numerous women who were close to Jesus. Mary's influence on Jesus shows in his sensitivity to people.

Solid spiritual growth requires that men and women influence one another. Each offers something unique to the other. Neither men nor women can come to wholeness without the other. Even pagan religions have gods and goddesses. Little wonder, then, that our faith offers us Mary as one whose influence teaches us about her son.

Jesus gifts us with Mary, his mother. She is an ordinary Jewish woman. She grew up in an ordinary family situation. She learned about life and love from her parents, Joachim and Anna. Her personal sense of worth came from the loving care of these two people. She learned much about Yahweh from their faith. She became espoused to Joseph and was ready to marry when God engages her for a special task.

"Do not be afraid, Mary, for God has been gracious to you; You will conceive and give birth to a son, and you are to name him, Jesus." (LK 1: 31) Words spoken in a few seconds, but they changed Mary's life. She will conceive by the Holy Spirit. Her experience was of no help in understanding this astounding message. All Mary received was a word from God. Her positive response gives some indication of the quality of her faith. "I am the Lord's servant. May it be as you have said." (LK 1: 38)

Her life from now on would require one "yes" after another. Her child would bring her joy and pain, worry and wonder. She would not always understand what he was about. His words were sometimes a puzzlement to her. Throughout her life she would be asked to continue to accept things she could not understand. The faith of her original "yes" is followed by a faith that says "yes" to fresh demands from God. Jesus would bring both joy and sorrow to this woman who said "yes" to God at the Annunciation.

As she listened to Jesus preach, she must have treasured the words and wondered at his power. As he healed people, she must have been proud of his service to the poor and needy. Yet, as rumors about him flew like a flock of sea gulls, she must have feared for his safety. When he was finally arrested and condemned, her heart must have yearned to hold him again in her arms. But that desire found fulfillment only when they placed his dead body in her arms. How the memories of his life flooded her mind as she held him ... how she had listened to his prayers and held him close because he was so precious to her. How something of herself died with him on the cross. It seems finished now. Her Jesus is dead and at peace. She believes even as the tears stream down her cheeks.

She gathers with other fearful people who knew him. He is buried now and they seem so afraid of what might happen. So she is with them, these "strong" men made so weak and fearful by his death. How they needed the support of someone who could accept their weakness. As soon as they could, some of the women went to the tomb.

Quite unexpectedly they returned. They knocked at the door shouting something about an empty tomb and Jesus being alive! Who could believe such talk! But even as doubts arose, hope poked her little head through their heavy hearts. When they went to the tomb they discovered that it was indeed empty. Unbelievably it is true! HE IS RISEN! As the facts become clear, Mary's heart can only repeat words she spoke those many years ago: "My soul tells out the greatness of the Lord ... for the Mighty God has done great things for me. His name is holy!" (LK 1: 46 & 49) What had seemed like an ending was simply God's surprising beginning.

Doctrine And Life

The Church has given Mary many titles. Litanies honor her name. Doctrines declare her motherhood and proclaim God's love for her. What is spoken of Mary has implications for our lives.

God preserved Mary from sin. God wishes to save us from sin too. The power of God is at work in us to keep us from the destructive power of sin and temptation. The same God who touched Mary with power wishes now to touch us with the power of the Holy Spirit. The love lavished on Mary is lavished on us. Mary, who held Jesus in the womb of her body is model for our holding Jesus in the womb of our lives. Our ministry is to give birth to Jesus in our life and our world. We are so gifted because God chooses to do such things. Mary's "yes" to God seeks to find an echo in our daily "yes" to Jesus and his gospel.

Mary was assumed into heaven, to be intimate forever with the God to whom she gave flesh. We too, after death; seek to be intimate forever with the God whose ambassadors we are on earth. Even now, we imitate Mary as we seek intimacy with Jesus in our present life. Mary serves as a model for what we are called to be.

Mary teaches us to pray. Her Magnificat contains both the tradition of her people and the spirit of her heart. God is praised for the greatness that gave Mary such gifts of grace. Pray with this woman of faith:

> *My soul tells out the greatness of the Lord, and my spirit has rejoiced in God, my savior. For he has looked with favor on his servant, lowly as she is. From this day forward all generations will count me blessed, for the mighty God has done great things for me. His name is holy; His mercy sure from generation to generation toward those who fear him. He has shown the might of his arm, he has routed the proud and all their schemes; he has brought down monarchs from their thrones and raised on high the lowly. He has filled the hungry with good things, and sent the rich away empty. He has come to the help of Israel, his servant, as he promised to our forefathers; he has not forgotten to show mercy to Abraham and his children's children for ever.*
>
> **Luke 1: 46-55**

Mary's words echo the words found in the mouth of Hannah. (1 Samuel 2: 1-10) Such praise comes from a heart that trusts God. Her prayer shows a clear-sighted awareness of God's power and care. Her prayer reflects the scriptures that were part of her everyday life. What had been promised to Abraham is fulfilled in her time. God does not forget people who are faithful and rely on this God of faithfulness.

How different is Mary's reliance on God and our too frequent reliance on self. How quickly the glory of rulers fades. How soon the popularity of movie stars and athletic heroes disappear. They seemed like gods for a while – and then they are no more. But a faithful, ordinary person like Mary remains part of our lives. God's wisdom chooses little people who know that God is the source of their life and joy. Such people cannot be destroyed because the source of life dwells within them. Mary teaches us that serving God is the way to real life.

Mary is not falsely humble, denying the gifts of God in her. Instead she revels in God's graciousness to her. Her clear vision of God and acceptance of the way God calls her shows what faithful love can do. She stands in awe (reverential fear) of this marvelous God. She praises

191

this God who never forgets the people who have been chosen by this same God. Let the spirituality of the Magnificat find a home in your heart. Quietly let the words lead you in prayer.

Marian Devotion

Devotion to Mary is part of our Catholic heritage. Art and poetry have sung her praises throughout the ages. Churches have been erected in her honor. All seek to capture the beauty of this Jewish woman of faith. Every solid devotion to Mary bears the imprint of Jesus: "while honoring Christ's mother, these devotions cause her son to be rightly known, loved and glorified and all his commands observed." (Constitution on the Church – #66) The final criteria for healthy devotion to Mary is that it brings us to Jesus and his gospel.

When any devotion or apparition leads people away from Jesus and the gospel, it is suspect. When they speak words of fear and guilt and impose condemnation on peoples, they are suspect. When they are based only on emotion or promote wild prophecies of doom and gloom, they are suspect. Mary is a woman of faith. She believes in God and God's mercy and love. She listened to and followed the words of her son, Jesus. If any apparition or vision speaks another kind of gospel, it is suspect. Mary is NOT the savior. She is one of us whom God loves in a special way. Her life and her self-giving are models for us. True devotion to Mary will reflect the gospel of Jesus.

> *... she belongs to the offspring of Adam; she is one with all human beings in their need for salvation. Indeed, she is clearly the "mother of the members of Christ ... since she co-operated out of love so that there might be born in the Church the faithful, who are members of Christ, their head." (Augustine) ... Taught by the Holy Spirit, the Catholic Church honors her with filial affection and piety as a most beloved mother.*
> **Constitution on the Church**
> **# 53**

If we were to summarize some of the criteria for healthy devotion to Mary and ways to evaluate apparitions, we might use the following:

1. The devotion/apparition must be in accord with scripture and reflect scriptural ideas.

2. The devotion/apparition should have a sound Christology and lead people to Jesus.

3. The devotion/apparition should be liturgically sound.

4. The devotion/apparition should be resurrectional – pointing to new life in Christ.

5. The devotion/apparition should be ecumenical i.e. should not create a barrier to others who believe in Jesus.

The Rosary

Devotion to our Lady has early origins in the Church.

Elizabeth proclaimed her "blessed". As early as 431 AD the Council of Ephesus declared her to be the Mother of God. The Hail Mary, in its entirety, is a product of the 15th century. It is found in a poem written by a Servite, Venerable Gasperini Boro. The Hail Mary was already incorporated in Franciscan breviaries at Paris in 1515. Pius V introduced it for all breviaries in 1568.

Despite this late development of the Hail Mary, something resembling the rosary was introduced by an Irish monk around the year 800 AD. He suggested replacing the 150 psalms recited by the monks by saying the Our Father 150 times. Some folks found that too much, so they recited a third of that number – 50 our Fathers. Some people carried pebbles in their pockets to keep count. Then strings with knots made their appearance. Finally, strings with beads replaced the knots. These strings of beads were called the PATERNOSTERS. They were commonly used in the middle ages. In the 13th century the Angelus replaced the Our Fathers.

In the latter part of the 14th century a Carthusian monk, Dom Henry Egher of Kalcar (Cologne), separated the Psalter of our Lady (150 Aves) by inserting an Our Father before each decade. Near the middle of the 15th century, Dom Dominic Helion of Prussia introduced the practice of meditating on the mysteries during the recitation. In the 1470's a

Dominican priest, Alan de la Roche and others, combined all these elements and gave us the rosary as we know it.

Besides this Dominican rosary of 15 decades, there are other forms of the rosary. The *BRIGITTINE ROSARY* has six decades plus one Our Father and three Hail Marys. The seven Our Fathers honor the seven sorrows and joys of our Lady. The 63 Hail Marys reflect the 63 years of Mary's life according to the revelations of St Bridget.

The Franciscan Crown rosary has already been described. The *ROSARY OF THE SEVEN SORROWS* developed in the 17th century. It honors the sorrows of our Lady. The *ROSARY OF THE SEVEN JOURNEYS* of our Lady reflect on the journeys of Mary and is a prayer for people as they travel. The *SCRIPTURAL ROSARY* incorporates scriptural texts into the recitation of the Dominican rosary. The rosary is one of the most widespread devotions to our Lady in the past 500 years.

Other prayers and devotions also honor Mary. The Angelus, the Salve Regina (Hail, Holy Queen) and psalms form a part of the devotion to Mary. Many feasts honor our Lady. Lourdes and Fatima are shrines of our Lady. Our Lady of Guadalupe has special meaning for the Americas. All these devotions teach us about the wonderful gift that God has given in Mary. Above all, they are meant to bring us to intimacy with Jesus, Mary's son and son of God.

Franciscans find it easy to honor Mary. Her readiness to trust God and accept the consequences serve as an example as we follow the gospel. She did not retreat from her commitment when it was tough. Neither will we. She did not shrink from identifying with Jesus when it could have been dangerous to do so. Neither will we. Even when it seemed that God had abandoned her and her son, she remained faithful. So will we. Little wonder that Francis loved her as he struggled with his call from God. Her positive trust and faith gave Francis hope in his own journey. She will do the same for us.

It was not her wish – his coming on earth.
She accepted it from the word of God's messenger.
She believed and she accepted the Word.
The Word was made flesh – in a cave.
Not a mother's choice for birth, but
part of being faithful to the word.
They were threatened and fled.
She would not have wanted it so,
but she would be faithful to the Word.
Then there were the three days of searching
and concern and his words – that she could
not understand – but she remained faithful
to the consequences of the Word spoken
twelve years before in the
silence of her room.

Then he left her for his ministry.
She was often alone as she heard of
his healings and preaching and the
whispered threats against him.
Even now, she was faithful – when he was
not around to assuage her concern.
Then came that awful day of condemnation
and his suffering and ... death.
So final! He is dead! My son is dead!
And still she is faithful and stands with
him at this moment of great agony of mind
and heart – true to the Word spoken in
the silence of her room
so many years ago.

And then he is alive again. The agony of
loss and pain is replaced by homecoming and joy.
She is silent now too – listening to the
words he spoke to others after breaking out
of the cave of his tomb.
Faithful now too – walking with those who
would continue his work.

The Word was made flesh and dwelt among us.
The Word-made-flesh spoke the Father's word
to all people everywhere.
The gospel word is our way of life.
Mary teaches us how to be faithful
to all the consequences of that word,
spoken in the silence of our hearts.
Teach me, Mary, teach me how to be faithful!

Reflection Questions

What quality in Mary is most attractive to you? Why? What is the foundation of Mary's place of honor in the Church? How would you describe Mary's faith? What is your response to apparitions of Mary? What criteria do you use to evaluate solid devotion to Mary? What are some of the signs that a devotion to Mary may be unhealthy? Does Mary's faithfulness find an echo in your life? What is most attractive to you in the words of Mary's Magnificat? How would you describe the spirituality of the Magnificat? Can a real devotion to Mary leave Jesus out of the picture? What role does the feminine influence of Mary have in our faith-life? What is your opinion about the role of Mary in the life of a Franciscan? How did Francis perceive Mary? Why did Francis find Mary so attractive? Describe the consequences of Mary's "Yes" at the Annunciation. How does your "yes" to Jesus compare with hers? How faithful are you in following the gospel-call? How can Mary be a help to you in being faithful to the gospel? Do you have a devotion to Mary? What are the results of your devotion to Mary?

SECULAR FRANCISCAN RULE

13. As the Father sees in every person the features of his Son, the first born of many brothers and sisters, so the Secular Franciscans, with a gentle and courteous spirit, accept all people as a gift of the Lord and an image of Christ.

    A sense of community will make them joyful and ready to place themselves on an equal basis with all people, especially with the lowly for whom they shall strive to create conditions of life worthy of people redeemed by Christ.

14. Secular Franciscans, together with all people of good will, are called to build a more fraternal and evangelical world so that the kingdom of God may be brought about more effectively. Mindful that anyone "who follows Christ, the perfect man, becomes more of a man himself," let them exercise their responsibilities competently in the Christian spirit of service.

Rule – Chapt 2 # 13-14

"A gentle and courteous spirit" has a nice ring to it. It invites people to embrace one another without distinction. Jesus is the source of such a spirit. He practiced it in his life on earth. God sees the image of Jesus in all of creation, especially in people. Gentleness and courtesy are the Father's way of dealing with people and creation. What the Father does, the Rule invites us to do. To "see through" creation and discover the image of Jesus. As people who are "pure of heart" we approach others with a gentle and courteous spirit, seeing Jesus in them.

Theologically, this is a sound approach. But practically it can be difficult to implement. People can just as easily be annoying, cruel, rude, a nuisance and a pain-in-the-neck as they can be clear images of Jesus! People who violently kill and maim others, people whose cruel and inhuman actions make then unattractive are hardly candidates for teaching us about the image of Jesus. People who think we are useless or poke fun at us or put us down are not easily seen as examples of the presence of Jesus. It can be most difficult to consistently show gentleness and courtesy to everyone we meet. There is no magical way to achieve a gentle heart nor any simplistic way to become courteous.

One way of beginning such a process is to examine our "platform of perception." How do we ordinarily perceive people? What standards do we use in measuring people? What expectations do we have of people? How aware are we of the process by which we categorize people? How do we perceive and judge ourselves? Getting in touch with our "platform of perception" gives a starting point for growth. The Rule invites us to adopt the perception of Jesus. Our beginning point will be both a knowledge of Jesus' perceptions and our own. Then we are in a position to compare the two.

Obviously, gentleness and courtesy begin with respect for self and others. If we perceive no good in ourselves or in other people, respect will be absent. If we are insecure, it is difficult to be thinking of the needs of others. Courtesy and gentleness require an "other-centeredness" that is difficult for people who are short on self-acceptance.

Any human community is composed of IMPERFECT people who are trying to do better. There will be need for forgiveness and understanding in any community. There are a lot of clumsy starts and stumbles along the way. Community-building is work. It doesn't just happen. It springs from a real love for one another, but it is a LABOR of love. We cannot afford the luxury of being people whose minds are "all mixed up and permanently set."

On the contrary, we need the kind of openness that allows for change and fresh approaches to people-problems in community. Gentleness and courtesy can be a big help on this journey.

A Gentle Heart

A gentle heart perceives things/situations/people as they really are. The gentle heart has no deceit, uses no coverups, has no unrealistic expectations in dealing with life. The gentle person responds to real life with realistic responses. The gentle person responds in a way called for by the situation. A gentle person does NOT get steamrolled by aggressive people. If strength and anger are a realistic response, the gentle person will show strength and anger. If supportive words or a hug is the realistic response, a gentle person gives them. But whether in anger or in a quiet response, the gentle person does not destroy the dignity of another person. Gentleness sees past the weakness and brokenness, the aggression and violence, the sarcasm and bias, to the real need of the person. Getting to the underlying needs allows the gentle person to be realistic in responding to people.

A person with a quiet self-confidence and wholeness can threaten people. Gameplaying and mockery are ineffective in trying to evade the reality such a person brings. We know that such a "whole" person will not be put off by attempts to hide our real self. The gentle and courteous person will look through the mask to the underlying reality we may fear to acknowledge. But gentleness and courtesy will allow the "whole" person to wait until the time when discovery will be opportunity rather than threat. Even so-called "whole" people have regular experience of their own weakness and brokenness. They do not feel in any position to judge – only to walk with the weakness and brokenness of others.

Bombastic, self-opinionated, cruel or unthinking people do not create such an atmosphere of acceptance. People who are stiff and rigid, insecure and fearful are unlikely to be able to handle openness and honesty. People who think they know-it-all or have little self-knowledge, cannot create an atmosphere of trust. For them gentleness and courtesy are a threat. We all have our "blind-spots" that we want to evade. We may not want to explore them. But a community that is gentle and courteous can invite us to take the risk and move toward greater wholeness. A fraternity needs to be a place where everyone works "to create conditions of life worthy of people redeemed by Christ." (Rule #13)

> ... *take our appeal to heart; agree with one another; live*
> *in peace; and the God of love and peace will be with you.*
> *Greet one another with the kiss of peace.*
> **2 Corinthians 13:11-12**

Some Help

There is no simple way to grow in gentleness and courtesy. There is no easy way to "exercise their responsibilities competently" without hard work. Serving one another is not exactly what our society influences us to do. We face the need to struggle together as we try to develop such qualities in ourselves and our communities.

These questions may help in that process. Use them gently and courteously. Don't let them paralyze you. Rather, let them challenge you to move to a fuller living of the gospel. If you find they are more bothersome than helpful, move on and walk as you can.

1. What attitudes dominate your daily life – getting or giving?

2. What is your approach to people – gentle and understanding or close-minded, judgmental and prejudiced?

3. What is your most common attitude – to serve and help others, or to be served and helped by others?

4. Are any of your ideas and attitudes so cemented and infallible that nothing will change them, or are you aware that new experiences and ideas may require change?

5. Do you "have to" be right all the time or are you open to working with others to discover fresh ways of looking at things or doing things?

6. How does gentleness and courtesy show in your everyday life?

7. What rating would you give yourself for creating an atmosphere of trust and acceptance?

8. What specific contributions do you make in building a better community spirit?

9. How do you react to rude or discourteous people?

10. Do you avoid reflection on certain areas of your life?

11. What do you do to add warmth and a spirit of hospitality to community gatherings? Do you make any effort to welcome new people and get acquainted with them? At work? In social gatherings? At fraternity meetings?

12. Are you faithful to prayer? Do you really know the gospel attitudes and values of Jesus? How could you improve?

13. How much time do you spend with scripture? Do you think it is enough for someone whose life and lifestyle is supposed to be based on the gospel?

14. What are you doing to become more COMPETENT in serving others in the spirit of Jesus? Do you think good will can substitute for competence? Is it an "either-or" situation or a "both-and" situation?

This list can be a beginning for reflection. You might want to share your answers with others. Remember that we have a common goal – intimacy with Jesus. We have a common need for one another – for we are good, imperfect people. Allow others to serve you as you strive to return the favor.

Outreach

A community without an outreach is on the road to death. Ministry to others is a natural consequence of healthy community growth. We learn many of the ways of compassion and understanding within the community. But our gifts are not limited to use within the small community. The gospel calls us to reach out beyond ourselves. When we do this, we do it as competently as we can. In ministry situations, it is not wise to put blind people on the list of car drivers.

All people are gifted in some way. All people have limitations. Good knowledge both of capabilities and limitations are important for healthy ministry. But such knowledge is on-going. Many gifts are only discovered when a situation calls them forth. So we will need to take risks even as we try to be practical about our capabilities. Keep the door open to discovery even as you try to be realistic about your "competencies."

Service to others makes us vulnerable. We are not in charge when we serve others. Such is the risk of gospel living. Jesus talks about this "towel and basin" ministry at the Last Supper after he washed his disciples' feet.

After washing their feet he put on his garment and sat down again. "Do you understand what I have done for you?" he asked. "You call me Teacher and Lord, and rightly so, for that is what I am. Then if I, your teacher and Lord have washed your feet, you also ought to wash one another's feet. I have set you an example; you are to do as I have done for you. In very truth I tell you a servant is not greater than his master, nor a messenger than the one who sent him. If you know this, happy are you if you ACT UPON IT."

John 13: 12-17

The ministry of "feet-washing" is a symbol for the kind of service we give. It can put us in vulnerable positions. We are not in control. But when we choose such service we are being faithful to the gospel. As our competence in the "towel and basin" ministry increases, we become better servants of Jesus to our brothers and sisters. The Spirit of Jesus enables us to do such things. Happiness is ours if we "ACT UPON IT!"

FRANCISCAN FOCUS

Clare Of Assisi

Clare is Francis' most faithful friend and follower. She is the daughter of Ortolana and Favorone di Offreduccio, a rich family in Assisi. She is one of three daughters. Her sisters are Catherine (Agnes) and Beatrice. She grew up in revolutionary times in Assisi. Clare's family belonged to the nobility. The nobility were the object of the revolution by the peasants. When the revolution grew violent (1198-1205), the family moved to Perugia. Clare's uncle, Monaldo, became a Perugian citizen. The family committed itself to fight for Perugia against Assisi. Perhaps some family members fought in the battle during which Francis was taken prisoner. The family remained in Perugia until about 1205. Assisians may have had some ambiguous feelings about the family when they returned from the "enemy" town.

Clare received a good education. She was probably better educated than Francis. She was a wise women with a sensitive heart. Though she was ten years younger than Francis, she was attracted to him. In her teen years she heard of his escapades and often went to hear him preach. His words struck a sympathetic chord in her heart. For over a year (1210 ff) she met with him to discuss his vision of life. His vision became her own and she decided to follow this gospel way of life.

In March, 1212, she left her home during the night and went to Francis. At the Portiuncula Francis cut her hair and gave her a rough tunic like his own. At first she lived at a Benedictine convent. Later she moved to San Damiano. Her flight from home caused quite a furor in the family. They tried to take her home by force, but were unsuccessful. Her two sisters joined her with a similar reaction by the family. The family was not happy at losing the daughters. Interestingly enough, when Clare's father died, her mother also joined Clare. Clare died on August 11, 1253.

Clare grasped the vision of Francis better than most. Her sense of poverty was sharp and clear. She knew that Jesus alone is the source of life. She defended the privilege of poverty with strong and persistent conviction. To be absorbed in seeking possessions could only be a roadblock to intimacy with Jesus. Neither bishops nor popes could swerve her from the path of poverty. Her wisdom and dedication made her the confidante of many people. She was indeed a beautiful flower in the garden of Francis. She deserves a special place in the hearts of those seeking to be faithful to the call of gospel living. Listen to her words.

> *What you hold, may you always hold.*
> *What you do, may you always do*
> *and never abandon.*
> *But with swift pace, light step*
> *and unswerving feet, so that*
> *even your steps stir up no dust,*
> *go forward securely, joyfully, and swiftly,*
> *on the path of prudent happiness,*
> *believing nothing, agreeing with nothing*
> *which would dissuade you from this resolution*
> *or which would place a stumbling block*
> *for you on the way,*
> *so that you may offer your vows*
> *to the Most High in the pursuit*
> *of that perfection to which the Spirit*
> *of the Lord has called you.*
> **Francis & Clare – Brady/Armstrong**
> **Paulist Press – Page 196**

QUESTIONS

1. Describe, in your own words, how Mary is a model of biblical spirituality. You may want to review chapter 8 to refresh your mind on the ideas of biblical spirituality.

2. What human qualities of Mary are most attractive to you? Why?

3. What criteria/standards would you use to evaluate whether devotion to Mary is solid and healthy? What signs would indicate an unhealthy devotion to Mary?

4. Write a commentary on the Magnificat (Luke 1: 46-55) Try to illustrate how this prayer offers a solid spirituality.

5. What role does Mary play in your spiritual life? How does she help you in following the gospel?

6. What qualities, in your opinion, are most important in community life? Why?

7. Give some concrete examples of how you SERVE others in your daily life. Do you feel competent in giving this service? How might you do better?

8. How would you describe a "gentle and courteous" spirit? What would hinder the growth of gentleness and courtesy?

9. Explain how good fraternity/community life enables us to serve one another and grow in a gentle and courteous spirit.

10. How would you understand St Clare's sense of the "privilege" of poverty?

SCRIPTURE reading/reflection

✝ John 15: 1-10

St John shares Jesus' word about the vine and the branches. Jesus contrasts the faithful and unfaithful follower. One bears fruit, the other becomes withered.

Share your reflections on the meaning of this text for your life. How does Mary serve as a model for fulfilling these words? What attitudes of the Magnificat are found in these words of Jesus? What is the goal or purpose of "bearing fruit"?

Woodcut by Fritz Eichenberg

CHAPTER 10

FRANCISCAN LIFESTYLE

We Americans coin many phrases. Among them is the term: LIFE-STYLE. Webster's new world dictionary defines it as follows:

Lifestyle ... the consistent, integrated way of life of an individual as typified by his manner, attitudes, possessions etc.

If it were possible, I'd love to spell out the lifestyle of a Franciscan. It would be great to be able to say how many material things a Franciscan ought to possess. It would be satisfying to pinpoint the attitudes a Franciscan ought to have on every subject. But such a detailed account is simply not possible. As usual, there are more questions than answers about the lifestyle of a Franciscan. Since we are pilgrims, our world keeps changing. Yesterday's answers may not fit today's problems. So I will simply share some ideas that relate to the subject of the "lifestyle" of a Franciscan.

Lifestyle

In order to create a Franciscan lifestyle that is "a consistent, integrated way of life ... as typified by our manner, attitudes, possessions etc", we'll be asking a lot of questions. Some may not have answers. But we will continue our search, because we are pilgrims. We will "keep on keeping on." We will move on even when there is no God-given blueprint. Some people will want to offer us an answer book. They refuse to move until God gives a blueprint. But we know from Abraham's experience that God doesn't always give blueprints and roadmaps.

Other folks will want to offer dogmatic answers. People flock to such a secure way of traveling. It is especially attractive to people who are insecure. They seem to delight in pre-packaged material. But our way may be less secure from a purely human point of view. However, trusting God even without a blueprint is much more gospel oriented.

Franciscans TRUST Jesus and rely on the Spirit of Jesus as they travel. They RELY on the gospel and the way of Jesus as they follow the vision. Franciscans take the GOOD though imperfect steps of the wanderer. Sometimes they walk forward fearfully or uncertainly – but they walk! From human standards they may seem to take too many risks. But if their journey is nudged by the gospel, they rely on God's faithfulness as they walk.

Our lifestyle does not develop a strategy for imposing guilt on ourselves or others. We will offer alternatives to things that seem to be destructive of life and/or people. If anyone is disturbed by the demands of our alternative, we will walk with him/her. We will help bridge the gap between the gospel and his/her lifestyle. Since we follow the gospel imperfectly, we are in no position to judge others. Our approach will be gentle rather than condemnatory. A genuine response to the gospel will bring joy and peace. Others may be attracted to these qualities in gospel-people.

We have words to share and dreams to hope in. We may sense that some folks are trapped by possessions or boxed in by a lifestyle that is confining. We can understand how easily we humans get caught in such traps. We will approach folks with gentleness and courtesy. Consistency in gentleness and courtesy is no little thing. Integrating life and the gospel does not happen automatically or without pain. We believe it is possible because Jesus has gifted us with his Spirit.

This chapter is full of reflection and questions. It is an attempt to come to grips with the consequences of a Franciscan lifestyle in today's world. The lifestyles of today may need to be challenged. The lifestyle of Francis may need to be studied more seriously. However we go about it, we need to face the challenge that living a gospel lifestyle requires of us. We will make choices that are consistent with the gospel of Jesus.

> *The great majority of North American Catholics were poor immigrants, and their church was the church of the poor. But after one or more generations we forgot the*

*very real poverty of our ancestors and became true sons
and daughters of the middle class. ... We try to convince
ourselves that today's poor are poor because of their own
fault and that all REAL Americans belong to the middle
class.*

*It is at this moment that our Father, St Francis, comes
to our aid. He makes us understand poverty. Poverty is
evil, and in any society where there is much poverty we
have to conclude that it is an evil society. In his day, St
Francis showed that society had to CHANGE. In the
midst of injustice, Francis preached the Kingdom of
God, i.e. he preached community. He called young men
and women of his time to come together and form
communities with the poor so that poverty could be
overcome!*

Cardinal Paulo Arns OFM
Maryknoll – September '82

People who live through an economic depression have unique ideas
about money and possessions. I remember how my father was distrust-
ful of banks. Even though he did part-time work for a bank as an
assessor, he didn't trust the system. The depression had made him wary
of the banking establishment. It wasn't a matter of right or wrong, but
simply a "feeling" about such things. When he died, we found a small
safe that he kept in the house. It contained some money "just in case
..." If you explore your own experiences, you may find similar attitudes
about money and security. It is not easy to trust when experience has
brought loss and suffering. Our attitudes may not be logical but they
are very real.

Lifestyles have a variety of names. The lifestyles of the "Jet set" and the
"Swingers" differ from that which stereotypes the motorcycle crowd.
Fundamentalist attitudes and lifestyle on a "born again" campus are
quite different from the lifestyle of more liberal groups on university
campuses. Film stars and rock groups have a quite different lifestyle
than the "rednecks" or old-time politicians. Religious fanatics develop
a lifestyle filled with holy cards and belief in the latest "visionary",
while others deepen a lifestyle based on the compassion found in the
gospel. The lifestyle of the rich and famous is noted for its extravagance

while sports heroes bask in notoriety and big salaries. With such an abundance of lifestyles, Franciscans are faced with many choices.

A gospel lifestyle is something we CHOOSE. It is not imposed from the outside, but springs from within the heart. The gospel gives us a way of perceiving people and events and the world around us. It helps us choose life-giving things that are of primary value to us. The gospel does not allow us the numbness of remaining static but nudges us to changes that are dynamic. The events and experiences of life are evaluated from the viewpoint of the gospel. Few things are ever infallibly settled. As we grow in our understanding of Jesus and his gospel we "review the situation" from this fresh perspective. Pilgrims can never quite "settle in" and remain satisfied with their progress. There are always many miles to walk before we sleep!

The process of living a consistent, integrated gospel life is unending. I remember my first trip to the Rocky Mountains. When we began the drive up the mountain, I was astounded at the view. Trees and woods were brilliant in a fall painting of reds and yellows. As we moved upward, the view offered still greater perspective. I saw the same trees, but now they were part of a bigger forest. I had to climb higher to see that pattern. As we climbed still higher, the trees and road and cabins blended in a new vision of relationship. There seemed a connectedness with all I had seen before. The widening perspective repeated itself as we reached the top. Then the grand design seemed even more overwhelming. I think our gospel pilgrimage is like that. We don't lose what we have learned in our past experiences. But as we grow we see them differently. Sometimes we understand them better when they are linked with our present experiences. Learning never ceases – nor does the delight of discovery grow boring.

A Franciscan lifestyle calls for trust as we climb our path to intimacy with Jesus. Evil often seems to triumph in our world. Massacres, mass slaughter and holocausts bombard our experience. Inhumanity and murder become almost commonplace and we can grow cold and defensive. In our anger and frustration at such outrages, we feel like we could "kill" the perpetrators. What we see in others we know could happen in us. We are capable of such destructive feelings. It is no simple thing to deal with the volcanoes and demons in our own heart. It may seem overwhelming to deal with the demons unleashed in our world!

212

Franciscans are not "handwringers", moping about how awful things are. Such powerful evil within and outside ourselves only pushes us to work harder to bring life to these situations. We present to the world the life-giving power of Jesus. He came to bring life and light, not death and darkness. He came to give his life for others not take life away from others. He came to teach us how to forgive not how to hate and kill. As evil seems to escalate so will we escalate our attempts to live the gospel. Rather than feeling helpless, we acknowledge God's call by greater fidelity to the gospel. The light cannot be overcome by the darkness. The life of the Spirit cannot be overcome by all the death-squads in the world. We will work harder to be salt and light, not fearfully, but proudly. We will confidently offer a gospel lifestyle that respects people rather than destroying them.

We are faced with many "isms" in our world. We feel helpless in many situations. Many things are beyond our individual control. But God works well when we are helpless. God calls us to faithfulness – not necessarily to success. We may not always win, but we will seek to be faithful to the gospel. That is our idea of "success". Our personal helplessness can also make us more aware of our need for community. Individualism can leave us isolated, lonely and hopeless in the face of problems too big to handle. Jesus call us together, to "communion" with each other. Together we face the realities of evil with the confidence of a faith-community that relies on the Holy Spirit. Franciscans know that the local fraternity/community is important for a consistent, integrated way of life.

Today's "isms" challenge us to be genuine about our Franciscan life-style. Consider a few of these "isms".

Sexism/Racism

... common diseases. Both of them flow from a narrow, prejudicial point of view. They label people with nothing more than gender or skin color as data. Such judgments are narrow, unfair and sometimes – unconscious. Character, skills, virtues and personality count for little to a racist or sexist person. People are judged and categorized without personal relationships. Sexism and racism assume things about people independent of the facts. Gender and/or skin color is the only data for judgement. Blind and narrow-minded, these folks believe themselves to be wise and broad minded. Prejudice separates people. It creates suspicion and mistrust. It separates sexes and races, creating an atmosphere where everyone loses. It is a closed-world, totally unfitting to a Franciscan lifestyle.

How do we accept one another and our role as man or woman? How well do we affirm the differing gifts we bring to one another? What personal sexist/racist ideas need change? How equal is our acceptance of one another? How do sexist/racist images hinder our knowledge of God? How sexist/racist is our language? Attitudes? Behavior? How well do we work with people of another race or gender to build a better world? Is sexism and racism a sin?

Consumerism

The acquisition of things for my own use is a common practice. I can easily be convinced that I have a real need for something I "want". The more popular and common it becomes, the more certain is my conviction that I cannot live without it. The advertising industry spends millions of dollars to convince me that I cannot live without it. Their creativity convinces me that I must buy their product. Ads tell me that intimacy will be mine if I use the right perfume – and I truly need intimacy. I will be respected by all if I own a luxury car – and I truly want to be respected. I will be happy if I buy the latest camera that allows me to record important family events – and I truly enjoy the memories of happy occasions. I will lose my teeth if I don't brush with a certain toothpaste – and I don't want to lose my teeth. Living in a consumer society means we are subject to developing attitudes based on the possession and accumulation of things. In fact, as Tevye says of the rich in <u>Fiddler on the Roof</u>: "When you're rich they think you really know" An uncritical attitude in a consumer society can create problems for a gospel lifestyle.

We will be faced with the reality of our society as we try to be true to our Franciscan lifestyle. So we will be challenged by many questions.

How well do we sort out our "needs" from our "wants"? Have we begun to believe that accumulation of things makes us a better person? How do we define success and failure in our lives? If people are hurt because of excessive profit-taking, what is our attitude about that? What proportion of what we own is really needed and what is not necessary? How well do we share what we have with others? What is our basic attitude in this regard? Do you think God wants us to be destitute? How does a faith- community best deal with the problem of consumerism? What values do your children/friends absorb from the way you deal with money and the accumulation of things? If you lived a simple lifestyle, how would it look? Do you think a simple lifestyle looks the same for everyone? Is there a common INNER attitude for all who live a simple lifestyle? What is it?

Leisure/Solitude

A Franciscan lifestyle will have a particular stance toward leisure and solitude. No one attains intimacy with another without investing time with the "other". A lifestyle that would profess that Jesus is important will need to take the time such a relationship requires. To listen to the Spirit and reflect on the gospel means being quiet and allowing our inner heart to hear. Cherishing solitude is a natural part of our lifestyle. A genuine lifestyle that allows for intimacy will nudge us to find creative ways to "take time" for Jesus. Each person will construct the structure that best serves individual needs.

We will share our individual ideas of prayerfulness. Such sharing offers a variety of ways of approaching the Lord. Each individual contributes his/her uniqueness through such sharing. It widens our awareness of the many ways the Spirit chooses to work in everyday life. Sharing our ideas and experiences of solitude and prayer is a good way to be accountable and balanced in our prayerfulness.

In a workaholic world, the use of leisure is an important element of a Franciscan lifestyle. We are accustomed to time-clocks. Work can become a necessity for economic survival. The demands of the business world do not always allow us to "take time" for life. Work and salary often become the foundation of our self-worth. Not to work or to work less than we do seems unthinkable to many people. Even our recreations are often so intense that they continue the stress load. Psychologically, when we take no time off from a dominating dedication to work, we become human robots. We are uneasy unless we are busy. We can't imagine just "doing nothing", much less talking to one another about serious things. Keeping the Sabbath day of rest comes hard to a society steeped in a "never stop" mode of living. I imagine psychiatrists are happy that we keep such a pace. It does help business. Words like stress, burnout, breakdown are commonly used in the marketplace.

A Franciscan lifestyle will invite us to give better direction to our lives. If we are able to simplify our lifestyle, we will begin to diminish our "wants." Fun times will be a normal part of life. The American dream will be wisely tempered with a good sense of priorities and humor. Celebrations will enliven us. Quiet times will be treasured. I especially loved what one of my Capuchin brothers told me on my silver jubilee: "Lester, have at least 25 celebrations this year – and enjoy every one of them!" When you celebrate – celebrate! Don't diminish the joy by worrying about what you have to do at home. Be where you are and enjoy it!

The ideal is not easy to achieve.

On what do you base your worth as a person? Does work dominate your life or support it? How does our economic system support a vibrant life? How does our economic system hinder living a vibrant life? What are the priorities in your life? Could someone else discover them by watching how you live? Why or why not? How important is leisure for you? How well does your use of leisure refresh you? Do the people around you get set aside or put down because you are too busy or irritable? What can you do about this? What kind of experience of solitude have you had? Has it been helpful? Painful? Scary? Delightful? What are you doing to learn good ways to use solitude? How well do you celebrate? Do you need artificial stimulants to have a "good time?" What does such a need say about your lifestyle? How much of your inner heart do you share with others? What are your greatest fears about doing this? How would you evaluate an economic system that keeps folks so busy they have no time for one another? Could you work to make changes – even small ones – in your own job? These questions only begin a process of seeking. Take the time to invest in the search.

Forgiveness/Reconciliation

Church folks talk about "hating the sin but loving the sinner." It may be a great motto, but how does one manage it? When someone hurts me, I get angry at "them" and not just at their "sin." I think other folks may feel that way too. At the moment of impact it is difficult to start making beautiful distinctions. I have found, however, that if I take time to simmer down, I can begin to sort things out. Little by little I begin to look at the issue without the personal hurt of my initial reaction. When I hurt, I want to strike back. Forgiveness is not what I want to do. A gospel lifestyle requires traveling the road of forgiveness.

Instead of nourishing my desire to defend or get revenge, I start a different process. I CHOOSE to try to forgive. That's about as big a step as I can take. But I choose to lean that way rather than the riled-up position of revenge. In serious matters this is not easy. It seems almost impossible. If I am the person who has been hurt, I feel downright self-righteous about how I feel. I have every right to be angry! Until this stance begins to soften, forgiveness is not even an option. But if I stay in such a stance, it begins to destroy something in me. No matter how righteous my negative response, it starts eating away at any form of peace. It makes it difficult to pray to a Jesus who calls us to forgive our enemies.

When we begin the process of healing, we may begin with a very small step. We decide, despite our feelings, that we will choose the process of forgiveness. We may not be able to do much more at the beginning. We may not even feel like forgiving. We may feel hypocritical about saying: "I forgive you." But if we want to follow the forgiveness path, we begin by beginning. Forgiveness does not mean we agree with what happened. It means I want to lift the hurt from the relationship.

Doris Donnelly offers a healthy process to follow. Please realize that forcing a "let's shake hands and make up" tends to ignore forgiveness in an attempt at reconciliation. It does not work.

1. Look honestly and realistically at the hurt. Don't deny and evade the reality of it.

2. Invite Jesus into the situation to help with the healing. We are often incapable of forgiveness without the help of the Lord. Ask his help and invite him into the situation.

3. Acknowledge the reality of the hurt and suffering. If you ignore this reality, you will simply "band-aid" the problem without getting at the basics.

4. Forgive the hurt – directly, precisely without holding back. Don't pussyfoot about it. Be direct in your forgiveness. You know how you hurt or were hurt. Deal with the situation honestly and directly.

5. Reconcile the situation – which is possible only AFTER real forgiveness. Don't waffle on forgiveness and try to jump to reconciliation – it doesn't work!

Sometimes the person who hurt you (years ago?) may have died. In such cases allow Jesus to be present to you both – and say the words in his presence. With living persons, direct physical presence is best. But we can never demand that the other forgive. We can only let go of the burden of hurt from our own heart.

Do I harbor unforgiveness? How does unforgiveness affect my lifestyle as a gospel-person What do I let loose of when I offer forgiveness? How willing am I to seek forgiveness when I have hurt others? Why is it important to draw Jesus into the process of forgiveness? Why is the way of forgiveness a part of a Franciscan lifestyle? How does forgiveness happen when we are hurt by a group of people? Can a gospel person refuse forgiveness? Why is forgiveness necessary before real reconciliation takes place? What does unforgiveness do to the person who harbors it? Is anger at being hurt a sin? Give reasons for your answer! How can we begin the process of forgiveness when we still feel angry? If we feel incapable of beginning to forgive, is there any way to get help? What role would a good faith-community play in the process of forgiveness and reconciliation?

Acceptance

Our lifestyle covers many things. We are called to learn to accept people of all kinds. Many time people get trapped in debilitating situations. Divorced people often feel left out of life. There is a sense of failure and awful loneliness. Franciscans accept divorced people. People with AIDS may die. No matter how they contracted AIDS, Franciscans accept people with AIDS. People with chemical dependence slowly kill themselves with drugs or alcohol. Franciscans accept people with chemical dependencies. People with terminal illness often struggle with the finality of such news. Franciscans accept and support their search for acceptance. The list could go on and on. For the Franciscan, no one is a "nobody."

Acceptance does NOT mean approval. It does not serve addictions by softening the consequences. Tough love will often be necessary. Intervention by competent people may be called for. Rehabilitation programs may be required. But a Franciscan lifestyle requires realistic acceptance of the person and competent handling of the "problem." It is not easy – but it is part of our lifestyle. People feel unworthy when chemicals, breakdowns, destitution, or illness take away their dignity. Our lifestyle requires us to offer the acceptance that gives them dignity.

What is the difference between acceptance and approval? Why is "softening the blow" for someone addicted to drugs or alcohol unhealthy? How would you describe "Tough love?" Why is intervention necessary when people deny their problem? Why is competence needed in an intervention? If people never suffer the consequences of their actions, will they deal with their problem? Are there problems in your life that you try to deny are happening? Are you willing to face them? Will you seek help? How would "acceptance" by someone else be defined if you were the person with the "problem?" Does the gospel idea of "love" put any time limit on love?

What A Lifestyle!

There is always more. But I hope these reflections give some sense of what Franciscans seek to embrace. We are ordinary people who believe in the gospel vision of life. We fail frequently, but refuse to abandon the journey. We are less faithful than we try to be, but we continue to seek greater fidelity. Above all, each day makes us more aware of our need for Jesus and his Spirit.

> For those whom God knew before ever they were, he also ordained to share the likeness of his Son, so that he might be the eldest among a large family ...

With all this in mind, what are we to say? If God is on our side, who is against us? ... Then what can separate us from the love of Christ? Can affliction or hardship? Can persecution, hunger, nakedness, danger or the sword? We are being done to death for your sake all day long, as scripture says: "We have been treated like sheep for slaughter." – and yet, throughout it all, overwhelming victory is ours through him who loved us! For I am convinced that there is nothing in death or life, in the realms of the spirits or superhuman powers in the world as it is or the world as it shall be, in the forces of the universe, in heights or depths – nothing in all creation that can separate us from the love of God in Christ Jesus our Lord.

Romans 8: 29-39

Our profession as Franciscans calls us to reflect on our style of living. We are called to be light to the world. We are asked not to hide our gifts from others. We are commanded to forgive others. We are quickly aware that a gospel lifestyle requires a lifetime of commitment. It requires an intimacy with Jesus who is our source of light and power. God trusts us. God delights in our attempts to be faithful. Continue to bring delight to the heart of God.

SECULAR FRANCISCAN RULE

15. Let them individually and collectively be in the forefront in promoting justice by the testimony of their human lives and their courageous initiatives. Especially in the field of public life, they should make definite choices in harmony with their faith.

16. Let them esteem work both as a gift and as a sharing in the creation, redemption and service of the human community.

RULE – Chapter 2 #15-16

Jesus is direct and sharp when it comes to justice for people. Scandalizing the "little ones" deserves death with a millstone. Jesus is angry with the self-righteous who never lift a finger to relieve another's burden. Jesus clearly spoke out for the ways of justice and concern.

Like anyone else, Franciscans can think in terms of "us" and "them." "We" are the good folks. "Them" are the bad folks who need change and reform. "We" are blessed by God while "them" are ignorant and cursed. "We" are wise in the ways of God. "Them" know nothing of God. Such condescending and arrogant attitudes find no place in the teachings of Jesus. Quite often Jesus clearly condemns such attitudes.

Sometimes folks are sincerely self-righteous and arrogant. Our sincerity masks the dark side of such attitudes. We sincerely believe we are "saviors" for those poor, misguided people who know nothing of Jesus. We walk smugly through life, wondering why people are turned off by our attempts to save them. When we discover such attitudes there is no need for a guilt trip. What is needed is a clear, radical and interior conversion. This is part of what Franciscan life is all about.

What we need is: ✛ Better gospel insights ✛ Greater compassion ✛ Better understanding of personal limitations ✛ How love shows itself in real situations ✛ Who is the savior ✛ Our own brokenness ✛ Our need for conversion ... to mention but a few.

> *Anyone who loves me will heed what I say; then my Father will love him, and we will come to him and make our dwelling with him; but whoever does not love me does not heed what I say.*
>
> **John 14: 23-24**

God is passionately in love with us. Our response to that love affects the way we experience it. But it does not change God. Different situations influence us in different ways. Sometimes we wonder whether God loves us when things are going badly. Sometimes we know God's love when things go well in our lives. In both cases God's love is at work. But we experience and respond to it in different ways. God's faithful love is the foundation of our worth. This gives us courage to take the initiatives that justice requires.

Our pursuit of justice touches a great deal of daily life. When we see injustice, whether on a schoolground or in an office, our task is to address it directly, gently and courteously. If people receive inhumane treatment, we will speak out against it and offer alternatives. Some economic systems trample the rights of people. Such systems need to be changed. Even if it takes years, Franciscans will continue the work to change unjust systems. Sometimes we confront power far greater than our own. But we will persist because we are committed to the path of justice. Seeking the ways of justice is often hard, frustrating, confusing, unsuccessful, even fearful, ministry. Change comes slowly and often meets with powerful resistance. Without the staying power of faith and the support of a solid faith-community we could easily give up. Those who would be in the "forefront in promoting justice" will quickly experience the risks, pain, rejection and even violence such a role can bring.

But fighting injustice is only part of the battle. Positively, we need to build the atmosphere in society that allows people freedom to grow to their full human potential. Such an atmosphere can aid both the oppressed and the oppressor. It is filled with acceptance, the ability to confront with love, the willingness to change one's own oppressive attitudes, the readiness to stick with it for the long haul. Both success and failure will meet our efforts. If our search for justice is built on faith in Jesus, we will persist. Depending on the Lord, walking the ways of gospel-faith, we will seek to build the Kingdom of God wherever we walk. All things are possible with the Lord.

There are many ordinary places for us to "do justice." We can create a climate of growth for our spouse, our children and our friends. We can build just structures in our parish and in our place of employment. We can enter into the struggle for justice with the poor and the homeless. We may be in a position to create greater justice within our prisons and in civil government. To "feel with" the victims of injustice will be part of our training for justice. We are not so naive as to expect that people are so good they never do anything stupid or evil. Neither will we be so pessimistic that we expect everybody to act in aggressive and destructive ways. The proverb says it well: "There is so much bad in the best of us, and so much good in the worst of us, that it ill behooves any of us, to talk about the rest of us."

When you work for justice, get your facts straight. Discover the truth of the situation. Listen to the different viewpoints and feelings. Get a good sense of what justice requires in this situation. Then initiate solid action to deal with the injustice or, at least, to begin a process of dealing with it. Sometimes injustice springs from ignorance. Correct it with education. Sometimes people are unaware of their injustice. Help them to become aware. Sometimes people are fearful of what they will lose if they practice justice. Try to help them overcome such fears. Sometimes injustice springs from uncontrolled grasping for power and/or greed. Hard work will be required to address such situations of injustice and oppression. If we are to be a people in the "forefront in promoting justice," be ready to pray a lot, share a lot, and discover how powerlessness feels.

Working for social justice will be more genuine if we also work at keeping our own house in order. Individually and as a community we must confront injustice in our own hearts and in our community life. Injustice drowns out love. But when love and justice combine, mercy blossoms. Our human struggle to create an atmosphere of justice is part of the Franciscan lifestyle.

*Therefore, since you have accepted Christ Jesus as Lord,
live in union with him. Be rooted in him, be built on him,
grow strong in the faith as you were taught; let your
hearts overflow with thankfulness. Be on your guard, let
no one capture your minds with hollow and delusive
speculations, based on traditions of human teaching and
centered on the elemental spirits of the universe and not
on Christ.*

Colossians 2: 6-8

Work

In a later chapter we will take a long look at work. For now a few
reflections are in order.

All of us do some sort of work. We have the God-given responsibility
to care for the earth. Work helps to fulfill this responsibility. We share
in the continuing work of creation. We are privileged to be able to work.
It ought to give us dignity.

But it is dangerous to make work THEE sign of our worth. If the ability
to work is the ONLY source of our self worth, a dangerous value is at
work. We become worthless when we are no longer able to work. Such
folks are perceived as useless and worthless because they don't "carry
their weight." Such an attitude is anti-gospel. Self-worth is not earned
by work or wisdom or success. It is given because God loves us. God
does not cease to love us when we have a stroke or when we retire or
when we are fired. Important as work is, it must never be the only
criterion of self-worth.

Work is one way we share with God in God's continuing creative
power. We draw from the earth, and from our creative resources, things
that support sound human growth. The inner vision of a blind person
offers insights that eyes often miss. Handicapped persons often reveal
an inner faith that shines through crippled bodies. The honest and
genuine expression of feelings of the retarded reveal how healthy the
world of emotions can be. Work is not simply producing "things." It is
art and music, poetry and photography. It is a life of reverence and
respect, joy and delight. Such work stands side-by-side with cement

225

masons and architects, taxi drivers and teachers. Work opens the human spirit to the wonders of visions and creates the marvels of great buildings. God allows us to work with the creative power that is given by the creator. Our task is to nourish it and help it enhance human life.

In that sense, wages, profits and economic systems are meant to serve this creative power, not control it. You and I are privileged to continue the creative work of God. We work in order to create a world where people can live in harmony.

> *Those brothers (sisters) to whom the Lord has given the grace of working should do their work faithfully and devotedly, so that, avoiding idleness, the enemy of the soul, they do not extinguish the spirit of holy prayer and devotion to which all other things of our earthly existence must contribute.*
> **Francis & Clare – Brady/Armstrong**
> **Paulist Press – Page 140**

FRANCISCAN FOCUS

Patron Saints – Elizabeth & Louis

St Elizabeth of Hungary and St Louis of France are the lay patrons of the Secular Franciscan Order. The feast of Louis is on August 25th and that of Elizabeth on November 17th.

Elizabeth was born in 1207, a contemporary of St Francis. According to custom, she was engaged to Louis of Thuringia at the tender age of three! As she grew up she developed a tender concern for the poor. Her in-laws didn't like her, but Louis loved her dearly. Elizabeth had to deal with a simmering feud with her mother-in-law throughout her married life. Louis supported her many efforts to help the poor. When famine struck, Elizabeth opened a soup kitchen for the needy.

When Louis died, Elizabeth's in-laws forced her off the throne and out of her home. With her four children she was left penniless and homeless. Her trust in God grew during this tough time. She developed a prayerfulness that brought her peace. She continued to serve her "poor ones" as best she could. It seems that Francis himself introduced her to the Secular Franciscans. She felt right at home in this way of life. She was eventually restored to her rightful position. She then provided for the care of her children and spent her last years nursing the sick in Marburg. She died in 1231 at the age of 24.

✛ ✛ ✛ ✛ ✛

Louis of France (no relation to Louis of Thuringia) was born in 1215. His mother, Blanche, shared her strong faith with him. He was crowned king of France at age 12. His mother governed in his name until he came of age. Sometime during this period he became a Secular Franciscan, possibly influenced by his Franciscan teachers. Bonaventure and Aquinas were honored guests at his table. He was a good father to his 11 children.

Louis governed France for many years. During a serious illness he promised to lead a Crusade to the Holy Land if he recovered. Upon recovery he fulfilled his promise. He was captured during the siege of Damietta. The Saracens promised him freedom if he would deny Jesus. He refused. But his courage impressed his captors and they released him.

Louis returned to France. He worked hard to apply the gospel to the business of governing. The artificial life of the court pained him. Injustice among some of his officials met with Louis' anger. Privately he lived a very simple life.

He embarked on a second Crusade in 1270. He caught the plague while visiting the sick and died in 1297 at the age of 82. Both he and Elizabeth dealt with real life with a heart influenced by the gospel. Amid family problems, court intrigues and personal suffering, they served the Lord well.

QUESTIONS

1. Write out YOUR description of a Franciscan lifestyle. It is not necessary to cover everything, only the elements that are important to you.

2. What positively disturbed you in this chapter i.e. made you want to change something in your lifestyle? Share what it is and what you are doing about it.

3. How would you implement gospel-justice ideas in your life? How would your actions influence others?

4. What is the value of sharing both faith AND weakness? Describe what your own experience of sharing means to you.

5. What quality in other people makes it easier to share? What quality makes it difficult?

6. Love, hope, faith and justice need to be integrated in a Franciscan lifestyle. Explain why these qualities need one another?

7. Describe the process of forgiveness-reconciliation. If you have a personal experience of this process, please share it. What would be most helpful to enable you to forgive and seek reconciliation?

8. Why is community support important for those who work for peace and justice? What does the community do that is so important?

9. Describe areas in your life, in your home, in your parish, in your city where you see a greater need for sensitivity to justice issues? What are you doing about it?

10. Describe the various "isms" of this chapter in your own words. Which one causes you the most problems in trying to live a gospel lifestyle?

SCRIPTURE *reading/reflection*

✝ John 8: 1-11

The story of the woman caught in adultery is a familiar one. As you read it, listen to it as though for the first time. BE the woman – imagine her feelings. BE the people – how do they feel? How do the words of Jesus sound when you are the woman? the people? How do the words of Jesus reveal his lifestyle and attitudes? Enter into all the feelings – fears, righteousness, compassion, embarrassment.

Write out the things that impress you the most in this story. What does it teach about our Franciscan-gospel lifestyle?

INDIAN PRAYER FOR PEACE

OH, GREAT SPIRIT WHO DWELLS IN THE SKY, LEAD US TO THE PATH OF PEACE AND UNDERSTANDING. LET ALL OF US LIVE TOGETHER AS BROTHERS AND SISTERS. OUR LIVES ARE SO SHORT HERE, WALKING UPON MOTHER EARTH'S SURFACE. LET OUR EYES BE OPENED TO ALL THE BLESSINGS YOU HAVE GIVEN US. PLEASE HEAR OUR PRAYERS, OH, GREAT SPIRIT.

CHAPTER 11

THE REAL WORLD

A bird flew out of forest into sky.
What does that mean?
It left the cool, the green darkness
for the love-colored cliffs of light
between day and night.

It left the fruited branch
of its poor clinging
for the bright, treeless air.
And in its flight it multiplied its singing.

Tell me, my dullness fastened to your branch,
is there no lesson there?
Mountain Sparrow – Jessica Powers

Many of us struggle to pray. Sometimes our patience is too short for good listening. Sometimes we are too busy to pray. So many other things need to be done. Anxious to get on with life, prayer is relegated to the back burner of our lives. Often it becomes a final resource when we need help. We are active people, involved in myriad tasks that leave little time for prayer. Intellectually we acknowledge our need for prayer. Practically, we may choose many other things rather than prayer.

We do good things. We help with religious education or work at a soup kitchen or shelter for the homeless. We plan liturgies or visit the sick. Who can quarrel with the value of good works? Prayer doesn't seem to produce anything tangible. Who wants to leave the "fruited branch ... for the bright treeless air."? Who wants to sing and leave all those needs and needy behind?

At its very best, prayer requires us to stand naked before God. We hold back nothing for ourselves. We are vulnerable to God, open to any working of the Spirit. Such prayer acknowledges that we can DO NOTHING, but with God all things are possible. It is not even "doing your best and God will do the rest." It IS "without me you can do nothing!" To stand thus exposed makes us aware of our dependence on God. It strips away the entanglements of our impulses and compulsions to be "doing something." It acknowledges Jesus as Lord.

Prayer invites us to destroy the idols of our life. Sometimes knowledge of the latest techniques of prayer becomes an idol. Sometimes making work "my prayer" becomes an idol. Sometimes we see no need for God and that attitude becomes an idol. Dogmatism about prayer can become an idol. Our belief in the power of technology can become an idol. Convincing ourselves that we don't have time for prayer can be our false god. Fear of standing naked and exposed before God and ourself can be an idol. We have many ways to give power to things that are not God. We have plenty of "strange gods" in our lives.

These false gods are attractive because they possess a grain of truth. Some of them seem to be beautiful ways to serve God's people. That is why they trap us so easily. Some of them find support from society, and it is hard to go against the tide of opinion. As I walk the path of prayerfulness, I need to recognize these false gods. I will bring them into the presence of the real God and see how small they are. I will reveal myself to the real God and allow God's transforming Spirit to change me.

> *But my people did not listen to my voice,*
> *Israel would have none of me;*
> *so I let them go with their stubborn hearts*
> *to follow their own devices.*
>
> *If my people would but listen to me,*
> *if Israel would only conform to my ways,*
> *I should soon bring their enemies*
> *to their knees and turn my hand*
> *against their foes.*
>
> *Those hostile to the Lord would come*
> *cringing to him, and meet*
> *with everlasting punishment,*

while Israel would be fed with the
finest flour and satisfied
with honey from the rocks.

Psalm 81: 11-16

St Francis sensed the need for humility in his life. An attitude of listening, joined to a readiness to learn, is important for prayer.

> *... if you were so subtle and wise that you have all knowledge and knew how to interpret all tongues and minutely investigate the heavenly bodies, in all these things you could not glory. For one demon knew more about the things of earth than all men together. ... these things would be an obstacle to you and none of them would belong to you nor could you glory in any of these things. But in this we can glory – in our infirmities and bearing daily the holy cross of our Lord Jesus Christ.*

Francis and Clare – Brady/Armstrong
Paulist Press – Page 29

Prayer reveals the truth about God and ourselves. The light of God unveils the fact that God alone is God – there is no other. God loves us, holds us close to his cheek, loves us unconditionally. As we accept our reality as creatures, God gifts us with intimacy. But it is not easy to be totally honest before God.

Some Obstacles To Prayer

We have inherited a philosophical distinction of body and soul. This separation comes from Plato, not from Jesus. Our bodies are seen as the weak, sinful side of our self. Anything connected to the body is less than good, while the soul winds up with a good image. Sex is connected with body, so it is obviously no good. Penitential practices often were used to keep the body in control.

Without trying to solve the philosophical arguments, this body-soul dichotomy has been a problem for Christians. If we accept the argument that the body is bad, how can we use the body in prayer? Can a comfortable body contribute to good prayer? Is it possible to be a whole person in prayer without using the body? Can our masculine and feminine qualities contribute to good prayer? Such philosophical schizophrenia can be an obstacle to prayer. We are one person, not a divided human being.

Some of us were taught only prayers of intercession. We keep asking for things from God. We were taught this practice as children and continue it into adulthood. Prayer of praise and thanks were not always part of early training. Some of us remain in the state of "give-me" praying. Praise and thanks are given short shrift in our prayer life. Yet they reveal maturity in prayer. If we wish to grow in prayerfulness, we will need to move beyond using ONLY intercessory prayer.

Of all the obstacles to prayer, nothing matches a heart that refuses forgiveness. Anyone who clings to resentment and unforgiveness will find prayerfulness next to impossible on a consistent basis. Jesus asked us to forgive others before joining in community worship. Our attempts at individual prayer will be hindered when our heart is angry or hateful. An unforgiving heart is a mockery when we come before a forgiving God. It's as though we are hiding clubs and knives under our coats instead of standing in openness before God. First we pray and then we hope to get revenge! Such a stance in not likely to enhance our ability to pray. We may have feelings of hurt or anger when we come to prayer. Honest prayer will acknowledge such feelings and seek help to deal with them. We need God's help to begin to forgive. But if we cling to our resentment and anger, growth in prayer will be stymied.

If our world is one of rigid and narrow ideas it will affect our ability to pray. Intimacy with Jesus tends to widen our horizons and encourage our search for new insights. However, if we are fearful and aggressive, we may find it difficult to have the openness that good prayer requires. We are faced with a God who loves to continue revealing fresh insights and ideas. God loves to share the richness of the Spirit with us. If we have decided we know-it-all, our prayer may easily stagnate.

Whatever hinders our growth as whole persons will hinder our growth in prayer. We humans are limited. God continues the revelation given through Jesus. Both as a community and as individuals we continue to grow in our knowledge and love of Jesus and one another. Life requires that we change and change often. The wonder of discovery will con-

234

tinue until we die. Each stage of life unveils another dimension of God's ability to be present in fresh ways. Openness is no little thing. But it is important that we seek the path of openness, allowing for God's continuing revelation.

> *There is much more that I could say to you, but the burden would be too great for you now. However, when the Spirit of truth comes, he will guide you into all the truth; for he will not speak on his own authority, but will speak only what he hears; and he will make known to you what is to come. He will glorify me, for he will take what is mine and make it known to you. All that the Father has is mine and that is why I said: "He will take what is mine and make it known to you."*
> John 16: 12-15

Jesus At Prayer

Jesus prayed with his neighbors in the Synagogue. He took an active part in their communal prayer. Jesus prayed in the desert, in quiet places that afforded solitude. He prayed with his disciples, inviting them to join him in prayer. He prayed before raising Lazarus, praising his Father for what God would do. He prayed when he was afraid in the garden of Gethsemane. He prayed words of hope at the Last Supper, sharing intimate thoughts with his friends. No place was too insignificant for prayer. No person too unimportant to pray for. Sometimes he questioned events, as in his prayer in the garden of Gethsemane. At other times he spent days in prayer, as when he was led into the desert. He prayed before healings and during healings. Prayerfulness was an atmosphere in which Jesus lived. He sensed the presence of his Father wherever he walked. Such intimacy both led to prayer and was a consequence of prayer.

As a result Jesus DID the will of his Father. He grew sharp and clear in expressing the Father's message to the people. His interpretation of life was colored and dominated by the influence of his Father, his "Abba." He was fearless in being faithful to that influence. Whether angels came to defend him or not, Jesus would be faithful. He could not imagine life without his Father. Such love diminishes the power of fear to influence decisions.

Prayer teaches us that God-is-with-us. It enables us to listen to God. It strengthens our ability to follow the gospel. It enables us to stop clutching and clinging to things, ideas and attitudes that keep us from God. As we let go of our baggage, we are free to be faithful to the word of God expressed in Scripture. Prayer nourishes our gospel life. Our attempts at gospel living move us to pray. Prayer is a lifetime engagement. The power of Jesus infiltrates our life as we surrender ourselves to God in prayer. We become one with the beloved, joined in a bond of unity given by the Holy Spirit.

> *From his full store we have all received grace upon grace; for the law was given through Moses, but grace and truth came through Jesus Christ. No one has ever seen God. God's only son, he who is nearest to the Father's heart, has made him known.*
>
> **John 1: 16-18**

Some Random Thoughts

Prayer on the personal level will be influenced by our whole life. Our images of God, our experiences of praying with people, the books we read and the workshops we attend will have their influence on us. Our faithfulness to the gospel or our lack of it will influence our prayer. But the bottom line in this search for intimacy with God is this: WE LEARN TO PRAY BY PRAYING!

God desires us to be whole people. When we need healing, God wants to heal us. When we are lonely, God desires to create intimacy with us. There is no limit to God's compassion and love. God is not stingy or incompetent. God willingly works within the structure of our limitations. Above everything else, God desires union with us. Whatever can assist that goal, God will do.

On our part, we need to accept our human condition. We are NOT God! We are NOT perfect. We are NOT all-knowing. We are NOT all-powerful. All our anxieties, fears and perfectionism has a way of closing us off from God. God can transcend such things, but we need to trust God. As we grow in the union that prayer brings, we walk more peacefully with our brokenness. We work to overcome it, but our reliance is on God as savior rather than ourselves as saviors. As intimacy in prayer develops, words diminish in our prayer. Prayer becomes more gentle and less forced, more quiet and less noisy and full of words. God seems to "fit" our lives and we feel fine in such an encompassing presence.

God can do whatever seems best – even if we are not clear on how things will work out. We can more easily live with ambiguity as our trust in God grows.

Darkness and dryness in prayer are not punishments from God. They may help to purify our spirit but their goal remains the same – God's desire to possess us totally. Such times call us to faithfulness when there is little reward for faithfulness. We discover whether we are faithful in order to get something for ourselves or whether we are faithful because we love God. Desert times create something new in us that is revealed only down the road of life. It is not a time for wallowing in guilt. It is a time to learn dependence on God, without whom we can do nothing. The desert is a place of reality. The seed is in the ground. It is invisible. We are asked to believe that God is at work without getting any proof. It's called FAITH.

> *Have no fear, little flock, for your Father has chosen to give you the kingdom. Sell your possessions and give to charity. Provide for yourselves purses that do not wear out and never-failing treasure in heaven, where no thief can get near it, no moth destroy it. For where your treasure is, there will your heart be also.*
> **Luke 12: 32-34**

Prayer will be flavored by the feelings and insights of daily life. Experiences of failure empty us of ideas of infallibility – and we come more humbly to prayer. Experiences of success deepen our awareness of God's gifts to us – and bring us to a prayer of thanksgiving and praise. Headaches and physical pain will flavor our prayer as will healing and vitality. Some days prayer will be prosaic. On other days prayer will be enthusiastic. Sometimes we will only be able to manage vocal prayer. On other days we may plunge deeply into contemplation.

Always God is in the middle of our prayer, speaking to us through the flavor of everyday life.

Leadership

Many groups engage in prayer. The leadership of such groups is uneven. Some leaders give sound direction – others have little sense of what real prayer-leadership means. Since community prayer is so important, assessment of the leadership is also important. There are some elements to consider in such an assessment.

1. If group leaders (or the groups themselves) seem to ASSAULT the participants, forcing conformity – that is a sign of poor leadership. The Spirit promotes freedom and respects individuals. The Spirit invites but does not force.

2. Sincerity is not a sufficient quality for leadership. A sincere leader can do stupid things very sincerely. Prayer can be used as a club to keep people in line. Beware of the sincere leader who allows for no freedom for participants or allows only ONE WAY of prayer.

3. Dependence on the leader is unhealthy when it is overdone. A good leader shares authority rather than cornering it for him/herself. Healthy leadership leads others to be able to walk on their own rather than becoming dependent on the leader. Beware the leader(s) who seems to monopolize power and authority in the group.

4. Leaders who seem to program peoples' response in prayer are more concerned with their own ideas than the work of the Spirit. Beware leaders who expect certain responses and manipulate the group to get them. Often they will poke fun of any response that does not fit "their idea" of a good response. Again, we are faced with leaders more intent on control than on prayer.

5. I might ask myself if I am really changing my life because of this community prayer. If no conversion is taking place in my life, I might seriously question the value of this group's prayer practices. Solid prayer naturally brings about change in our lives. We learn new ways to respond to the gospel.

6. Does the leadership and/or the group allow friendships to grow naturally in the group? If so, it is healthy. But if the group or leaders

tend to isolate people from one another, we face some serious leadership problems.

7. Do the leaders/group take my life situation into account? If I am forced to fit a certain mold no matter what, poor leadership and group development is at work. Or if there is a growing dependence on the group or its leaders, I need to wonder about the leadership. Good leaders allow and encourage initiative and freedom.

Good leadership creates a sense of freedom and support. Poor leadership creates a sense of conformity and dependence. Good leadership invites people to share. Poor leadership demands that they share. Good leadership delights in individual growth. Poor leadership is threatened by the uniqueness of individual growth. Good groups delight in the members' growth in the Lord. Poor groups want members to meet a rigid standard of growth. Good groups encourage initiative and independence. Poor groups tend to be authoritarian and demand conformity.

All groups are imperfect. But gentleness and courtesy, respect and support are signs of healthy groups. A healthy group understands imperfection without letting people wallow in it. With loving kindness they invite members to move ahead in their attempt to follow the gospel. You are invited to be a gently persuasive person as you deal with others in any group you join.

Prayer Forms

Prayer has many forms. The goal of prayer is to develop intimacy with Jesus. Jesus engages us where we are and within the framework of everyday activity. Jesus deals with all our realities. If we choose to wear a mask before Jesus, our prayer may be empty and dry – unreal. If we hide our feelings of anger or hatred and try to sanitize our prayer, our prayer may be arid – unreal. God knows us. Prayer invites us to come before God honestly, just as we are at any particular time. Such honesty is a process of growth. We gradually get in touch with our personal reality and inner self. As that happens our prayer grows in depth. No ONE form of prayer will fit every situation of life. These few forms are shared simply to offer a taste of prayer forms that might help.

In the area of prayer as in many areas of the spiritual life, it is good to have a spiritual companion. Such a companion can help us on our faith journey. It is good that a companion be competent in understanding the spiritual life. A good companion will have a reasonable understanding of human nature, an acceptance of people and some awareness of obstacles in the spiritual journey. Knowledge, prayerfulness and experience are helpful qualities in such a person. As you feel the need, seek out a competent spiritual companion and guide. Together you can help to nurture the work of the Spirit in your lives.

Contemplation

Contemplation is a common human experience. When I studied in California, I would often go to the ocean. I would sit on a rock, back to the beach, and listen to and watch the waves. Their sounds and rhythm took me "out of myself." I was caught in them and became a part of them. Nothing else seemed to matter. The sound of the waves covered over any sounds of people and animals on the beach. The awesome power of the ocean absorbed me. It was simply me and this vast body of water – alone with each other. I was amazed when I looked at my watch and realized how time had flown by. I had engaged in contemplation. Think of the birth of your first child. For a moment you can hardly believe it – this is YOUR child. This tiny, squirming, crying, beautiful creature was created by you and your spouse. Your child helped you forget everything else in focusing on this new life. You engaged in contemplation. Remember the death of someone you loved with an all-embracing love. You looked at the body, dead and lifeless, and in the midst of your sorrow and loss you are flooded with memories. All the moments you spent together; things you had done together, even arguments you may have had. For a moment you are "out of yourself" and in the world of your life together. You engaged in contemplation ... you and the beloved were together again.

Contemplation is not an action you take to produce a result. It simply happens. It is not controlled nor even planned. Contemplative prayer invites us to find the space that allows contemplation to happen. But the prayer itself is not within our control. Quite the contrary. We surrender to whatever the Beloved wishes to do. We are simply present and attentive to the Beloved. It is powerfully real, but no words can adequately describe it. It is presence rather than action or, better, the "action" of presence. We enter contemplation solely for the sake of the Beloved. We seek nothing else than surrender of our "self" to the one we love. We expect no results. We program no consequences. We are present and let any results or consequences happen as the Beloved desires.

Contemplation requires quiet attentiveness. We need to put aside concerns and dreams, worries and anticipations. As far as possible we leave the intruding elements of life aside for the moment. Whatever helps us do this can help our contemplation. Ask Jesus to quiet your heart and mind. Allow yourself to be aware of the presence of the Holy Spirit in the depths of your being. Contemplation is freedom to "be with." No agenda is needed. Total presence to God is what we seek. Total surrender to this loving God is what we desire. Then we are simply quiet. If anything intrudes, we acknowledge it and hand it over to the Lord. Then we return to being present to God. Long or short, five minutes or an hour – this is God's time to have us completely. When our contemplative time is finished, we offer thanks and gently go about our other business.

Scriptural Prayer

The gospel is our way of life. The bible is a natural place to go to listen to God. It is the word of God written for our benefit. Scripture can be a healthy resource for prayer.

Create some space for yourself. Try to get a place and time when you will be undisturbed. Ask the family to give you a half hour without being interrupted. The richer the silence, the better it is. So take some time to settle down. Some people find that music can settle them down. Others have some gentle exercise that settles them down. You may have other means to quiet yourself. Use whatever works for you. Some days take more time than others – allow for the differences of different days.

Once you are quiet within, take a comfortable position so that your body is at ease. Then open the scriptures. Select a text you wish to use. It might be a text from the liturgy or a part of the bible you are presently reading or a story from Luke or words of Paul. Let it be reasonably

241

short. Ask God to help you pray. Then, without prejudice, read/listen to the scripture. Read slowly and attentively. Linger with the words. If a word or phrase strikes you, stay with it – repeat it again and again. Don't interpret it, but simply let it soak into your heart. Stay with it as long as it seems to be touching you.

If nothing seems to happen – read the text through again and again. Listen with faith. Don't be nervous because nothing seems to be happening. Perhaps this word is being impressed on your memory for use at some future time. Your simple task is to listen and let the power of the word do whatever it wants.

At the end of about 20 minutes gently thank the Lord for his word to you. Perhaps you will feel moved to lift up people in prayer for a time. An Our Father may conclude your prayer. Gently return to the other business of your life. As with contemplation, allow the word the freedom to touch you however it wishes. You may find it helpful to write a few reflections that came during prayer. Use a prayer journal if that is helpful. Some people jot notes in the margins of their bible. Do whatever is helpful to you.

ANOTHER FORM OF SCRIPTURAL PRAYER (Sr Mary Reuter)

1. DESCRIPTION OF AN EVENT ... select an event from your daily life that you consider to have been formative or growthful to you. DESCRIBE what happened.

2. QUESTIONING...

    A) What changes took place for you? (E.g. in your understanding, choices, attitudes, relationships with others or with God?)

    B) What evoked the change?

    C) What changes took place in the other person involved, as far as you can tell?

3. SCRIPTURAL CONNECTION ... what event, person or theme from scripture relates to your event? (I.e. who in scripture experienced a situation similar to yours?)

A) What are the similarities?

B) What are the differences"

C) What insight does the scripture text bring to your experience?

4. CONVERSION ...

A) What do you want to say to God about your experience?

B) What might God be saying to you through your experience and reflection?

C) What do you intend to DO as a result of this experience and reflection?

5. CELEBRATION ... Write a sentence prayer of gratitude to God for what has happened.

Group Scriptural Prayer

Scriptural prayer can be used by couples or in groups. You might follow a format similar to this:

Married couples might do it while sitting together or while lying in bed together. Feel each other's presence and quietly be aware of the presence of God. Have one person read a short scriptural passage out loud. Read slowly and reverently. Allow for silence after the reading. Then share with one another what the words meant to you. No theological abstractions, but simply: "I heard this ..." or "This struck me ..." or "To me it meant ..." or "I felt ..." Keep the reflections in the first person and keep them SHORT! Speak only for yourself. Don't preach! This is NOT a discussion or scriptural exegesis but a simple sharing. The partner simply listens – no remarks are necessary. After both have shared, a bit of silence allows the words to soak in. Then read the same passage aloud again. Then silence. Then a second sharing – which goes deeper because of the first sharing. The same process can be used a third time.

Each round builds on the previous one. The personal sharing may open a new insight into the scriptural word(s). At the end the prayer is closed with a simple prayer of thanks. Sometimes you may wish to sing a suitable song. You may take some time for intercessory prayer.

If a group uses this prayer, the same process is used. Have someone read a text – silence – then spontaneous, PERSONAL ("I" not "We") sharing – silence ... then have someone else read the same text and repeat the process. The same can be done for a third time allowing anyone who wishes to share their reflection on the word. Close as indicated above and allow for spontaneity in prayer and song.

This prayer simply allows the word to impress itself on us. Hearing the response of different people widens our understanding of that verse of scripture. The repeated reading and reflection allows for a deeper, richer listening with each reading.

Centering Prayer

Centering prayer is a simple prayer. It is a prayer of longing that allows us to move into God's presence. As with other forms of quiet prayer, choose a place where you will not be disturbed. Be physically comfortable. Close your eyes. Settle down and gently turn your attention to the Lord. Tell God that you believe in the presence of the Holy Spirit. In trust we hand ourselves over to God.

Choose a word – a love-word – that expresses your sense of being with the Lord. Keep it short, no more than three words e.g. "Lord Jesus", "Abba", "Father", "Love" etc. Choose a word that is meaningful to you. This word keeps us attentive to God. It is a simple sigh of love reminding us of the presence of God.

During Centering prayer whenever anything else intrudes, we use our word to return to the Lord. Sometimes we have to use the word constantly. Other times it is used sparingly. Some days it may not be needed at all. It makes no difference. For this twenty minutes we allow God to do whatever he wants in us. It is a pure gift to God. Our attention is completely on God. This time is CENTERED on God and not ourselves. Our "word" helps keep us focused on this loving God.

When the twenty minutes are finished, end the prayer very gently. We have gone deeply into prayer even when we don't feel anything. Come out gently. Interiorly, pray the Our Father very slowly – listen to the words. Though we may not experience immediate results, consistent centering prayer will bring peace and a gentled spirit. After 30 days or so you may wish to examine, with a spiritual companion, the results of this prayer.

To summarize: 1. Be in faith and love to God who dwells within you. 2. Let your love-word be gently present, supporting your time with God. 3. When other things intrude, use the prayer word to gently return to God. 4. Conclude your prayer with the Our Father or some other suitable prayer.

The Jesus Prayer

The "Jesus prayer" is a very ancient prayer of the Church. The words of this prayer are simple:

> LORD JESUS CHRIST, SON OF GOD,
> HAVE MERCY ON ME, A SINNER.

You can say it anywhere – driving, between classes, in the kitchen, at the checkout counter, between interviews or meetings, any break during the day. Some people find it helpful to connect it to their breathing. Breathe in with the words: LORD JESUS CHRIST and breathe out with the words: SON OF GOD, HAVE MERCY ON ME, A SINNER. You can shorten the phrase if you wish. But use it slowly and gently. Find your own best pace. It is a gentle way of remembering the presence of Jesus and acknowledging it consciously.

Reflection

Such brief summaries of these prayer forms do not do them justice. There are fine books and tapes that can help you explore them in greater depth. In addition, they are only a few of the many forms of prayer. The list is long, too long to explain on these pages. Liturgical prayer is a beautiful way to praise God. Vocal prayer, recited or sung, is a beautiful form of prayer. The "Prayer of Christians" serves well as a prayerbook that is filled with the Scriptures and arranged for everyday prayer. Proper use of the rosary and reflection on the mysteries can be a solid form of prayer. For some people, use of symbols and bodily gestures can form a way of prayer. The Stations of the Cross can offer insight into Jesus' love for us and be a solid form of prayer. The Eucharist is prayer.

Our way of life REQUIRES us to <u>pray daily!</u> It is fundamental to a gospel life. Our prayer form may change from day to day. One day the Eucharist may be our prayer. On another day we may only manage to cry out to God for help. What is needed for consistent growth is consistent prayer. Life will often dictate the form our prayer takes. Prayer is meant to bring us to intimacy with the Father, the Son (Jesus) and the Holy Spirit. As intimacy grows it will affect our life. In one sense, the way to assess the quality of one's prayer is to assess the quality of one's life. Prayer changes us into gospel people. It WILL SHOW in our life if we are faithful to daily prayer!

> *In very truth I tell you, whoever heeds what I say and puts his trust in him who sent me has eternal life; he does not come to judgement but has already passed from death to life.*
>
> **John 5: 24**

> *This is how we can be sure that we are in him: whoever claims to be dwelling in him must live as Christ himself lived.*
>
> **1 John 2: 5-6**

Reflection Questions

What form does your daily prayer take? What is your most exciting experience of prayer? What makes it most difficult for you to pray? How do you feel about community prayer? How does your prayer change your life? How does prayer affect the life of someone who professes to follow the gospel? What qualities would you expect in someone who prays regularly? What is most discouraging about your attempts to pray daily? What value is a spiritual companion with whom you can share your inner journey? What form of prayer is most attractive to you? Why? How would you assess the quality of a leader or a group dedicated to the gospel life? What moments of contemplation have you had? When St Francis spent the night in prayer, what form of prayer do you think he used? What is the best way to assess the quality of your prayer? How often do you use the scripture as your way of praying? How could you help someone else to pray? Why is silence important for some forms of prayer? How would you explain why prayer and gospel-action are partners? How willing are you to try some new forms of prayer? DO IT!

SECULAR FRANCISCAN RULE

17. In their family they should cultivate the Franciscan spirit of peace, fidelity and respect for life, striving to make of it a sign of a world already renewed in Christ.

By living the grace of matrimony, husbands and wives in particular should bear witness in the world to the love of Christ for his Church. They should joyfully accompany their children on their human and spiritual journey by providing a simple and open Christian education and being attentive to the vocation of each child.

RULE – Chapter 2 #17

Family life today faces many problems. It is quite a feat to balance firm guidelines and parameters for growth while creating an atmosphere of healthy freedom. Job and community obligations can strain family relationships. Attentiveness and dialogue are needed to keep a balance between personal, family, social, community, job and parish obligations.

Society is not always helpful to the family. The impact of drugs in our society can wreck people's lives and devastate families. Unhealthy ideas about sexuality can wreak havoc on the fabric of family life. Training for job skills without concomitant training for life leaves many people unprepared for inter-personal relationships. The temptation to take easy and instant solutions creates frustration when human problems defy instant solution. The divorce rate, child and spouse abuse, anger and violence and a host of other societal problems are not helpful for building solid family life. The "isms" we spoke about have an impact on family life as does early pregnancy and pro-life issues.

The Rule of the SFO does not claim to answer these problems. It does offer an alternative possibility. It asks family members to create a spirit of "peace, fidelity and respect for life." HOW to do this is the problem faced by families. How to show love for one another requires real wisdom and understanding. Sometimes people need to be left alone to work through difficulties – "Stand by but don't pry." At other times there is the need to plunge into the middle of the problem – to offer advice, a hug or whatever. Conversion can require that we lovingly confront people or offer tender affirmation. How will we respond to anger, depression or exuberance? Clearly, fidelity to the search for answers cannot be avoided.

How do we share a respect for life that extends from the womb to old age? How do we react to nuclear weaponry that could destroy all life? Peace is not something that just happens. It is accomplished by peacemakers who are committed to creating a world of peace. "And I shall break bow and sword and weapon of war and sweep them off the earth, so that my people may lie down without fear." (Hosea 2: 18) Needs differ so much. A cuddly baby has needs quite different from a 6'5" 250 pound football player or a 16 year old cheer leader. Creating a spirit of "peace, fidelity and respect for life" takes work, solitude, prayer, pain, tough love, gentle love, patience and a lot of stamina.

Franciscan families do not live in splendid isolation from the world. Hurts, suffering, communication breakdowns, anger, loneliness, powerlessness walk side by side with joy, delight, companionship, communication, acceptance and the laughter of ordinary family life. Discovering ways to make family life workable is an imposing task. Dictatorships in families may get things done but at a very high cost to people. Total democracy in family life can create chaos as shared ignorance drowns the wisdom of experience. Family groups need to talk together and listen to one another to make the family "a sign of a world already redeemed by Christ."

Parents establish the climate of the family. Their mutual love and respect (or lack of it) will influence the children. Whatever can be done to deepen the bond between spouses is worth the effort. Whatever ways they find to support each others' spiritual yearning will be worth the effort. Whatever they can do to face difficult issues together will be worth the effort. Whatever they can do to create space and time for one another and the family will be worth the effort. Whatever corners they can cut to allow themselves time alone and together will be worth the effort. Whatever they do to continue their personal growth and sense of self-worth is worth the effort. However they design ways to be part of their children's lives will be worth the effort. A good Franciscan community/fraternity will try to help parents in this search for balance.

Vocation

Parents who are open to the gospel will also be sensitive to the Lord's call to their children. Franciscan parents do not push and shove vocations on their children. But they are sensitive in helping the children see possible options for life. Parents can help children get facts about various vocations and walk with them through a good decision-making process. That is much different than forcing a choice on a child. The Lord calls people to many vocations. That includes marriage, priesthood, religious life, ministries in the Church, ministries outside the church, ministries as single people or ministries as couples. The key element is to have a sense of the way in which people can serve God. Whether marriage, church ministry, social ministry or whatever, God invites us to use our gifts for the benefit of God's people.

Family Failures

Franciscan couples and families do not always succeed in making marriage and family life a workable proposition. We are not immune to family problems, including divorce. Crises in families make us aware of human limitations. When Franciscan families face separation, divorce, substance abuse, law-breaking, mental or emotional breakdowns, the community/fraternity needs to offer support. As a community the Lord asks us to bear one another's burdens. We are not excused when the problems are messy and seemingly insoluble. It is part of a good Franciscan fraternity that human support and assistance are given to people in crisis. Fraternities will face tough decisions about the most effective kind of help to give. But we may not evade the issue.

Peace, fidelity, respect for life. Demanding qualities when violence, infidelity and putting a cheap value on life seem to pervade our world.

We obviously need the help of the Spirit of Jesus. It is this Holy Spirit who will enable us to create a climate where gospel values prevail.

> *... God is rich in mercy, and because of his great love for us, he brought us to life with Christ when we were dead because of our sins. It is by grace you are saved. ... it is not your own doing. It is God's gift not a reward for work done! There is nothing for anyone to boast of; we are God's handiwork, created in Christ Jesus for the life of good deeds which God designed for us.*
> **Ephesians 2: 4 & 8-10**

FRANCISCAN FOCUS

Francis And Prayer

St Francis understood that prayer touches the whole of life. Without prayer, gospel life lacks a dimension that is vital. Without contact with God in prayer we grow less sensitive to God's presence in our lives. Faithful prayer becomes a supportive partner for action. Action relies on the contact that prayer brings. St Francis often warned his followers never to diminish the spirit of prayer. His personal prayerfulness brought him in touch both with God and with the whole of creation. Faithful prayer helps us appreciate our world without becoming possessive of it. Faithful prayer connects us with others without trying to dominate their lives. We know the difference between creation and the Creator, between a loving God and a wounded people. But we also know how intimate is the connection between them.

For Francis, Jesus is God's love made visible. Jesus is God's presence made human in our world. Jesus is the sacrament that shouts out the presence of God among us. The Canticle of Brother Sun reveals Francis' exploding awareness of God's presence in the whole universe. Such a prayer can lead us to the same wonder at God's love revealed in creation.

St Francis affirmed again and again the importance of prayer. We ask his help to continue to affirm it in our lives, day in and day out. The American Indian People have a beautiful sense of this presence and our need to acknowledge it. This word from their spirituality speaks for itself.

> *A person's shadow has a life of its own. Each night, when we lie down to sleep, our shadow departs, going out to explore the world it is not free to explore during the day. It becomes intrigued by this marvelous and complex world and is reluctant to return home at daybreak. So it*

is necessary for the person, upon rising, to hum his shadow home. The shadow must obey the hum and each person has a special hum of his own.

If we are too busy or thoughtless, and do not hum the shadow home, the whole day will be difficult. Until the shadow comes home we are not whole. We say: "We are not ourselves today." Part of us is missing. Humming the shadow home is essential for inner harmony and unity. Not too many people seem to know their morning hum when you ask them about it!

QUESTIONS

1. Describe the form of prayer that is most meaningful to you. Share how it makes a difference in the way you live your everyday life

2. How do you feel about using your body in prayer, e.g. gestures bows, genuflections, dance etc? Where did your feelings come from? Why do you feel this way?

3. How can scripture be used in prayer? What value do you find in this form of prayer?

4. Describe contemplation in your own words. Share any contemplative experiences you may have had.

5. What qualities reflect good prayer and/or group leaders? What would be some danger signals of poor leadership?

6. Why is consistent, daily prayerfulness important for someone who is trying to follow the gospel way of life?

7. How can a local fraternity support couples in their married life and/or in their role as parents?

8. What positive things does Franciscan life offer to family life? Spell out the ways it could help parents, couples or children?

9. List some practical ways that you affirm people in your everyday life. How do you feel when you receive affirmation from others? (The more concrete and specific the affirmation, the better it is!)

10. What kind of support can a fraternity give to single people? What ways can single people serve the fraternity?

11. How does your fraternity offer support and acceptance to single parents? What help is given to dysfunctional families in the fraternity or to friends or relatives of fraternity members?

SCRIPTURE *reading/reflection*

✛ 2 Corinthians 6: 1-10
St Paul suffered much in his ministry of preaching the gospel. He readily shares his weakness and suffering with the Corinthians. The presence of Jesus enables him to continue despite the hardship.

Reflect on Paul's words. What helped him to be faithful when things were rough? If you listened to these words and applied them to prayerfulness, what lesson would you learn about the consequences of prayer?

CHAPTER 12

DISCOVERING REALITY

"If you stand by my teaching, you are truly my disciples: you will know the truth, and the truth will set you free." ... *"In very truth I tell you" said Jesus: "that everyone who commits sin is a slave. The slave has no permanent standing in the household, but the son belongs to it forever. If then the Son sets you free, you will indeed be free."*

John 8: 31-31 & 34-36

"Wrongdoers hate the light and avoid it, for fear their misdeeds should be exposed. Those who live by the truth come to the light so that it may be clearly seen that God is in all they do."

John 3: 20-21

Then he raised his voice in a great cry: "Lazarus! Come out!" The dead man came out, his hands and feet bound with linen bandages, his face wrapped in a cloth. Jesus said: "Loose him; let him go."

John 11: 43-44

Jesus spoke frequently to people about how to be free. Sometimes he cured physical illnesses that bound people. Sometimes he forgave the sin that chained them. Sometimes he shared a perspective that gave them a new lease on life. Sometimes Jesus confronted peoples' self-righteousness in order to bring them to freedom. Sometimes he affirmed them in the path they were following to freedom. In his teachings Jesus revealed many ways to freedom. He said that surrender and dying to oneself is the way to freedom. He said that serving one another and loving enemies is a way to freedom. He said that trust in his Father's care is a way to freedom. Jesus helped people depose idols so that they would be free to worship the true God.

Blessed is the servant who esteems himself no better
when he is praised and exalted by people than when he
is considered worthless, simple and despicable: for
WHAT A PERSON IS BEFORE GOD, THAT HE IS
AND NOTHING MORE. Woe to that religious who
has been placed in a high position by others and does not
wish to come down of his own free will. And blessed is
that servant (MT 24: 46) who does not place himself in
a high position of his own will and always desires to be
under the feet of others.
Francis & Clare – Brady/Armstrong
Paulist Press – Page 33

St Francis understood the message of Jesus. His own conclusions were similar to those of Jesus. Francis knew how easily we get bound up in ourselves. How easy it is to be possessed by possessions. What Francis wrote, he practiced.

Therefore, let us desire nothing else, let us wish for
nothing else, let nothing else please us and cause us
delight except our Creator and Redeemer and Savior, the
one true God.

... Therefore, let nothing hinder us, nothing separate us
or nothing come between us ... and love, honor, adore,
serve, praise, bless, glorify and exalt, magnify and give
thanks to the most high and supreme eternal God.
IBID – Page 133-134

Francis saw the link between poverty and freedom. To surrender to the Lord was the ultimate way to freedom. It meant that nothing but the Lord would direct life. He would not be hindered by material things nor burdened by self-seeking. The truth of the matter is clear. To lose oneself to the Lord was to discover the freedom the gospel speaks about.

It was the whole calculation, so to speak, of that innocent
cunning, that the world was to be outflanked and out-
witted by him, and be embarrassed about what to do with
him. You could not threaten to starve a man who was

258

ever striving to fast. You could not ruin him and reduce him to beggary, for he was already a beggar. There was very lukewarm satisfaction even in beating him with a stick, when he only indulged in little leaps and cries of joy because indignity was his only dignity. You could not put his head in a halter without the risk of putting it in a halo.

St Francis of Assisi
Chesterton – Image Books –
Page 103

We recognize a certain note as natural and clear as the note of a bird; the note of St Francis. There is something of gentle mockery of the very idea of possessions; something of a hope of disarming the enemy by generosity; something of a humorous sense of bewildering the worldly with the unexpected; something of the joy of carrying an enthusiastic conviction to a logical extreme.

IBID – Page 120

The Spirit guided St Francis in the way of freedom. Its' name was Lady Poverty and it left Francis unfettered. Its' name was Brother Juniper, and it rode under the banner of simplicity. It was named "Perfect Joy" and dancing was the sign of its presence. It was named "Intimacy" and Jesus was its source. It was named "Truth" and the way to it was lit by he who is the Light.

Francis learned to discard anything that could enslave him. He recognized the subtle temptations of power, choosing instead the way of a servant. He realized how easily possessions and wealth could lead to anxiety and worry. He chose poverty and trust in a provident Father. He was aware of how easily concern and responsibility for others could lead to belief in one's "saviorhood." Francis returned again to Jesus and acknowledged him as the one and only "savior." Such truth gave freedom to Francis. It allowed Francis to see people, himself and the created world with eyes that discovered God in all of them.

Freedom And Truth

Any dictionary can give definitions for these words. We might understand them by looking at their opposites. Opposed to truth are such things as: lies / half-truths / rationalizations / masks / deceit / white lies / rash judgments / suspicion / stereotypes / statistics / propaganda / personal infallibility and prejudice. Such words contain negative and destructive elements. They tend to hide and confuse, cause fear or anger, enable people to jump to conclusions without benefit of facts. They can create a climate of insecurity and distrust. When such "opposites" of truth dominate a situation, freedom can become a casualty.

My own experience taught me the subtleties of suspicion. I attended a workshop that was very intense. Several psychologists guided our small groups. I began to suspect that I was "being observed" by these people. The intensity increased as did my suspicions. About the fourth day the leader suggested we needed an evening to unwind and relax. So he invited us to his home. Even more suspicious, I figured this was simply a ploy to enable all the psychologists to observe us in "relaxed" surroundings. All evening I watched them. When I played pool I watched them. When I had a little wine I watched them. I never caught them watching me, but that just proved how clever they were. My suspicions created a miserable evening for me.

When I finally discovered (and accepted) the truth, it was the opposite of my suspicions. No "watching" was involved. The leader recognized our need to relax and simply wanted us to have an enjoyable evening. I had made my evening miserable by creating my own, false truth. It confined and shackled me. It gave me no joy. It made me more tense and insecure than I had been before. The TRUTH would have set me free, but I would have no part of it! When I finally accepted the real TRUTH, I was both embarrassed and free.

God's revelation offers me freedom. But my interpretation of God's revelation can shackle me. When I confine God to my own meager image of God I gain nothing. When I confine God's generosity, I may feel abandoned. When I presume that God doesn't trust me, I feel helpless. When I accept my interpretation of God as a harsh judge I am frightened of God. Patiently, God continues the work of knocking down the Berlin walls of my inner spirit. As God teaches me the truth about my brokenness, I discover a caring God who is always faithful. When I realize that I may not easily or ever overcome some weakness in myself, God's presence and truth gives me confidence to continue the journey.

> *To keep me from being unduly elated by the magnificence of such revelations I was given a thorn in my flesh, a messenger of Satan sent to buffet me; this was to save me from being unduly elated. Three times I begged the Lord to rid me of it, but his answer was: "My grace is all you need; power is most fully seen in weakness." ... So I am content with a life of weakness, insult, hardship, persecution and distress, all for Christ's sake; for when I am weak, then I am strong.*
> **2 Corinthians 12: 7-10**

Our society finds such a boast of weakness intolerable. Money might be a source of power. Political office may be a source of power. Weapons may be a source of power. But weakness? It seems to be nonsense! So we find true freedom eludes us while we boast of our power.

How many politicians are truly free? How many generals really believe they can guarantee our safety with their weapons? How many economists feel free as they predict GNP's and stock market fluctuations? How many of us feel free when we have unlimited power knowing that it is only a temporary situation? How does wealth make us free when we must spend so much time protecting and promoting it? How free are we when we face destitution? How free do we feel when old age creeps into our bones? How free do we feel when society forces us to act contrary to our inner spirit? How free are we when our only friendships have been "bought" rather than given? The litany could continue. As we reflect on these items, Paul's words begin to take on new meaning. God's friendship makes the difference – and that's the truth!

Another sort of litany speaks of how freedom happens. When we forgive people from our heart, we experience freedom. When we abandon feelings that could destroy others, freedom enters. When we use power to promote the good of others, we sense freedom within ourselves. When revenge gives way to reconciliation, gentle freedom comes. When I deal honestly with my feelings, I experience being freed of their domination. As I let loose of: false judgments / fear / magical, superstitious faith / refusal to acknowledge limitations / my "savior" complex / my suspicions etc etc – I find myself and know the truth. Such truth brings a sense of freedom.

Truth puts us in touch with reality. Where reality is, there is God. Gospel people embrace reality. Not easily, not without struggle, not without taking detours – but we try and keep on trying! Our freedom is not an isolated freedom. Community life reminds me that my freedom will take others' needs into account. Freedom will teach me to accept responsibility in relationships. It will help me realize that I am not a "lone ranger" but part of a faith community of imperfect people. My actions, freely chosen, will support others rather than ignore them.

> *You, my friends, were called to be free; only beware of turning your freedom into license for your unspiritual nature. Instead, serve one another in love, for the whole law is summed up in a single commandment: "Love your neighbor as yourself." But if you go on fighting one another, tooth and nail, all you can expect is mutual destruction!*
>
> *… If the Spirit is the source of our life let the Spirit also direct its course!*
> **Galatians 5: 13-16 & 25**

Jesus Stories About Truth/Freedom

The gospels offer many stories about Jesus and how he brought people to freedom and truth. A leper is cleansed and re-enters society a free man. A paralytic is cured and follows Jesus. Sin is forgiven and life opens up for the sinner.

In the gospel of Luke (7: 36-50) is the story of the penitent woman. Simon judges this woman of the street, and wonders why Jesus would associate with her. Jesus offers him a story about two men in unequal debt to their master. Both are forgiven. Who would love more, Simon? Simon's answer is right – and he convicts himself. The woman leaves Simon's house a free person. Simon still has some distance to travel before he is free of prejudice!

The story of the Prodigal son in Luke 15: 11-31 is another story of freedom. A son who loses everything in an extravagant spending spree learns about forgiveness from his father. Not only is he accepted back, he is accepted in a totally unearned way – he is family again! The father creates an atmosphere for both older and younger son to find a new perspective on life. For both sons the father desires the freedom of forgiveness and acceptance. Both sons have the possibility of new maturity because of a father who loves them both.

The "Kingdom" stories reveal another part of the integrity of gospel people. Discovery of a treasure influences people to sell everything to have it. In Matthew 13: 44-46 a man finds buried treasure in a field. In "joy" he sells everything to he able to buy the field. A merchant finds a pearl of special value, so special he sold everything he had to buy it. The truth about the Kingdom of God is that when we understand what it really is, we sell everything to possess it. The more clear the truth about the kingdom becomes, the greater our joy at the discovery. The "selling" of everything means nothing compared to the "treasure" and "pearl" that is bought. Entering the Kingdom is not a sad journey. Quite the contrary. The truth about the Kingdom makes it a joy to leave everything and claim it!

Of course, not everyone embraces the truth. In Mark 10: 17-22 we read about a good man who was unable to sell everything for the kingdom. The rich young man in the story was simply asking a religious question. All he expected was a non-threatening response. When the young man responded to Jesus he said: "But Teacher, I have kept all these since I was a boy." (MK 10: 20) Scripture says that Jesus' "heart warmed to him." Then he offered an invitation to sell everything for the pearl of following Jesus. "At these words his face fell and he went away with a heavy heart: for he was a man of great wealth." (MK 10: 22) Failure to embrace the pearl (Jesus' invitation to follow him) left him heavy hearted. It is hard to cling to things and be free.

An ordinary day for a Samaritan woman was quickly changed by Jesus (JN 4: 8-30). He asks for water. She is surprised. Jews and Samaritans don't do such things! So Jesus begins a revelation of truth that astounds her. From talk of drawing water without a bucket, the conversation turns to water you get without a bucket. Then on to her husbands. Then her astonishment that Jesus knows so much about her. Finally, she begins to think that he might be the messiah. Throughout the whole story Jesus leads her from one truth to another. Her response? She left her water-jar and returned to town: "Come and see a man who has told me everything I ever did. Could this be the Messiah?" (John 4: 29)

There is a poignant kernel of truth for Peter in the gospel of Luke (LK 22: 31-34). Jesus warns Peter about a weakness that will soon show – Peter will deny knowing Jesus. Obviously, such truth is more than Peter can acknowledge. "Lord, I'm ready to go with you to prison and death." (LK 22: 33) Then Jesus speaks a truth that will lead Peter to conversion: "I tell you Peter, the cock will not crow tonight until you have denied three times over that you know me." (LK 22: 34) How often Peter must have remembered the truth about his weakness. How Jesus knew and still forgave – and freed Peter!

> At that moment while he was still speaking, a cock
> crowed; and the lord turned and looked at Peter. Peter
> remembered the Lord's words: "Tonight before the cock
> crows you will disown me three times." And he went
> outside and wept bitterly!
> **Luke 22: 60-62**

Obviously, the way to truth and freedom is not always easy. We can fight the truth. We can kick against the goad. It is not glamorous to accept the truth about our weakness and neediness. But acceptance of the truth about ourselves is a way to freedom. Being in touch with reality offers a breakthrough to our real self as well as to God. Reconciliation, joy, love, gentleness are some of the consequences of real freedom. Sin enslaves. The truth frees. Preoccupation with self is confining. Openness to God and creation is expanding. Lack of love limits relationships. Passionate love multiplies relationships.

> If anyone imagines himself to be somebody when he is
> nothing, he is deluding himself. Each of you should

examine his own conduct and then he can measure his achievement by comparing himself with himself and not with anyone else; for everyone has his own burden to bear.

... Make no mistake about this: God is not to be fooled; everyone reaps what he sows. If he sows in the field of his unspiritual nature, he will reap from it a harvest of corruption; but if he sows in the field of the Spirit, he will reap from it a harvest of eternal life. Never tire of doing good, for if we do not slacken our efforts we shall in due time reap our harvest. Therefore, as opportunity offers, let us work for the good of all, especially members of the household of the faith.
Galatians 6: 3-5 & 7-10

The gospel reveals the truth to us. We can follow the gospel because Jesus has given us his Spirit. We need forgiveness and God forgives us. We need love and God loves us. We need someone to trust and offer us security and God faithfully comes to give light and life. We seek unity and communion and God offers us Jesus and the community of faith-in-Jesus. The pattern God offers us is the pattern we offer others.

... Do not set your minds on what you are to eat or drink; do not be anxious. These are all things that occupy the minds of the Gentiles, but your Father knows you need them. No, set your minds on his kingdom, and the rest will come to you are well.

Have no fear, little flock; for your Father has chosen to give you the kingdom. Sell your possessions and give to charity. Provide for yourselves purses that do not wear out and never-failing treasure in heaven where no thief can get near it, no moth destroy it. For where your treasure is, there will your heart be also.
Luke 12: 29-34

The Secular Franciscan Rule offers guidelines in our search for truth and freedom. Consider the following:

6. ... rebuild the Church ... devote themselves energetically to living in full communion with the Pope, Bishops and Priests fostering an open and trusting dialogue of apostolic effectiveness and creativity.

10. Let them follow the poor and crucified Christ, witness to him even in difficulties and persecutions.

11. ... Let the Secular Franciscans seek a proper spirit of detachment from temporal goods by simplifying their material needs ... strive to purify their hearts from every tendency and yearning for possessions and power.

12. Witnessing to the good yet to come and obliged to acquire purity of heart ... they should set themselves free to love God and their brothers and sisters.

13. A sense of community will make them joyful and ready to place themselves on an equal basis with all people, especially the lowly for whom they shall strive to create conditions of life worthy of people redeemed by Christ.

15. Let them ... be in the forefront in promoting justice by the testimony of their human lives and courageous initiatives.

Rule – Chapter 2

As the Rule moves us beyond our selfishness, we daily explore the ways of truth. As our concern for others grows, we see beyond ourselves and discover the face of God in people. As we sense our need to work together to accomplish the works of justice, we work harder to build a healthy community life.

Reconciliation

Shame, guilt and co-dependence are common words today. Books are written on these topics. Workshops are given on alcoholism, addiction, sexual abuse, dysfunctional families and a variety of related topics. Some of the data proposes astounding statistics. One out of every six (some say "four") women is the victim of sexual/physical abuse by family members and/or relatives. The majority of people who have been sexually/physically abused become abusers themselves. 97% of people in mental hospitals believe that God cannot forgive them for what they have done. Looking around at society and the pain of so many people, escaping through drugs, workaholism, alcohol and sexual dysfunctions seem understandable. None of us (or very few of us) escape being touched by these victims. Guilt and shame find plenty of customers.

Healthy guilt calls me to accountability for something I am responsible for doing. What I did was not good and I am capable of changing it. Unhealthy guilt accepts responsibility for something I am not responsible for. I'm bad and I can't change no matter how hard I try. Notice immediately that healthy guilt leads to conversion and life. Unhealthy guilt leads to depression and a sense of being useless and no-good. Healthy shame tells me that there are limits to what I can do. Even when I want to help or do some good thing I may not be able to do it because I am a limited human being. There are boundaries to what I can do. Unhealthy shame turns me into a bad person. I cannot acknowledge my limitations. I must be a bad person if I wasn't able to help someone or didn't deal well with a personal problem. I am good-for-nothing!

Imagine how often a child learns such things in a dysfunctional family. Parents get a divorce. The child begins to believe it is his/her fault that the parents divorced. If I had done this or that, mom and dad would be together. I am no good since I couldn't keep them from getting a divorce. A child is caught in a family cycle of alcoholism or drug abuse. If I were a better child, mom or dad wouldn't drink. If I didn't get them angry they wouldn't drink. If I were stronger and more obedient, they would stop drinking. I am no-good. If a child is sexually molested or physically abused, he/she thinks it must be "my fault." These adults wouldn't do this if I didn't deserve some punishment. I must have done something wrong to deserve this. I must be no-good if this happens to me. If a habit of personal sexual deviation is part of life, fear can keep it from being openly acknowledged so that I can get help. So the "beat goes on" and a sense of unhealthy shame, guilt, and unworth becomes reality.

Modern life helps create many prisons for us. We live in self-imposed confinement and see no way out. We accept responsibility when we are not really responsible. We develop a fear that if we are caught in our "sin" no one will be able to like us. We hide and slowly die. Abuse, addictions, and abandonment create for us a feeling that there is no light at the end of the tunnel. We have been abused, addicted or abandoned because we deserve it. No one really cares – and they shouldn't care for someone as bad as I am. How can a spouse or a friend or a parent really love such a bad person. The truth could help us to freedom, but the truth is too much to face.

How does reconciliation take place for such folks? Is Jesus helpless to enter such lives? Is there no path to healing? Reconciliation and healing are possible. Fr Peter McCall OFM Cap offers some possible steps to healing. There is no claim that they are easy, but it is a healing process that is possible. Anyone caught in the narrow world we described above will recognize the road to freedom that is offered.

1. "Feel the pain." So long as we deny the pathology there is no hope for healing. We need to "own" the pain and ask for competent help.

2. Others will NOT be able to heal OUR pain. We will have to acknowledge that it is a problem within us. It is not someone else's problem – it is our problem. Projecting it on others – unloving parents, abusing spouse, insensitive church people – none of this will do much toward solving the problem. Both the problem and the solution lie within ourselves.

3. Decide that YOU have something to say about whether you want to be healed or not. We don't mean you will be able to heal yourself. But we do say that you can move past the feeling of being the "victim." Maintaining a "victim" attitude resists real healing and continues to give life to unhealthy shame. We do not say that no one else had a part in what happened. They obviously did. We are saying that we have the option of not letting them continue to be the predominant influence on our life. If we can let go of the grievances we hold against others, we can enter into healing. We can't change what happened in the past. Neither can we escape the way it influenced our lives. But we CAN decide that we will not continue to give it power over us.

4. This step goes beyond the psychological element of healing. That has a value of its own. We are inviting you to a spiritual healing. We believe that IF we could have taken this step ALONE, we would

have done it long ago! IF we could be our own savior, we would have saved ourselves long ago. But we do need help. We cannot heal ourselves alone. We are not our own savior. We need someone to help us who is outside the problem and in a position to help. For us this someone is the Holy Spirit. We believe that the Spirit of Jesus can help us re-interpret our problem and find a better way to live.

We invite the Spirit of Jesus to show us options. We ask the Holy Spirit to help us let go of control over our healing process. We need to let go of all the controls that have kept us bound and shackled. We trust the Holy Spirit to offer possibilities beyond what we could ask or imagine. The Spirit may help us not only to re-interpret our response to the hurtful actions of others, but also to help us change our interpretation of WHY others did such things to us. It is called CONVERSION. It is the way to true reconciliation of mind and heart … and relationships.

I hope it is obvious that allowing competent people to be part of this healing is important. We have learned unhealthy guilt and shame, so we can unlearn it. It is not given to us by God, but God's power can help us break free of it. Choose to seek and accept the help of competent gospel people. If competent psychological help is available, use it. But do not remain trapped in the untruth of toxic shame and guilt. God wants more for you. God chooses the way of truth and freedom. Allow God to be part of the solution.

Real guilt and healthy shame make us aware of our need for God. It helps us realize what change we need to make in our lives. When we bring real guilt to the Sacrament of Penance, God lifts the burden of guilt and reminds us that walking with us is what God loves to do. The strength of God's Spirit will enable us to change and undergo real conversion. The Sacrament of Penance reminds us that the power of the Spirit can enable us to do what we could not do alone. There is something intimate about sharing our innermost self with a loving God. It is even more affirming to know that God loves us still. Such faithful love tells us that we need not remain bound by our sins. We can change!

> *But you are a chosen race, a royal priesthood, a dedicated*
> *nation, a people claimed by God for his own, to proclaim*
> *the glorious deeds of him who has called you out of*

269

darkness into his marvelous light. Once you were not a
people at all; but now you are God's people. Once you
were outside his mercy; but now you are outside no
longer.

1 Peter 2: 9-10

Reflection Questions

How would you describe freedom? Truth? What personal
areas of life do you try to keep from acknowledging? Do you
believe they might be "untreatable"? What scriptural story(s)
offer you hope when you find it hard to surrender to God's
ways? How does poverty enable us to be more free? What
role does the Holy Spirit play in our search for freedom? How
would you define "shame?" What is the difference between
shame and guilt? What elements of the SFO Rule seem to
offer support for our struggle to be free? What can you do to
help another person to be free from the slavery of guilt,
shame or addictions? How does Jesus deal with the issue of
guilt and shame? What role does faithful, consistent, tough
love play in helping others to overcome their "slaveries"?
What impact does divorce, addiction or abuse on the part of
parents have on children? What is one possible process of
achieving healing for guilt, shame and/or abuse? How does
the Sacrament of penance help us deal with these problems?
How firmly do you believe that Jesus wants to and can help
us to freedom? How do your images of God help or hinder
your ability to seek help from God?

SECULAR FRANCISCAN RULE

18. Moreover they should respect all creatures, animate and inanimate, which "bear the imprint of the most High", and they should strive to move from the temptation of exploiting creation to the Franciscan concept of universal kinship.

19. Mindful that they are bearers of peace, which must be built up unceasingly, they should seek out ways of unity and fraternal harmony through dialogue, trusting in the presence of the divine seed in everyone and in the transforming power of love and pardon.

RULE – Chapter 2 – #18-19

St Francis loved the whole of creation. The Canticle of Brother Sun reveals his delight in creation. Wind and fire, sun and moon, earth and clouds become sister and brother in God's universal family. The faith of Francis saw the presence of God in the universe – and especially in God's people. Because God is present, all things and all people deserve respect. We are brothers and sisters to creation because creation has only one Father.

The earth serves people. It provides housing food and fuel. It offers places of solitude and land for growing food. Fresh waters satisfy our thirst and rains nourish our plants. Sunlight warms the earth and draws the blossoms forth from tree and plant and flower. These resources are given to be shared by all of God's people.

The Rule asks us not to exploit the earth for our own selfish benefit. The food and resources of the earth are created so that ALL people can share in them. Hunger, destitution, starvation and homelessness are NOT what God wants for people. God desires that we share resources in such a way that no one will be hungry or destitute or starving or homeless. Whatever creativity we can use to accomplish this is part of our task.

Obviously we will have to deal with how well we use resources. We will look at the policies that control our use of wood, power, fuel, water, minerals, space, animals, land – all of our resources. Franciscans will not stand on the sidelines of these issues. We will be in the midst of the struggle. Business people will check the ways of production and distribution to make them more equitable. Consumers will be more selective about what they really need. Manufacturers will make better use of raw materials. Waste management people will find better ways to dispose of waste. Factories will seek to find ways to dispose of toxic wastes. In short, we believe that we are responsible for the earth. We believe that our role is to use imaginative ways to provide all people a share in the fruits of the earth.

Franciscans have chosen such a response to human need by their profession. We will fulfill that commitment by continuing to find better ways to share resources with all people. We could easily extend such sharing to our educational skills, our farming skills, our business skills and our distribution skills. All gifts are put at the disposal of God's people around the world. Exploitation of people or resources will not be heard of among us. We are committed to create a Kingdom where all people can live in peace and dignity. It is our way of life!

Peace

Peace is God's gift to us. The external peacefulness of a world free of conflict is only the beginning. Inner peace is another dimension of any peace-seeking. Many of the ideas we have already explored affect the ways of peace. Our personal sense of worth, our acceptance of others, our attempt to create a climate of growth – all contribute to peace.

> *Then the wolf will live with the lamb and the leopard lie down with the kid; the calf and the young lion will feed together, with a little child to tend them. The cow and the bear will be friends and their young will lie down together; and the lion will eat straw like cattle. The infant will play over the cobra's hole and the young child*

dance over the viper's nest. There will be neither hurt
nor harm in all my holy mountain; for the land will be
filled with the knowledge of the Lord, as the waters cover
the sea.

Isaiah 11: 6-9

The road to peace takes many steps. The cessation of violence is a
beginning – but it is not gospel-peace. Cease-fires, arms control and
co-existence are important but they are not gospel-peace. Negotiations
to end economic domination are good steps, but they are not gospel-
peace. Neither on a personal, national nor international level can these
things be called gospel-peace. But they are hopeful steps in that direction.

Peace is God's gift. "Peace is my parting gift to you, my own peace,
such as the world cannot give." (JN 14: 27) We seek peace from God.
We bear such peace to the world. Whatever it takes, however long the
struggle, despite all obstacles, we will seek the ways of gospel-peace
for all people. We will continue to work to create a world alive to the
needs of people. We will work to create an atmosphere of respect for
others. We will work to create a place where human dignity can be a
reality for all people. Methinks we have a lot of work to do!

Part of our work will take place in our community / fraternity life.
Franciscans seek the way of harmony through dialogue with one
another. When arguments and divisions enter our community, we will
deal with them honestly and dialogue about the issues. We will not get
into name-calling and personal vendettas. Issues can be negotiated.
Dialogue can solve issue-oriented problems. But personal violence to
one another tends to separation, not unity. We will not "let George do
it!" We will accept responsibility for doing what needs to be done to
establish peace and harmony. One look at St Paul's definition of the
qualities of love offers plenty of food for thought.

> *Love is patient and kind. Love envies no one, is never*
> *boastful, never conceited, never rude; love is never self-*
> *ish, never quick to take offense. Love keeps no score of*
> *wrongs, takes no pleasure in the sins of others, but*

delights in the truth. There is nothing love cannot face;
there is no limit to its faith, its hope, its endurance.
1 Corinthians 13: 4-7

So try to do it! Love enemies. Love friends. Love the healthy. Love the sick. Love criminals. Love the poor. Love the rich. Love yourself. Love your children. Love your spouse. Love your pastor. Love the terrorists. Love judges and teachers, gas attendants and phone operators. Love people who disagree with you. ... etc etc. We are called to love – and we will need a creative imagination to discover HOW to love all these people!

We need the help of Jesus. No doubt about it. Jesus makes demands that can be met only if we are united with him. Jesus is the foundation stone of our life of love. He IS the vine. Cut off from him we wither. United with him all things are possible. That is the truth that can make us faithful to the gospel.

Sister Death

Sister Death became a friendly relative for Francis. We often experience a sense of grief when we lose someone through death. We may experience fear when we consider our own death. St Francis invites us to diminish the power of fear-of-death by seeing death as our Sister. She enters our life to lead us to more life. We are too small for all that God desires to give. Sister Death opens us to embrace a new life with God. As we struggle with such ideas, Jesus walks with us. He himself walked through a painful death. He himself walked through feelings of abandonment. He himself experienced fear. But none of them separated him from life with his Father. Faithful unto death, the Father raised him to new life. What has been done for Jesus is the model of what will be done for us.

> *This perishable body must be clothed with the imperish-*
> *able, and what is mortal with immortality. And when*
> *this perishable body has been clothed with the imperish-*
> *able, and our mortality has been clothed with immortal-*
> *ity, then the saying of scripture will come true: "Death*
> *is swallowed up; victory is won! O Death, where is your*

victory? O Death, where is your sting?" ... But thanks be to God! He gives us victory through our Lord Jesus Christ.

1 Corinthians 15: 53-57

FRANCISCAN FOCUS

In a letter that St Francis wrote to the Rulers of the people, he invites them to be responsible leaders. Copies of this letter were sent to many modern leaders on the 800th anniversary of the birth of St Francis in 1982.

TO ALL LEADERS & REPRESENTATIVES OF THE PEOPLE

To all mayors and consuls, magistrates and rulers throughout the world, and to everyone who may receive these letters. Brother Francis, your little and despicable servant in the Lord God, sends his wishes of health and peace to all of you.

Pause and reflect, for the day of death is approaching. I beg you, therefore, with all possible respect, not to forget the Lord or turn away from his commandments by reason of the cares and preoccupations of this world. For all those who are oblivious of Him and turn away from his commands are cursed and will be totally forgotten by him. And when the day of death does come, everything which they think they have will be taken away from them. And the wiser and more powerful they may have been in this world, so much greater will be the punishments they will endure in hell.

Therefore, I firmly advise you, my lords, to put aside all care and preoccupation and receive with joy the most holy Body and most holy Blood of our Lord Jesus Christ in holy remembrance of him.

And you should manifest such honor to the Lord among the people entrusted to you, that every evening an announcement be made by a town crier, or some other signal, that praise and thanks may be given by all people

*to the all powerful Lord God. And if you do not do this,
know that you must render an account before the Lord
your God, Jesus Christ on the day of judgement.*

*Let those who keep this writing with them and observe
it, know that they will be blessed by the Lord God.*
**Francis & Clare – Brady/Armstrong
Paulist Press – Page 77-78**

Perhaps only a hopeful person like Francis would dare to write such a letter. His own faith in Jesus could not be contained – it had to be shared. Leaders of every persuasion are asked to be responsible both to God and to the people they serve.

QUESTIONS

1. Write out a definition of freedom (i.e. biblical freedom).

2. What things keep you from being free? Take time to reflect and discover any hindrances to freedom within yourself or in your life. Such reflection can help us discover areas where "conversion" is needed.

3. After reading this chapter, how would you define "sin"?

4. How does the Sacrament of Penance help us to achieve freedom? How do you feel about this sacrament? Be honest as you share your experience of the sacrament.

5. How can the faith-community / fraternity help in achieving greater freedom in our lives?

6. Read Chapter 2, # 4 to 19 of the Rule. Choose points that you consider most helpful in widening your vision of fraternity life. Why do you consider them helpful? How do they challenge you to new growth in Franciscan living? What help do they offer in achieving greater embrace of the truth about yourself or the fraternity?

7. How does reverence for creation touch the lives of people? What are some of the ways that creation is exploited today? What issues of exploitation are you addressing in your life?

8. How would you describe gospel-peace? What are some of the signs that it is present in a person or situation? What are some of the steps that lead to true peace?

9. How does unhealthy guilt and shame keep us from being free? In what ways do healthy guilt and shame help us grow more free and help our conversion?

10. Explain the consequences of dealing wisely with guilt and shame. How would hope and joy be a part of this process?

SCRIPTURE *reading/reflection*

+ 1 John 1-5

This letter of John contains a simple message. God loves us and invites us to love God in return. We can keep the commandment to love because we are born of God. Faith enables us to obey God's commandment to love God, neighbor and self.

After prayerful reflection apply the ideas of this text to the concept of "freedom." How does this text offer insight(s) into the meaning of "being free?"

 *PILGRIM'S PROGRESS*

Each of us follows the gospel in our unique way. The same is true of St Francis. His response to the gospel fit the person he was. Part of any charism is the blending of God's gifts and our human response.

St Francis

Writers speak of them as though they were "instant" saints. For "pedestal" saints, miracles are everyday occurrences. The problems of life are solved with one hour of prayer. Since we know how the saint's story ends, we impose revisionist interpretations on earlier experiences of the saint. Such a process does a disservice to the saint. It puts him or her outside our reach. Our lives are not like that, so we keep such saints at arm's length.

St Francis is a product of the times in which he lived. He was influenced by the spirit of Assisi. During his growing-up years, Assisi blossomed with ideas of revolt and revolution. As their wealth grew, the merchant class began to gain power as well. The nobility became enemies of the ordinary people. Their wealth and lifestyle often mocked the poverty of the peasant. Profits and power were replacing noble birth and royal privilege. Assisi was divided into many factions. Violence grew. Such violence forced some of the nobility, including Clare's family, to abandon Assisi for safer lodgings. The talk in the central market place centered on ways and means to gain power.

Francis listened and learned about the careers that brought honor. Knighthood was a priority for a man who sought such honor. His father's wealth supported his desires. Purchasing knight's armor was no problem for Francis. Knighthood, romantically understood, was eagerly sought by Francis of Assisi. It would be his road to glory.

As often happens, God used this "vision" of Francis to call him to a new way of life. On one of his trips to glorious knightly battles, Francis has a dream. The dream is filled with castles and swords and shields. It seemed to confirm his search for knighthood. But the words spoken at Spoleto did not support his search. Instead, God confronted Francis with talk about serving the Lord or the servant. The final word ... "Return to Assisi."

This was not what Francis wanted. Returning to Assisi meant facing his father and friends. He could already hear their mockery when he told them about "voices" that told him to return. Such actions were not calculated to get affirmation from his father or friends. Instead of joining the army and being on his way to glory in battle, Francis is back in Assisi because of his "voices." Though he was told in the vision that further directions would be forthcoming, they weren't. It seemed that Francis was being left high and dry by God.

This first of many desert experiences taught Francis to trust God without getting proof. It was a matter of faith. Francis escapes father and friends by wandering the countryside and living in caves. Doubt grows. Nothing is happening. Has he taken a wrong turn? Is he imagining the voices that spoke to him? Francis is confused by the silence of God.

Prayer for help was common for Francis during this time. He learned much about himself and his lifestyle in the days and nights of solitude. He became aware of the price of following the voice that called him. Discovery and fear walk side by side in Francis during this time. He remains faithful to the call, yet impatient with the long silence of God. Waiting is not easy. Hiding from his father and friends is depressing. Francis is learning what it means to depend on God.

As the search continues, his spirit gradually grows more calm. He begins to assess the issues involved in the call. There is more clarity about the price of following God's call. Francis allows God greater freedom to direct his life. His prayer becomes less anxious and more at ease in God's presence. The little church of San Damiano becomes a refuge for him. His spirit is learning to accept the way God is acting.

Then, praying before the crucifix in San Damiano, the long period of silence is broken. It seems to Francis that Jesus speaks to him from the crucifix: "Go, repair my house ..." Delighted, Francis immediately does what he thinks God wants of him – he starts fixing up churches. He becomes a beggar, asking for stones and mortar. He becomes a stonemason, repairing walls and roofs of dilapidated churches. How good it feels to know what God wants!

This first response is very human. We know God has something else in mind, but Francis didn't know that. So he did what seemed to be God's desire for him. His new experience of begging unveiled some fresh dimensions of life. Francis learned both the good and bad of people's response to beggars. The calluses and aching muscles revealed a body unaccustomed to physical labor. Even this "simplistic" response becomes a learning process for Francis.

It also brings him to another mistake. He takes cloth from his father's store, puts it on a horse and heads out of town. Selling both cloth and horse gives him money to buy needed supplies for fixing churches. But at least one priest would have no part of it. Francis' reputation and his father's brooding anger combined to scare the priest. He would not accept the stolen money. The trip had been a waste of time. So Francis threw down the money and walked away.

But his father would take no more! Furious at his son's theft and embarrassing way of life, Pietro drags Francis before the magistrate. No son of his is going to get by with stealing cloth! Francis claims he is serving the Church and demands trial by the Bishop. Still breathing fire, Pietro brings his son before the Bishop. Francis has no case. His theft is obvious to everyone. The Bishop can do nothing except demand that Francis return the stolen goods.

It is one of those moments when time stands still. Francis is calm. Aware of the power of symbols, he does something quite unexpected. In front of the crowd gathered for the trial, he takes off his clothes. He lays them at the feet of his father. Then, moved by a spirit bigger than his own, he makes a final commitment to the call of God. "... no longer will I say, Pietro Bernadone, my father. But now I will only say: 'Our Father in heaven.'" Francis cuts himself off from his past. He puts his life into the hands of his heavenly Father. With no staff or wallet, he begins a new life with nothing!

These steps in the growth of Francis were not logically planned. They simply happened. He responded in the creative way that seemed right to him. He will take the gospel seriously. The hurdle of fear and escapism that kept him confined had been overcome. Pietro had helped him come to this commitment. It happened. Even more unexpectedly, other men came to follow Francis. His direct response to a call to follow the gospel was attractive to others.

Followers brought about more changes for Francis. He had not planned on this. Alone, he could simply follow his heart. Now he was responsible for others. New questions arose. Should they become hermits or go about preaching the gospel? Should they seek the way of solitude or choose to minister among the people? Every time something ended something new began. It meant that Francis had to adjust to the new ways of God. With the coming of Clare, Francis gained a companion worthy of the call.

After consulting Sylvester and Clare, Francis decided that his community would combine preaching and solitude. It is the way of Jesus, who preached to the people but often left them for the solitude of prayer with his Father. The clinching argument for Francis was always Jesus. What Jesus did, Francis wanted to do. Action and contemplation became partners in his community.

As his Order grew so did the problems. Not everyone who followed Francis was totally committed to the gospel. Some thought Francis was too harsh. They wanted a mitigated way of life that was easier to follow. Others wanted even more penance to overcome an evil world. The extremes fought with each other. Francis was dismayed that his own followers should miss the message that seemed so clear to him. The struggle to guide this growing group was too much. Francis relinquished control of the Order. Others became the superiors. Even his Order was not his Order. It belonged to Jesus. What pain the struggle brought him. The crucified Jesus became more and more real to Francis. His own experience brought the cross. Another of God's surprises.

Side by side with these struggles was a growing intimacy with Jesus. Clare was a strong support for the dream of Francis. Her presence and love nourished him when he was overwhelmed by physical and spiritual pain. God provided new friends and new intimacy to strengthen Francis during times of struggle within himself and in the Order. One of the wonders of God's love for Francis is proclaimed in the Canticle of Brother Sun. Francis is nearly blind. Light hurts his eyes. Stomach and intestinal problems make life miserable. He has surrendered his Order to others. He is saddened when his original dream seems to be watered down. In the midst of this pain, his heart cries out the joy of the Canticle. Once again God surprises both Francis and ourselves with joy that blossoms in the midst of pain.

Intimacy with Jesus is at the heart of the dream. The gospel is the way to accomplish the dream. Quite naturally Francis wanted to experience what Jesus experienced in his living as well as in his dying. Francis asks to experience both the pain and the love of Jesus on the cross. God gives the gift of stigmata – and new intimacy follows. How clear an image Francis offers the world. The cross is the way to life. What looks like the end of everything is only the beginning of everything. The death of Jesus seemed to prove Jesus wrong and weak. Yet, within three days, death itself would he defeated by new life given by the Father. Francis, asking for the experience of Jesus' love and pain, acknowledges the cross as the way to new life. The Word is Francis' bread of life. Francis' life is his response to the Word.

Each situation leads to discovery. The Holy Spirit offers unexpected new life just when it seemed impossible. If we were to summarize the "pilgrim's progress" of Francis, it might look like this:

1. THE CALL ... offers a fresh outlook on life and is answered with joy and enthusiasm as well as idealism.

2. CONFUSION ... a stage that occurs when God seems silent. As the work of giving life to the dream continues, tiredness sets in. There is a tendency to grow weak in responding to the call. But it can also be a time when faith grows.

3. STRUGGLE ... the struggle to remain faithful sometimes brings disillusionment and frustration. Nothing seems to be going well. At this stage, cynicism sometimes replaces enthusiasm. The work of

building community, praying and being faithful seems so useless. It is not easy to face the reality of our weakness. Yet God is present in the middle of the struggle.

4. NEW CALL ... in the midst of dark and dry times we experience a new call from God. It may be a call to trust Jesus. Our sense of realism improves. We understand more clearly who is in charge. Prayer becomes more realistic as we acknowledge that Jesus is Lord. We realize that progress is slow and steady, not full of leaps and bounds toward holiness.

5. COMPASSION ... we grow in compassion as we suffer. We understand human brokenness because we experience it personally. We are more patient with ourselves and others as well as with the community. Gentleness grows as our response is more realistic. We grow in the ways of the Lord. We also understand God's ways with greater realism.

6. TRUST ... in Jesus grows in us. We know that we need Jesus for growth in holiness. Jesus invites us to closer union with others. Community becomes a place to discover the presence of God. It is also the place where both joy and sorrow can be confidently shared.

7. INSIGHT ... as we "see" with the eyes of faith, we also "see" any darkness in our lives. Though such insight makes us feel we are going backwards, the opposite is true. We have new insight only because of a deeper relationship with Jesus. The light of his presence unveils what was hidden and allows us to deal with it. This, in turn, leads to another call to conversion and new life.

8. REPEAT ... we may repeat the process at a new level. This is the pattern of life as gospel people. The deeper our union with Jesus, the greater our awareness of our littleness before God. The power of God transforms us. It is not our own doing, but God's love at work.

> *"Anyone who wants to be a follower of mine must renounce self he must take up his cross and follow me. Whoever want to save his life will lose it, but whoever loses his life for my sake and for the gospel's will save it.*

*What does anyone gain by winning the whole world at
the cost of his life? What can he give to buy his life back?"*
Mark 8: 34-35

Reflection

Following the gospel leads to many changes in our lives. We discover
the dream and the cost of the dream. We embrace the gospel and the
work of living the gospel. We sense God's love and God's call to
conversion. The pilgrimage is not boring but demanding. The journey
opens new horizons and requires the surrender of old ones.

The journey of St Francis often seemed to be at a crossroad. He dreamed
of knighthood and became a Knight of Lady Poverty. He felt the
melancholy of defeat in a Perugian prison only to discover the joy of
dependence in the caves of Assisi. He followed a natural tendency of
generosity only to be confronted by the need to embrace a leper. He
was disappointed with friends who did not understand the dream and
is surprised by Clare who delighted in it. He tries to control the dream
and the Order only to be asked to relinquish it to Jesus in order to be
free. When he is ready to fly down one path, the Lord leads him down
another path. Always crossroads. Always the call to follow the Lord's
way rather than his own.

Francis grows through such confusing starts and stops. Francis learns
to cut through rationalizations and discover God within and around
him. Francis grows in respect for all creation, for God is there. Kings
and Sultans, hungry people and rich people, the powerful and the
powerless, all receive respect from the Poverello of Assisi.

Francis could confront laziness and be angry with mediocrity. His goal
was to enable people to grow to a full life and not be satisfied with
lukewarm living. He could call people to accountability for their
stewardship. To misuse gifts is to offend the God who gave them.
Francis would stand still before God – so humble as to come to us under
the form of bread. Francis had a deep reverence for the Eucharist, the
presence of Jesus.

287

*Let the whole of mankind tremble, the whole world
shake, and the heavens exalt, when Christ, the Son of the
living God, is present on the altar ...*

*Look, Brothers, at the humility of God and pour out your
hearts before him. Humble yourselves, as well, that you
may be exalted by him. Therefore, hold nothing back of
yourselves for yourselves, so that he who gives himself
totally to you may receive you totally!*
**Francis & Clare – Brady/Armstrong
Paulist Press – Page 58**

Jesus is the foundation of the Franciscan life. The gospel is the way to
follow Jesus. Through the power of the Spirit, we can be all Jesus calls
us to be. Without Jesus, the gospel way of life is impossible.

Other Ways

Crises can be a way of leading people to conversion! Dissatisfaction
with life and uneasiness with our way of handling situations can
intensify the search for meaning in life. The passage from early adulthood to mid-life can rip away false ideas of invincibility. Moving from
family and home to life-on-our-own can be frightening. Life offers
many opportunities for change. In the middle of such change is God.
Through life-situations the Spirit of God manages to open us to a power
beyond ourselves. But the journey is not easy nor the results assured.
Crises can as readily lead to a breakdown as well as a breakthrough.

The EXODUS EXPERIENCE is a model of what life might be like.
Through Joseph, sold by his brothers, the Jews came to Egypt. Initially
the Pharoah favored the Hebrew people because of his love for Joseph.
But Joseph and the Pharoah died, and things changed. Oppression
became the daily fare of the Hebrews. God raises up Moses to lead these
slaves to freedom. Moses, stutterer and murderer, is chosen to lead the
people to a promised land. God is aware of the cries of the people. God
hears their cry and responds.

Freed from Egyptian slavery the Hebrew people wind up in the desert.
The harshness of the land forces the people to depend on God. But they

288

don't like it. They want other gods who will follow their instructions. A golden calf symbolizes their rejection of God. Grumbling against God, they do their "own thing" in the desert. But God calls them to return to faithfulness. He gives manna and water. He supports leaders. In the desert wasteland, the people learn to be God's people.

Then they enter the land of promise. The wandering is over and now they are blessed. But they seek new forms of slavery by asking for a king "like other nations have." God warns them about kings who will have a military build-up and will demand taxes and grow arrogant. But they refuse to listen. So they return to another "Egypt" of their own making. The cycle repeats itself.

Our lives may resemble this EXODUS experience. Called to follow the gospel, we may refuse. We may have our own ideas about gospel life. We may be trapped and enslaved by those ideas. God finally gets us to move from any "Egypt" we may create. The desert is our next stop. There we learn that God alone is God. We grumble and complain. We murmur about how good it was in "Egypt." We create a golden calf to replace God. We wander in the desert until we learn dependence on God. Then we enter a promised land. The vision is clear. We delight in all that God provides – until God provides light to see deeper into the heart of our darkness. There we discover another "Egypt" hidden within us. The cycle repeats itself.

Throughout the entire experience, God is present. The new insight into our darkness happens because intimacy with Jesus is growing. Our return to Egypt is different than the first time. It is part of a spiral toward deeper reliance on Jesus. Again and again the journey is made. Each time our surrender is more complete. Each time our sense of God's presence is deepened. The EXODUS EXPERIENCE is one way to reflect on our spiritual development.

Another way to approach the signs of "pilgrim progress" is spoken by Jean Vanier. We believe that it is necessary to be first and best. By themselves these are not evil things. What happens in reality may not be so easily dismissed. If we believe that success means being on top, being first, being best, then our efforts will focus on doing that. Such a process means some people will be on the bottom, will be last and will be the worst. The room at the top is limited. The energy we use to get there is great. Society's push brings us to exhaustion. Not only is it tiring getting there, it is tiring staying there. Fatigue and tiredness accompany the struggle. There is no time to celebrate or unwind. The inner clock keeps ticking, pushing us to greater efforts. How tiring it is! How easily we forget others and our own inner needs.

A pilgrim makes progress by seeking to go down the ladder. Instead of looking on others from the heights, we go down to walk with our own poverty. We walk with people in poverty. It is like God becoming human. God walks among people, enters their world, embraces their limitations. In Jesus, God goes down the ladder to be with us. A good pilgrim will recognize the covenant God makes with us through Jesus.

> *He was in the form of God; yet he laid no claim to equality with God, but made himself nothing, assuming the form of a slave. Bearing the human likeness, sharing the human lot he humbled himself, and was obedient, even to the point of death, death on a cross. Therefore God raised him to the heights ...*
> **Philippians 2: 6-9**

Pilgrims are honest. They plunge into their own brokenness at the call of Jesus. They have fears – fears of being abandoned, rejected, losing freedom. But we face these issues at the invitation of Jesus. Pilgrims deal with these realities and overcome fear because Jesus is with them. Pilgrims go down among God's poor ones. They meet the poor and make a covenant with them, like Jesus does with us. The poor can teach us wisdom and faith and hope. Undistorted by the rat-race to be first, we can share our inner self with each other. We learn dependence on God. We understand our need for each other and a caring community. We will teach each other how to love without trying to dominate or control.

Our choice to covenant with the poor brings life even though we may have expected disappointment by following the gospel. The burden of being trapped trying to move UP the ladder is gone. Jesus keeps his promise to help us find our life when we thought we were losing it. It is another way to reflect on a Pilgrim's progress.

Community Growth

Whatever we apply to personal growth can be applied to community growth. We come together in fraternity life through a call to follow the gospel. Faith in Jesus is at the heart of the Christian community. The honesty that helps us grow happens when we are part of an accepting community. We do not fear the covenant with the poor, for we are poor. We are free to share our brokenness because no one is unbroken. We are happy to share experiences of joy because sharing joy magnifies its power. We dialogue on the issues that divide us because shared ideas may bring greater wisdom than individual insights. We share our inner self because it is respected and kept sacred in the community.

It is not easy to build community life. Our imperfections keep getting in the way. Our individual viewpoints keep us from hearing other viewpoints. Trust doesn't just happen because we are Franciscans. It takes time and commitment to build an atmosphere of trust. We are often at different places in our lives. Someone is in Egypt, struggling with some personal slavery. Someone else has just walked into a promised land of discovery. Another person finds the idea of self-knowledge too frightening. At the same time someone else is hurting because of harsh words or some action of rejection. What a lot of "handing over" of self is required in community. How much energy we will invest in overcoming suspicion or hurt feelings or dishonesty or power struggles.

The community will experience the EXODUS experience again and again. Some problems persist beyond their time. Failure is not easy to handle. Community failure to act, when action is called for, can create disharmony. Disruptive members can destroy the best laid plans. People in community can be stupidly enthusiastic or lazily inactive. We will have more than our share of humanness. Still, we are committed to create a climate where humanness is understood and accepted.

On the other hand, we have good celebrations. We have prayer experiences that move us to tears of joy. We are gently surprised by the dedication of a brother or sister. We are impressed with the joy of one who suffers. We realize our strength as a people dedicated to Jesus, willing to "keep on keeping on" no matter what the price. We learn so much from the example of others in the community. It is good to know we are not alone on this pilgrimage to God. We learn about Jesus through the honest sharings in community. We learn to celebrate the ordinary gifts that life brings. We find joy in our covenant with the poor. Service brings us satisfaction. New members bring us happiness in seeing another person answer the gospel call of Jesus. When Sister Death calls someone home, we gather together both in grief at our loss and thanksgiving for eternal life. When our experience helps someone else, the gift is mutually satisfying.

The spiritual life, then, has many ups and downs. Tracing the progress of pilgrims is itself full of ups and downs. What we have shared can be of some help. One of these approaches may fit your journey. Though not an exhaustive exploration of pilgrim's progress, they may offer some help. Use them in whatever way seems healthy for you.

Collaboration

Working together is easier to talk about then to do. When people collaborate they are able to communicate well. They talk directly about issues that divide them. They supply creative ideas to issues they agree upon. They find the ways to work things out so that everyone involved can support the action that is taken. It demands a lot of give and take. Pet ideas are not easily abandoned nor even allowed to be changed. We like to protect what is ours. Collaboration will require the willingness to "talk it through" so that the issue can be addressed. The solution is more important than individual ideas about the solution. We can accommodate our ideas if a solution is found. Collaboration reminds us that the "problem to be solved" is the enemy. We are not enemies to each other.

There are some things to be aware of in seeking the way of collaboration in fraternity life or ministry. Some obstacles to good collaboration are:

COMPETITIVENESS ... a need to win. If I need to win, I cannot support your idea which may be better than mine.

NARROW VISION ... inability to see beyond our own little world. Creative ideas usually move out the horizons of life. If this frightens us because we live in a small world, collaboration will be difficult.

ARROGANCE/KNOWITALLISM ... this might be associated with the need to always be "right." If I think I know everything, how can I collaborate? No one can offer any better ideas than I already have.

BURNOUT ... stress has killed my creativity. I don't have the energy to talk about anything. I just don't care. Not much hope for collaboration here.

Coupled with these things are associated behaviors. I may be unwilling to deal with conflict or loss. If so, collaboration will be threatening. I find it hard to separate rejection of my ideas on an issue from rejection of me as a person. I find it difficult to share my honest feelings about an issue, so collaborators are left in the dark about my real feelings. I do not have the skills for collaboration and feel clumsy.

The good news is that we can learn the skills of collaboration. Gospel living helps us deal with arrogance and narrow-mindedness. Gospel living helps us learn how to share our real feelings. Gentleness will drive out arrogance. Burnout can be avoided by shared ministry. We are not trapped and helpless. The skills of good collaboration in community and ministry are learnable. Much of what we share in this book will help in learning the ways of collaboration. It is not a magical transformation. It takes an investment on our part. But we can improve our ability to work together.

Growth in collaboration has its own stages of development. We begin by being uncertain whether we can work with others. We may be rigid or loners. It may be that we really do work best alone. But good dialogue with competent people can help us discover how true this is. IF we choose to move toward collaboration, we may spend lots of time TALKING about collaboration. We are not ready to act, but we talk it to death. This is followed by some tentative attempts to collaborate. We're not ready for a life-time commitment to collaboration, but we try. Finally, we are willing to commit ourselves to collaboration – even when it is tough.

In its own way, the stages of development of collaboration can reflect our growth in gospel living. It can be a way of reflecting on a "pilgrim's progress." Community growth, personal growth and spiritual growth have similar signs of progress.

A basic quality of all growth is the strengthening of relationships. We grow in self-knowledge and acceptance. We develop a listening ability that draws us closer to others. We develop a more intimate relationship with God through our closeness to Jesus. In the ups and downs of gospel living, intimacy grows. Freedom and truth become partners on our journey. Individually and as a community we support one another in such growth.

> *Put on, then, garments that suit God's chosen and beloved people; compassion, kindness, humility, gentleness, patience. Be tolerant with one another and forgiving, if any of you has cause for complaint; you must forgive as the Lord forgave you. Finally, to bind everything together and complete the whole, there must be love. Let Christ's peace be arbiter in your decisions, the peace to which you were called as members of a single body. Always be thankful. Let the gospel of Christ dwell among you in all its richness; teach and instruct one another with all the wisdom it gives you. With psalms and hymns and spiritual songs, sing from the heart in gratitude to God. Let every word and action, everything you do, be in the name of the Lord Jesus, and give thanks through him to God the Father.*
>
> **Colossians 3: 12-17**

Reflection Questions

How would you define a "pilgrim"? In this chapter, what do we mean by "pilgrim's progress"? What experiences of Francis do you identify with? What "signs" of progress seem to fit your life best? What kind of response does God look for from us? Give reasons for your last answer. How do you experience the "call" of God? What is God trying to do when we experience the "desert" in our gospel life? What role does the experience of human weakness play in our gospel-life development? Why does a faith-community experience similar developments for solid growth? What qualities do people need for good collaboration? What kinds of experiences best help us learn respect for others? How would you describe the "Exodus experience" of your own life? When does our growth and development stop? What qualities hinder collaboration the most? How does poverty (not destitution) help our gospel-living? In all these ways of progress, when is God present? How has this chapter helped you understand your own position in following the gospel?

SECULAR FRANCISCAN RULE

20. The Secular Franciscan Order is divided into fraternities of various levels – local, regional, national and international. Each one has its own moral personality in the Church. These various fraternities are coordinated and united according to the norm of this Rule and of the Constitutions.

21. On various levels, each fraternity is animated and guided by a council and minister (president) who are elected by the professed according to the Constitutions. Their service, which lasts for a definite period, is marked by a ready and willing spirit and is a duty of responsibility to each member and to the community. Within themselves the fraternities are structured in different ways according to the various needs of their members and their regions, and under the guidance of their respective council.

22. The local fraternity is to be established canonically. It becomes the basic unit of the whole Order and a visible sign of the Church, the community of love. This should be the privileged place for developing a sense of Church and the Franciscan vocation and for enlivening the apostolic life of its members.

RULE – Chapter 3 #20, 21,22

The Secular Franciscan Order has a specific organizational structure. The basic block of this structure is the local fraternity. On it are built the regional (provincial), national and international structures. Each level serves the other in various ways. Through a good interchange of information and assistance, much good is accomplished for the SFO.

A FRATERNITY is the local community of Secular Franciscans. It is here that personal interchange is most obvious. It is here that affirmation is given and ideas exchanged. It is in the local fraternity that members learn about the Franciscan way of life. It is here that forgive-

ness happens and healing takes place. Interacting with one another, we learn to listen and we learn patience. Here we find support for our common call and loving confrontation to help us grow. Ministry flows from the local fraternity as does the shared joys of gospel living. Together we sharpen our understanding of the vision of St Francis.

Each fraternity has its own character. It will reflect the people who are part of it as well as the area in which it is established. In the interchange between these particular people, the fraternity will develop its charism and style. A fraternity is a place where imperfect people work together to make the gospel a livable reality. It is a place of study, formation, celebration, sorrow, parties, prayer, and good humor. Every person of a fraternity contributes to the climate of the fraternity. Common involvement in fraternity life is expected. Mutual responsibility for fraternity life is basic.

Relating To Other Groups

The local fraternity establishes relationships with other groups. Relationship with other Franciscan fraternities is natural and normal. Relating to other groups for ministry purposes makes good sense. Fraternities will find ways to cooperate with parish and diocesan groups for mutual benefit. The local fraternity is at its best when it realizes it is part of a bigger "church." Our contribution is not simply to make our local fraternity better but to make the world better. A good fraternity life will build such sharing with others into its lifestyle.

Within the SFO, the local fraternity relates to regional and/or provincial councils. These councils relate to the national Council which, in turn relates to the international Council of the SFO. Councils at each level serve as links to the wider world of Franciscan life. At each level members of the three Orders of St Francis work together to promote his vision. They help each other live the Rule more effectively. They keep all levels in touch with national and international information and needs. The various Councils can assist local fraternities in development as well as handling problems more effectively.

All Council members are SERVANTS of the SFO. The structure is meant to serve Franciscans in the pursuit of gospel living.

The Councils at various levels can also serve as a resource for one another. When ministry demands are too great for a local fraternity, regional groups can be called upon to help. When a local fraternity develops exciting programs to spread the gospel, it is shared with other Councils. One vital ingredient for such sharing is communication. Regular and open communication can help people at all levels. If the present structures are inadequate for this supportive role, we will seek better structures. It is important to serve each other as fully as possible.

Local Council

The people responsible for developing a local fraternity are the local fraternity COUNCIL. The local fraternity is "ANIMATED AND GUIDED" by the Council. Such responsibility requires more than following regulations. It calls for people who create a solid faith-community. It requires people on the COUNCIL who plan ways and means to deepen the scriptural growth of the membership. The COUNCIL decides on the acceptance of new people into the fraternity. It decides on accepting novices to profession. Council members are expected to have a "ready and willing spirit" of service to the fraternity. A good COUNCIL will learn ways to share fraternity work and ministry with the whole membership. But they remain responsible for animating and guiding the fraternity.

Serving the fraternity as a COUNCIL member is decided through election by the professed members. Once elected, people serve for the period prescribed by the Constitutions. It is fair to say that not everyone is qualified to serve on the Council. Some people have other gifts that could be burdened by council service. The committee choosing candidates for Council should do so prayerfully and wisely.

Council members will experience the joy of developing programs and plans that enhance gospel life. They will also have to deal with problems that arise in our imperfect, human fraternity. They will deal with acceptance of new members as well as having to confront inactive members. They are responsible and accountable for use of the common fund monies. They decide on the use of the common fund and how to support both needy members and the poor who are not Franciscans.

Perfect people are not required for Council elections. Skilled, dedicated people are.

The Council deals with ALL the members. It cannot favor people or factions. It is called to serve both people who physically participate as well as people who are homebound. It has the joy of celebrating with people and planning ways to help people grieve over members who die. Fraternity problems usually wind up at the desk of the Council. They cannot evade dealing with them. One helpful criteria is to see how the situation might better reflect the gospel of Jesus.

Fraternity Members

Fraternity members have the responsibility of supporting and assisting the local Council. When disagreements occur, members work to settle it one-on-one. But if that does not work, it is important to bring it to the Council. It is unhealthy to let personalities destroy or diminish the vitality of fraternity life. Fraternity members also bring ideas and projects to the Council – and willingly work to implement them. Fraternity members share their vision of Franciscan life with the Council. They help plan meetings that contribute to fraternity growth. They design fraternity ministries together with the Council. They respond to the Council's call for help or committee work etc. Though the Council has primary responsibility for the fraternity, sound growth happens best if there is collaboration by all.

Finally, an individual local fraternity is established according to the norms given in Canon Law. We exist within the Church and are governed by her laws. If you seek to establish a new fraternity, get the help of the Regional or provincial Council or its president.

The SFO fraternity is meant to be a "sacrament" for people. Its presence should reveal God's presence among the people where it is established. It should nourish its members to sound growth in gospel living. Working together, Secular Franciscans try to create a world fit for God's people.

FRANCISCAN FOCUS

St Francis prayed often on his mountain, La Verna. The solitude of the mountain brought real intimacy with Jesus. In September of 1224, two years before his death, Francis was praying on this mountain. His walk with Jesus had brought him to a beautiful intimacy. He asked Jesus for two gifts. Francis sought to experience the love that Jesus experienced in his life. Francis also asked to experience in his body the pain Jesus endured on the cross. The response that God gave is recorded in the Fioretti.

> *St Francis began to contemplate with intense devotion the passion of Christ and his infinite charity. The fervor of his devotion increased so much within him that he utterly transformed himself into Jesus through love and compassion. While he was thus inflaming himself in contemplation ... he saw coming down from heaven a Seraph with six resplendent and flaming wings. As the Seraph ... came closer to Francis, he noticed that he had the likeness of a crucified man, and his wings were so disposed that two wings extended above his head, two were spread out to fly and the other two covered the entire body.*

> *... Francis was very much afraid, and at the same time he was filled with joy and grief and amazement. He felt intense joy from the friendly look of Christ, who appeared to him in a very familiar way and gazed at him very kindly. But on the other hand, seeing him nailed to the cross, he felt boundless grief and compassion.*

> *... During this marvelous apparition, all of La Verna seemed to be on fire with very bright flames which shone in the night and illumined the surrounding mountains and valleys more clearly than if the sun were shining over the earth.*

... Now when, after a long time and a secret conversation, this wonderful vision disappeared, it left a most intense ardor and flame of divine love in the heart of St Francis; and it left the marvelous image and imprint of the passion of Christ in his flesh. For soon there began to appear in the hands and feet of Francis the marks of the nails such as he had just seen in the body of Jesus crucified. ... For his hands and feet seemed to be pierced through the center with nails, the heads of which were in the palms of his hands and in the upper part of his feet outside the flesh and the points extended through the back of the hands and the soles of the feet so far that they seemed to be bent and beaten back. ... Likewise, in his right side appeared the wound of a blow from a spear, which was open, red and bloody.

Omnibus of Sources
Franciscan Herald Press
Page 1449/1450-51

The feast of the Stigmata of St Francis is celebrated on September 17th. May God draw us to such a desire for intimacy with Jesus. "My God and my all."

QUESTIONS

1. Outline your perception of the stages of growth in St Francis' conversion process. How did each stage prompt further growth in Francis?

2. Outline the stages of growth for YOUR life. What experiences, events, people, feelings have brought you to where you are. Get in touch with the way God is working in your life!

3. What/Who is the foundation of a Christian community? What are the consequences of your answer for fraternity life i.e. what will be required of people because of the foundation you choose to build on?

4. What stages does a fraternity go through as it becomes a faith-community? Where is your fraternity at in this process? Is the process ever complete? Give reasons for your answers.

5. Describe how the EXODUS experience applies to your life?

6. Describe the spirit of your fraternity. Some questions to help you:
   ✛ How does the Council lead? ✛ What Franciscan qualities show most clearly in the fraternity? ✛ How do members cooperate with the Council? ✛ What programs of growth help build fraternity life? ✛ How would you evaluate the common prayer of the fraternity? ✛ How active is the fraternity? What ministries are part of fraternity life? ✛ How are individual members helped/supported in their Franciscan life? ✛ What learning opportunities does the fraternity provide? ✛ Does the fraternity show a good sense of collaboration? ✛ How does the fraternity work with other groups?

7. Who are the people of your local fraternity Council? What are their responsibilities? Do you make any effort to get to know them? What more could you do?

8. How do the Councils at regional, (provincial), national and international levels relate to each other? What services do they provide? How can they help the local fraternity?

SCRIPTURE *reading/reflection*

✛ 1 Corinthians 1: 26 to 2: 5
St Paul writes to a church torn by conflicts and factions. He deals with the conflicts and points out how divisive they have become. People are taking sides and tearing the community apart. Paul urges them to remember the gift God gave them when they were called to follow Jesus. They were not called because they were so wise or noble. It was God's gracious gift to them. Paul asks the Corinthians to rely on the Spirit of God as the source of their unity.

Reflect on this text. Write out the points you consider important for fraternity life. How do they affect YOUR life in fraternity?

CHAPTER 14

SACRED SECULARITY

For many years Christians considered: the "secular" world an enemy. Books and sermons spoke of dangers in being contaminated by the "world." Worldly and secular things were a danger to the good Christian. The title of this chapter, SACRED SECULARITY, may spark some warning lights in my reader's head.

To turn off the lights, let me explain. I do NOT intend to sanctify the elements and values of the "world" that are counter to the gospel. Neither will I canonize greed nor self-seeking. Nothing that is anti-life will draw my approval. Anything contrary to the gospel will not be praised or supported. I do NOT intend to support attitudes that prefer profits to people nor those that value possessions above relationships. These things and their companions remain a stumbling block to gospel people.

On the other hand I will NOT applaud Christians who withdraw from the problems of the marketplace on the plea of seeking holiness. I will NOT praise people who walk away from oppression and injustice and call it "God's problem" or "Poor folk's problem." I will NOT support people who believe the gospel is too weak to confront the "power of the world." Neither will I identify with anyone who tries to live a disembodied spirituality that mocks the incarnation. Ivory towers will not seem hospitable to me nor will people who talk a lot and never DO anything.

We are not greenhouse plants safely shut off from real life by insulated glass. We are not pampered people afraid to get dirt under our fingernails. We live in the world. We have a responsibility for the world. We are meant to bring the gospel message to the world. That is impossible if we avoid the world.

> *But everyone should be quick to listen, slow to speak,*
> *and slow to anger. For human anger does not promote*

*God's justice. Then discard everything sordid and every
wicked excess, and accept the message planted in your
hearts, with its power to save you.*

*Only be sure you act on the message, and do not merely
listen and so deceive yourselves.*
James 1: 19-22

*What good is it, my friends, for someone to say he has
faith when his actions do nothing to show it? Can that
faith save him? ... if it does not lead to action, it is by
itself a lifeless thing.*
James 2: 14 & 17

A good spirituality combines prayer and life, action and contemplation, solitude and compassion. If it must do battle with secularism
(counter-gospel elements), it will do it in the world. Solid spirituality
does not run away from the world and leave it to its own devices.
Gospel people will tackle evil in all its forms. We will do this even if
the odds seem insurmountable. We believe that the power of Jesus is
greater than any other power. On that basis, we may not win all the
battles, but we will never cease to engage the enemies of Jesus. The
rhythm of solitude and support, prayer and action, affirmation and
confrontation will be the song of our lives. We will remain in the world
because we offer a lifestyle people need to see. We will be salt, bringing
a gospel flavor to life on planet earth. We will be light, offering a vision
of shalom and justice for all people. Unwilling to hide God's gifts under
the bed, we risk revealing them and sharing them. To proclaim the good
news to the world, we will be in the world.

Secular Franciscans live in the world. They earn a living there. They
recreate there. They go to hospitals there. They have dances and parties
there. They experience light and darkness there. Their friends are there.
It would be suicide for a Christian to evade the world under the plea
of holiness. God chose to plunge INTO the world at the incarnation.
How strange if God's people tried always to escape it! Franciscans will
not abandon the world to its own devices. That could be disastrous for
the world and for us. Our road to God leads through our life in this
world.

If Franciscans are to "go forth as witnesses ... among all people" (Rule #6), the marketplace is where we go. Limiting our witness to fraternity meetings would be too meager. Continually snuggling in a cozy fraternity womb is not the witness called for by the Rule. Our community life is needed to support our witness in the world. We need people who challenge and support us. We need a group that will accept us and listen to our struggles as we bear witness to the gospel. We pray together and share the difficulty or excitement of witnessing to the gospel. Jesus is with us. He is the source and foundation of our hope. With Jesus we face the non-gospel elements in the world. We will persist in creating a world that reflects gospel ideals and values.

Consider some of the things we deal with in our world.

1. Governmental policies can diminish or degrade people. Sometimes it deprives people of dignity. The gospel requires us to promote better policies that support human dignity.

2. Some sexual practices and promotions strip men and women of their dignity while offering them the attraction of money. Sometimes people have no other resource than using their own bodies to survive. We need to be attentive to programs that can help deal with such human problems that denigrate God's gift of sexuality.

3. People in prison are often forgotten by the criminal system. While punishment that encourages reform is reasonable, this is often not done. We support serious efforts to make prisons humane places. This is a gospel demand even for hardened criminals. We will struggle in dealing with our own feelings as well as dealing with the prison system. We may be unpopular with many who cry: "put 'em away and throw away the key!"

4. Working with the elderly, the handicapped, AIDS victims and others outside the "mainstream" of life is very demanding. Homeless people include families, children and people with two jobs. They might be us. Sacred secularity calls us to attend to their needs and work to change economic systems that contribute to such "problems."

5. Divorced people, single parents, latch-key children, un-wed mothers, many single people, live lonely lives. Their sense of rejection and personal failure is high. Crisis seems a daily companion

and hope an impossible dream. Sacred secularity expects us to be gospel people for them.

6. Educational systems sometimes become warehouses that shove people through without preparing them for life. Sacred secularity gets involved in developing and designing effective educational programs.

7. Many ministries need help to deal with the urban problems of housing, fair employment practices, concern for ethical representation, healthy practices in the workplace and many other issues. Sacred secularity tells us to plunge into such ministries as competence and time allows.

8. People need time for leisure and the re-creation of their spirit. Places of retreat and solitude, recreation and enjoyment need to be supported. Sometimes people need other people to give family members a break from caring for a spouse or a parent or a bedridden relative. Sacred secularity will not allow us to stand by and do nothing.

9. Our world has found many ways to kill. Guns and knives do it quickly. But starvation or denial of medication can do it as surely though more slowly. People can die of loneliness, isolated and dead long before physical death. Life is fragile and frustrating for many people who are denied hope for anything more than survival. People can work themselves to death or go off to war and die. Life can be terminated in the womb or cut off in the prime of life by violence and oppression. We are a people of life. Our God is a God of the living, not the dead. At whatever cost, we will oppose actions and situations that keep people from a full life. Sacred secularity demands this of us. "We have this command from Christ: whoever loves God must love his fellow-Christian too." (1 John 4: 21)

You can add to this list. Each of us cannot deal with ALL the issues listed here. We are called to address an issue where our gifts and personality fit best. We are a holy people and our earth is a holy place. As the song puts it: "This is holy ground ... for the Lord is present and where he is, is holy."

Implementing the gospel in the marketplace is risky business. We do not have simplistic answers to the world's problems. We do have a vision from Jesus that offers a worldview to guide our actions. We will not escape the pain of limitations and failure. But we will never allow them to keep us from persisting. Sacred secularity is not for the faint-hearted and feeble Christian. It requires a great deal of common sense and uncommon wisdom. It is done by ordinary people empowered by the Spirit of Jesus and his gospel.

If nothing else, the scope of our task is staggering. David and Goliath seem like small-time confrontation when we realize what we are up against. Ever so quickly we are called to prayer. We are called to Jesus. We are called to the reality of knowing how little we are and how great is our need for the Holy Spirit. Dealing with so many issues in our world, we realize why we are called to community. How alone and isolated we would feel if we had to tackle these issues by ourselves. How clearly Jesus calls us to build solid, faith-filled communities. The pattern for gospel people is clear. A) Listen to the Word, both the scriptural word and the Word-made-flesh. B) Break open the word with one another as well as breaking bread in our Eucharistic celebrations. C) Implement the word in the marketplace of our lives. We need to know the facts and data of our world as well as knowing the person and revelation of Jesus.

St Francis And The World

St Francis chose this gospel path. When he faced the problems of people as well as his own life, his response was to go to the gospel of Jesus. The gospel gave him the building blocks of a solution. Each experience of Francis gave new life to the power of the gospel. But one experience had a special impact on his life. It was not a prayer experience. It was not when he shared the gospel with his brothers. It was not when he spent such beautiful time with Clare.

One of the most meaningful experiences for Francis was his contact with the leper. His fear of touching these diseased people was great. His training and experiences had taught him to loathe these people. He was willing to help from afar, but not close up.

> *The Lord granted me, Brother Francis, to begin to do*
> *penance in this way. While I was in sin it seemed very*

309

*bitter to me to see lepers. And the Lord himself led me
among them and I had mercy on them. And when I left
them, that which seemed bitter to me was changed into
sweetness of soul and body. Afterward I lingered a little
and left the world.*

Francis & Clare – Brady/Armstrong
Paulist Press – Page 154

Our path to God will resemble that of Francis. We may begin with
discussions, consciousness-raising and dialogue. Sooner or later we
will be "led among" our personal lepers and we will show mercy to
them. Our fears will be changed to compassion. We may linger a while,
but sooner or later we will abandon the world's view of the lepers of
our time. When we do, we will walk among them. For God so loved us
that Jesus came among us to share his ways of life and light. Jesus is
our model.

Walking among the poor will reveal our inner poverty. We will relate
to our own poverty and to the poor. We will learn from both. God is
there. We will discover God among those who know God well. We will
be taught faith by those who know their need of God, the "little ones."
Walking together we will work to create a new heaven and a new earth
for God's people.

Look at the consequences of the presence of Jesus. Sinners receive a new
vision of life. A prostitute escapes death and finds new reasons to live.
Nicodemus gets new information for his intellectual pursuit. Zaccheus,
little man and tax-collector, finds a new way to deal with life. A widow
regains her dead son. Martha and Mary find joy in the raising of
Lazarus. Hard-hearted lawyers are confronted with a call to change
their views so that they help people. Lepers find their skin healed and
go from being outcasts to being part of society. Self-righteous people
are confronted by a new viewpoint that challenges their views. Ordinary folks have a new hope because someone cares about them. Pilate
learns a lesson about the source of authority. Sick people find someone
who cares rather than condemns. A blind man not only receives sight,
but vision as well. A synagogue audience is given a message with
authority and a revelation that seems impossible. Devils experience the
power of one who comes from God. Forgiveness gives sinners new
hope and a sense of dignity. The sacred secularity of Jesus is obvious

310

on the pages of the gospel. He plunged into life with the same vigor that he plunged into prayer. Jesus IS our model.

Franciscans will SUPPORT AND STRENGTHEN ANYTHING THAT IS LIFEGIVING. We will resist and oppose anything that devalues or destroys life or the ability to live a human life with dignity. The areas of action for implementing this conviction are unlimited.

Nursing homes sometimes isolate and alienate patients. We will confront this issue and try to make such homes more life-giving. Abortion destroys both life in the womb and respect for life. We will work to build respect for life. We will work to help those faced with life-threatening issues. Housing discrimination, redlining, poor housing and allied problems diminish people's right to healthy housing. We will work to develop good housing and public housing policies. Divorce and separation creates a feeling of isolation and failure. We will walk with people and accept them in order to bring them new life. Immigration quotas and our desire to protect a selfish lifestyle keeps many people in economic and political slavery. We will work to design and develop more humane and compassionate policies and practices. Hunger around the world and in our own country destroy bodies and diminishes the spirit of life. We will share resources so that people might live without the specter of hunger and its consequences. The use of military and political power often brings violence and death rather than security and freedom. We will work to use power in a way that serves people, allowing them freedom and responsibility to direct their lives and political process.

The social implications of the gospel cover the planet. But while we look "out there" and respond to real needs, we also "look within" our family and "down home" relationships. Support and affirmation are needed in marriage and family. Justice and responsibility must be practiced in fraternities and parishes. Issues of conflicts between individuals must be addressed with compassion and justice. Relationships must be nourished and an atmosphere of gentleness be a part of friendships.

Sacred secularity does not leave any area of life untouched. If our actions, attitudes and values bring death to ourselves or others, they need conversion. This is the "radical interior change (conversion)" spoken of by the Rule.(#7)

> *The dignity of the human person also requires that every person enjoy the right to act freely and responsibly. For this reason, in social relations especially, a person should exercise his rights, fulfill his obligations and, in the countless forms of collaboration with others, act chiefly on his own responsibility and initiative. ...*
>
> *For any human society that is established on the sole basis of force must be regarded as simply inhuman, inasmuch as the freedom of its members is repressed, when in fact, they should be provided with appropriate incentives and means for developing and perfecting themselves.*
>
> **Pacem in terris – John XXIII**
> **#34**

A Caution

Many groups in society provide programs of self-development and fulfillment. Some of them focus so much on self and concern for self that "self" is made the center of the universe. Self-searching that is overdone can lead to a lopsided view of people and the world. On the other hand, lack of self-knowledge is no great virtue. We need to know ourselves and achieve a realistic self-acceptance. Such progress allows us freedom to serve others without fear of "losing" ourselves.

Use good, common gospel-sense in relying on such programs. Perpetual focus on self tends to narrow our world. The gospel seeks to expand our horizons. Don't allow any program to destroy what the gospel seeks to give. What is true for an individual is true for a fraternity. A fraternity needs to know itself. It needs to know both the strength and weakness of its membership. It needs to deal both with the limitations and potential of its membership. But a "forever focus" on fraternity life that ignores the bigger church and world is an unhealthy fraternity life. Reaching beyond ourselves is often the way personal or fraternity issues find a resolution. Avoid a narrow vision that limits dialogue and is often nothing more than shared ignorance. The gospel does not seek isolation. It requires building relationships in a catholic (universal) sense.

Beware, too, of people or groups who have all the answers. It evades the work of searching or the struggle it takes to surrender to the Lord's way. The gospel pushes us to search, to sell what we have and buy the pearl. No sale is necessary if we have packaged and ready-made answers. The gospel proclaims healthy values and attitudes. The way we implement them in life-situations demands lots of listening and openness to more effective solutions. Don't become trapped in a "one-way" spirituality. John XXIII has a telling phrase in MATER ET MAGISTRA: "... in their conduct they should weigh the opinions of others with fitting courtesy and not measure everything in the light of their own interests." (#239)

Reflection

This chapter only opens the door to the meaning of sacred secularity. You need to discover its meaning for your life. It happens in the reality of the world in which you live, work and play. It happens among friends, with co-workers, family members, parish groups, bingo and card parties, wherever people touch your life. We are imperfect people seeking wholeness. Forgiveness and reconciliation will be well known among us. Personal relationships will be supportive as well as stressful. We need Jesus and other people to help us along this path. We do fail to communicate. We need to discard prejudice and bias and self-right-eousness in order to listen. We deal with people who are ugly and attractive, rude and courteous, ungrateful and gracious. People enter our lives who are exciting and boring, energetic and lazy. War, oppression and violence will enter side-by-side with shalom, support and gentleness. Creativity in relationships is not a luxury. It is a necessity. God can help us, for creativity is God's way of sharing life with us.

The gospel brings tension into life. I could avoid this tension quite simply. I could ignore my neighbor. I could refuse to forgive my enemy. I could avoid compassion. I could isolate myself from people. I could keep my sense of unworthiness. I could run from the "world." I could nestle in a cocoon of prayer and evade justice issues. I could label people in order to avoid contact. But I would also be dead! The tension created by following the gospel is a life-giving tension. When I am disturbed by the gospel, it moves me to do something. Action brings life with God and God's people. It brings life. Jesus is true to his promise to give life and light to faithful followers. Hope and tenderness blossom under the light of Jesus. St Francis offers this advice:

> *And by this I wish to know if you love the Lord God and me, his servant and yours, if you have acted in this manner; that is, there should not be any brother in the world who has sinned, who after he has looked into your eyes, would go away without having received your mercy, if he is looking for mercy. And if he were not to seek mercy you should ask him if he wants mercy. And if he should sin thereafter a thousand times before your very eyes, love him more than me so that you may draw him back to the Lord. Always be merciful to such as these.*
> **Francis & Clare – Brady/Armstrong**
> **Paulist Press – Page 75**

The gospel attitude of Francis is clear. When we choose to follow the Franciscan way of life, this is what we embrace. The power of the Holy Spirit makes it possible for us to "keep on keeping on." St Paul echoes the words of Francis.

> *Therefore, now that we have been justified through faith, we are at peace with God through our Lord Jesus Christ, who has given us access to that grace in which we now live; and we exult in the hope of the divine glory that is to be ours. More than this: we even exult in our present sufferings because we know that suffering is a source of endurance, endurance of approval, and approval of hope. Such hope is no fantasy; through the Holy Spirit he has given us, God's love has flooded our hearts.*
> **Romans 5: 1-5**

Reflection Questions

What does "sacred secularity" mean to you? What areas of your life are untouched by the gospel? How do social issues and the gospel relate to one another? What is more important – social action or prayer? Is that the wrong question to ask? How do you relate prayer and social justice? What is the role of community life in our attempts to implement the gospel in "secular" society? What issues get more attention from you: Social peace and justice ideas in the larger world –or– peace and justice in your personal relationships? Describe some issues of our world that you have the gifts to deal with. What are you actually doing about it? Why can groups too focused on self-improvement be unhealthy for a Franciscan? What role does self-knowledge play in our ability to implement sacred secularity? What personal ideas or viewpoints will you need to surrender in order to follow the gospel? What kind of tension does the gospel create in your life? What are you doing about it? What can the "poor" teach you? Do you bring God to others or discover God in others? or both? Why is "one-wayism" a danger to the integrity of gospel living? What gospel text speaks most clearly to you about sacred secularity? How does the incarnation (God becoming human) influence your ideas about sacred secularity? Explain why prayer and action are both necessary for consistent growth in gospel living. Is a gospel-discussion alone enough for implementing our gospel life? What help does it offer?

SECULAR FRANCISCAN RULE

23. Requests for admission to the Secular Franciscan Order must be presented to the local fraternity whose council decides upon the acceptance of new brothers and sisters.

    Admission to the Order is gradually attained through a time of initiation, a period of formation of at least one year, and profession of the Rule. The entire community is engaged in this process of growth by its own manner of living. The age of profession and the distinctive Franciscan sign are regulated by the statutes.

    Profession by its nature is a permanent commitment.

    Members who find themselves in particular difficulties should discuss their problems with the council in fraternal dialogue. Withdrawal or permanent dismissal from the Order, if necessary, is an act of the fraternity Council according to the norm of the Constitutions.

    RULE – Chapter 3 # 23

The Rule continues to spell out the responsibilities of the local Council. The Council is responsible for the admission of new members to the fraternity. Not everyone who seeks to join the SFO is called to join. The Council is responsible for determining the absence or presence of the call. There are some criteria that can assist them. The list is not meant to be exhaustive.

Positive Signs

Among the elements needed in applicants for the SFO are these:

1. A solid desire for spiritual growth.

2. A spirit of optimism and hope. Pessimists and chronically depressed people do not easily fit the spirit of St Francis.

3. A good sense of humor. People who are dead serious about everything are not good candidates for the SFO.

4. A sense of dedication to learn about and follow the gospel. Gospel living is demanding. A strong dedication to this pursuit is important.

5. It is helpful if people have some idea about St Francis and his life. This will grow and develop, but some initial knowledge seems reasonable to expect.

6. Though the desire for holiness is important, people also need a good sense of mission and ministry i.e. service to others. Applicants need to be open to serving others. A good fraternity will expect them to participate in fraternity ministry(s).

7. Applicants need to be open to personal conversion. The Rule calls for a "radical interior change" to be carried out daily.

8. Applicants should have a good sense of responsibility for their lives and growth. The Secular Franciscan way of life is not a baby-sitting proposition. We help one another, but we expect a mature response in following the gospel.

9. Faith in Jesus is fundamental in applicants. Again, we help one another to develop this relationship. But people joining the SFO need some foundational faith.

10. Members of the Franciscan fraternity need to be Catholics who are faithful to their beliefs and practice them. Non-Catholics can certainly follow the spirit of Francis. However, membership in a local fraternity requires applicants to be Catholic.

Council members would do well to dialogue with applicants about these criteria. Such dialogue can help the Council make wise decisions about applicants.

Negative Signs

The other side of the coin is to have some criteria that indicate the lack of a call to the SFO. Again, good common sense must be used in applying these criteria.

1. People who already belong to a religious Order or another "Third Order", are not allowed to join yet another similar group.

2. Non-Catholics may not be received to membership. However, they may associate with a fraternity without becoming full members. Good dialogue can determine the kind of participation that is healthy.

3. People whose present life and lifestyle is obviously counter to the gospel may not be accepted into the SFO. Unless there is a desire for real conversion, such folks hardly make suitable candidates for a gospel way of life.

4. One spouse in a marriage needs the support of the other spouse to join the SFO. Exceptions are possible. Basically we want to avoid causing marital problems because of the SFO. Here again, open dialogue with everyone concerned is very helpful in finding a good solution.

5. People whose reputation is one of gossiping and criticism of everyone from God to the poor is NOT a fit candidate for the SFO. People who are super-critics, who show irresponsibility in financial affairs, people who exhibit poor responsibility in family life or are anti-social personalities make poor candidates for the SFO.

6. People with serious addictions who make no effort to deal with the addictions. If they have no will to change, it is foolish to allow them to join a community that requires change!

7. Be cautious about accepting people with strange devotions or devotions that absorb their lives. If the devotions are not approved by the Church, they are certainly NOT viable candidates for the SFO.

8. Though all of us have various problems in relationships, the SFO should not accept people who are unable to establish and maintain friendships. If they lack communication skills and are not willing

to learn, it is better NOT to accept them into fraternity life. Our life requires reasonable communication and sharing. If people are not able to do this, fraternity life will be too demanding.

9. People with rigid and unbending attitudes will find our openness and expanding horizons difficult to accept. It is better NOT to accept them than to allow them to become dictators in the fraternity. Again if they truly DESIRE to change, council members will take that into consideration.

10. It seems to me that people who use power and/or violence to get their way will NOT he suitable for gospel living. We all make mistakes. But when a candidate reveals a quality of being power-hungry or likes to dominate, the Council members need to be very cautious about accepting him/her.

As with any criteria, common-sense application is necessary. Even more important, Council members must get to know the candidates personally. It is unfair to the fraternity and the formation director to lay the decision-making burden on their data and insights. The entire council is responsible. Hence, council members have a serious obligation to get to know candidates for the fraternity. When honest doubt remains, it is generally good to give the fraternity the benefit of the doubt. Honest and gentle, direct and compassionate dialogue with candidates should be the hallmark of the Council. The Council dialogues with the candidate to determine whether or not God is calling him/her to the SFO.

Formation

Admission to the SFO is a process. Initially, people may simply come to "look us over." We share general information with them. If they wish to begin formation, they attend formation sessions for a period of time. When they feel ready, they ask for admission to the novitiate. The final step is to apply for profession. Good dialogue between Council and applicant will promote good decisions.

One element of good formation is the fraternity itself. The WHOLE FRATERNITY is responsible for the formation of new members. The lives of professed members offer an example of what Franciscan living looks like. Professed fraternity members need to participate as actively as possible in the formation program. Everyone in the fraternity will influence new people. It is important for professed members to be aware of that influence and make it a positive one.

The Council is responsible for providing a good formation program for newcomers. When a good program is lacking, it will show in the fraternity. Fraternity life stagnates. New members wander haphazardly toward profession. No sense of direction generally indicates no direction is present. The nature and intensity of the formation program will have consequences for a fraternity. It is important and essential to invest both time and energy in a good formation program. Fraternity members need to participate in it. The time of formation prepares a person to accept our way of life. No fraternity can neglect formation or do it with indifference and expect to have a vibrant fraternity life.

Newcomers have a right to expect good formation. They want to experience Franciscan life so they can make a good decision about joining. When we speak of formation, we want to be attentive to the continuing formation of the professed. Everyone is in formation. We are all learning the ways of following the gospel. The Council takes special care that a good formation program is available to newcomers. If fraternity members have never had solid formation, they should be encouraged to participate in some formation-type learning. The presence of professed members at formation sessions is a healthy sign of a desire to continue their own formation. It also gives them a chance to relate to the new folks.

Some fraternities assign professed "Sponsors" to each novice. The sponsors take special care to be available to the novice. It is a good practice to follow.

After at least a year of formation, the Council must decide to accept or refuse admission of novices to fraternity life. A good formation program will help people make this decision. Regular contact on the part of Council members will help them decide on the suitability of novices. This decision needs to be made prayerfully and with integrity. There should be clear data that is used to make these decisions. If the information indicates that God is NOT calling someone to our way of life, that is communicated. The reasons should be shared with the novice. Good dialogue and prayer together is part of good communication. We need to love each other enough to share opinions and ideas honestly and with empathy.

At best, our decisions are good but imperfect. When it seems clear, after consideration, the decision is made and followed. Waffling is not helpful to anyone. If a novice is accepted for profession, the affirmation of the Council decision should also be shared.

It is a good practice to do quarterly evaluations with the novices. It can offer them an insight into how the Council perceives their development. It is a fair way to help the individual if particular areas of growth need to be addressed. It is unfair to refuse admission if there are changes that can be made but are difficult because of time constraints. The role of the Council is to help people grow during formation. Quarterly dialogue can help accomplish this goal. It is also a help in moving toward a wise decision about admission to profession. Councils would do well to initiate something of this sort as part of their policies for formation.

Profession

Novices who are accepted into the SFO make a profession of our way of life. Generally this profession is a permanent one. Becoming a gospel person is a lifetime task. Our commitment to it will be permanent. However, special circumstances may call for exceptions. Follow the process in the Constitutions or Statutes when this occurs.

People are accepted into an individual fraternity. Though there can be exceptions, this is the ordinary policy. The head of the local Fraternity is the president. Therefore, it is the president who accepts the profession of a novice. The president is officially designated to receive people at the profession ceremony. If the president cannot do so, someone delegated by the president may receive the profession.

The profession ceremony should be a joyful fraternity celebration. After the profession, the novices should receive some symbol of their commitment. It might be a ring, a crucifix, a Franciscan "Tau" cross or some other symbol decided upon by the Council. Family and friends are welcome at professions. Novices should encourage their family, friends and relatives to join him/her. Courtesy and hospitality should be obvious at the profession ceremony.

Change Of Status In The SFO

The circumstances of our lives often change. Professed Secular Franciscans often face such changes. If relationship to the SFO changes, the commitment may change as well. At other times, moving to another area requires transferring to another fraternity. Here are a few possible situations and what a responsible Secular Franciscan can do in each case.

1. When people move to another locale for whatever reason, they inform their former fraternity. On arrival in the new area, they apply for admission to the local fraternity in that place. They need to get a record of their profession for the new fraternity The fraternity secretaries can take care of this need. The transferee becomes a member of the second fraternity upon acceptance of the transfer by the fraternity Council of the new fraternity.

A local fraternity may require the transferee to attend some formation or other sessions. It is the right of a fraternity to require such things. It offers the opportunity for getting acquainted. It can provide time for sharing the practices and policies of the new fraternity.

In addition to physical moves to another place, problems relating to health can change the relationship between the fraternity and the individual. For whatever reasons it is important for the Council and the individual to clarify the situation. Together they can determine the level of participation that is both feasible and practical.

2. After profession, some Secular Franciscans decide to withdraw from the SFO for a variety of reasons. Some may join a religious Order. Others may enter into marriage and require a review of their commitment to the SFO. Some grow lazy in their commitment and drift away. Community gatherings are missed. Communication

breaks down. Hurts happen. Such erosion of commitment needs to be addressed by the Council.

Drifting members should be called to accountability. The Council has both the right and responsibility to do this. But it should be done directly and with loving dialogue. If there is little or no hope that the erosion of commitment will stop, the Council may decide to dismiss the member. At other times the individual may seek to be dismissed from the SFO.

Such decisions are to be put in writing. It clarifies the issue both for the Council and the individual. A member who wishes to withdraw should make that request to the Council in writing. The Council frees the individual from commitment to the fraternity. Good communication makes a big difference in dealing with these situations.

3. Members sometimes go through a disillusionment stage with gospel living. They begin to absent themselves from community gatherings and/or participation in fraternity ministries. The Council has a duty to seek communication with the individual. Oftentimes good dialogue can deal with the issues quickly. At other times it may become frustrating when communication is attempted but there is no response. The Council must follow through and try to discover what the facts are. The same is true when a member is present but a source of friction in the community. Sometimes people do things that are destructive of community life. The Council should deal directly with such folks. The offer of a "grace period" may be of help, allowing time for change. But if the destructive behavior continues, the Council may need to consider dismissal for such an individual. In all cases, hearsay data is NOT sufficient. The Council must have direct and real data to act upon. Justice must be practiced. But indecisiveness does justice to no one! It is wise to communicate concerns in writing. If dismissal follows, that dismissal should be in writing.

These can be tough issues for a Council to deal with. But the Council is responsible to and for the fraternity. When members consistently renege on commitment; then their presence is a source of irritation and friction among the members; when a member is obviously unfaithful to our gospel life as spelled out in the Rule, the Council must take action. It will be caring, compassionate, honest action, but act they must. The good of the fraternity as well as the individual is at stake.

The details of dealing with changes in status for Secular Franciscans are spelled out in the Constitutions. If there are doubts about how to proceed, contact a knowledgeable member of the regional or provincial Council.

> *You, my friends, were called to be free; only beware of turning your freedom into license for your unspiritual nature. Instead, serve one another in love. ... What I mean is this: be guided by the Spirit.*
>
> *... the harvest of the Spirit is love, joy, peace, patience, kindness, goodness, fidelity, gentleness and self-control. Against such things there is no law. Those who belong to Christ Jesus have crucified the old nature with its passions and desires. If the Spirit is the source of our life, let the Spirit also direct its course.*
> **Galatians 5:13, 16 & 23-25**

FRANCISCAN FOCUS

A healthy Franciscan fraternity promotes a balance between solitude and activity, dialogue and silence, confrontation and affirmation. St Francis links solitude and fraternal love in his "Rule for Hermitages." Thomas Merton had these words about this "Rule."

> ... It has been observed that the genius of it easily reconciles things that seem at first sight irreconcilable. Here St Francis has completely reconciled the life of solitary prayer with warm and open fraternal love. Instead of detailing the austerities and penances which the hermit must perform, the hours they must spend in prayer etc, the Saint simply communicates the atmosphere of love which is to form the ideal climate of prayer in the hermitages. The spirit of the eremitical life as seen by Francis is therefore cleansed of any taint of selfishness and individualism. Solitude is surrounded by fraternal care and is therefore solidly established in the life of the Order and the Church. It is not an individualistic exploit in which the hermit, by the power of his own asceticism, gains the right to isolation in an elevation above others. On the contrary, the hermit is reminded, above all, that he is dependent on the love and good will of others. This is certainly a very effective way of guaranteeing prayer, since it shows him how much he owes it to others to become a true man of God.

The Rule for hermitages reflects the good sense of St Francis. In his straightforward way he incorporates the idea of hermitage in the middle of community life. The service of the Brothers provides the hermit with the opportunity for solitude. Hopefully, we can do the same for one another.

The Rule for Hermitages

Those who wish to live religiously in hermitages should be three brothers or four at most. Two of these should be mothers and they may have two sons or at least one. The two who are mothers should follow the life of Martha, while the two sons should follow the life of Mary (LK 10: 38-42), and they may have an enclosure in which each one may have his small cell in which he may pray and sleep. And they should always say Compline of the day immediately after sundown; and they should be eager to keep silence, and to say their Hours, and to rise for Matins; and let them seek first of all the kingdom of God and his justice.(MT 6:33) And let them say Prime at the proper time, and after Terce they may be free from silence, and they may speak and go to their mothers. And, whenever it pleases them, they can seek alms from them as little "poor ones," for the love of God. And afterward they should say Sext and None and Vespers at the proper time.

And in the enclosure, where they live, they should not permit any person to enter, nor should they eat there. Those brothers who are the mothers should be eager to stay far from every person; and because of obedience to their minister, they should protect their sons from everyone, so that no one can talk with them. And the sons should not talk with any person except their mothers, and with the minister and his custodian when it pleases them to visit with the blessing of the Lord God. The sons, however, should sometimes assume the role of the mothers, as from time to time it may seem good to them to exchange roles. They should strive to observe conscientiously and carefully all the things mentioned above.

Francis & Clare – Brady/Armstrong
Paulist Press – Page 147-148

QUESTIONS

1. What does "Secular" mean to you when used in the term "Secular Franciscan Order?" One way to clarify is to describe both what it is and what it is not.

2. How does our contact with the world and people help us grow in holiness? Gives reasons and/or examples to support your answer.

3. Why is prayer important for someone involved in sacred secularity?

4. In your opinion, what gospel qualities are most needed in American society? Where are they most needed i.e. what areas of American life are most in need of such qualities?

5. How do you integrate prayer and action in your life? Share some of the ways that have helped you accomplish this integration. Share things that hinder such integration.

6. Describe the process by which someone becomes a member of the Secular Franciscan Order.

7. What are some positive criteria by which to judge a call to the SFO? What negative criteria would indicate the lack of such a call?

8. Who has the right and responsibility for accepting members into the local fraternity? Who is responsible for the formation of new members in the SFO?

9. If the status of Secular Franciscans changes after profession who is responsible for dealing with the situation? What process is followed for: Dismissing people from the fraternity? Calling people to accountability for their Franciscan life? Handling the transfer of people to another fraternity?

SCRIPTURE *reading/reflection*

✛ James 2: 1-9

St James is a practical writer. In this text he deals with a common experience for Christians. It is easy to show favoritism. Working with lovable people is easier than working with annoying people. Sometimes we delight more in serving the rich than in serving the poor.

Reflect on this text. Then share a personal experience when you showed favoritism or practiced prejudice in dealing with people. What does St James ask of you in this text?

CHAPTER 15

THE CREATIVE TOUCH

"Fill the earth and subdue it" The Bible, from the first page on, teaches us that the whole of creation is for people; that it is their responsibility to develop it by intelligent effort and by means of their labor to perfect it. If the world is made to furnish each individual with the means of livelihood and the instruments for growth and progress, each person has, therefore, the right to find in the world what is necessary. The recent Council reminded us of this: "God intended the earth and all that it contains for the use of every human being and all people." All other rights whatsoever, including those of property and free commerce, are to be subordinated to this principle.

Populorum Progressio – Paul VI

St Francis expected his followers to work with their hands. Before resorting to begging, they were to try to support themselves by work. He saw idleness as an enemy of the soul and a hindrance to spiritual growth. On the other hand he warned his followers not to become workaholics and extinguish the spirit of prayer. The issue of work is important on our gospel journey.

We are commissioned by God to care for the earth. We are stewards of God's creation. Work is one way in which we fulfill this command. Work is a gift to God's gospel people. The earth exists for all people. Work gives us the opportunity to care for the earth as well as ourselves and our families.

It must be added that when one is motivated by Christian charity, he cannot but love others, and regard the needs, sufferings and joys of others as his own. His work,

wherever it be, is constant, adaptable, humane and has
concern for the needs of others: ...
Mater et Magistra – John XXIII
 # 257

Work is not a punishment. It is an opportunity to collaborate with God in the continuing creation of the world. God is a dynamic God always at work creating and re-creating the world and its people. God leads people to new discoveries. God unveils cures for illnesses and unveils dimensions of space. God loves discoveries that bring life to people. The inventive creativity of God's people brings delight to the heart of God. Sadness comes when that inventiveness is misused to create instruments of death. In human life, work plays an important role.

The Rule asks Franciscans "to esteem work as a gift and as a sharing in creation, redemption and service of the human community" (Rule #16). Francis would delight in this vision of work, for it reflects his spirit.

Some people see work as a necessary evil. One must work to earn money to support oneself and the family. Earning money allows us to buy things we need and want. Other people see work as a way to fill time. Doing nothing all day is boring and depressing. Still others view work as an opportunity for creativity, using skills and talents to create new products and services. For some, work itself is boring. This is especially true of monotonous and repetitive work. Our attitude depends on where we work, what we do, what it pays, what benefits we receive or how stimulating it is.

The word "work" is used in many ways. Doing the dishes and launching satellites is called work. Fixing cars and styling hair is work. Assembly line welding and professional sports are called work. Nursing is work and so is counseling. Hoeing in the garden is work and studying is work. Carpentry and computer programming is work. Painting or taking care of the baby is work. Caddying at a golf course or walking the dog can be work. Preaching can be work and so can committee meetings. The list is endless, limited only by human ingenuity.

Our attempt to talk about work in a way that touches so many different situations is difficult. The best I can do is offer some reflections. It is your task to apply these ideas to the work YOU do.

Reflections On Work

Our attitude to work is important. Attitudes influence our perception of the work we do. Gospel people see work as a gift. We are partners with God in caring for the earth and its people. Work allows us to share in that "care." Work allows us to share in the redemption of people. Through work we offer people the service of perceiving work in a gospel context. Work is a service to the human community. It brings us in touch with people-needs that work can fulfill. Ideas such as these presuppose an attitude that approaches work positively. Developing this attitude is a personal responsibility.

Simplistic answers to the "how-to-do-it" are not helpful. The suggestion of saying a Hail Mary with each bolt you turn may sound good. But if you turn a thousand bolts a day, the Hail Mary's will not make the work creative and meaningful. Assembly line kind of work needs a different solution than a policy-making job requires. A worker who is part of the entire production of something, seeing it through from beginning to end, can find satisfaction. Someone who has only a small part in the production may find much less satisfaction in work. People who do counseling will take a different approach than a garbage collector. Some work may be so inhuman that it is difficult to develop a positive attitude about it. Such work may need to be eliminated or done by machines.

Creativity can be stretched a great deal with some jobs. We may be called to redeem a job from dehumanizing effects. Safety regulations may need to be sharpened. Working conditions may need a more human touch. Dialogue between workers and employers may need to be strengthened. Profit sharing may be a way to bring meaning to work. Scheduling may make a job more acceptable. Within the workplace there are many ways that "redemption" can take place. God's people have a right to work, to work in safety and to be able to achieve a just reward for work. A good system of accountability can be helpful when justly applied.

Developing programs for alcohol and drug abuse help both worker and employer. Adding a few comforts to the workplace can make working more enjoyable.

Overwork diminishes our capacity for good relationships. It can interfere with spouse and family relationships. If so, a bold critique is needed. Perhaps it calls for a job change. Gospel people see relationships as primary. If work subverts that priority, we need to deal with the issue. Sometimes work produces lethal products whose only use is to destroy people. We must question whether we can continue to support such things with our labor. If the product is not lethal but can have both good and bad effects, we may struggle about what to do. Easy answers are not available in our imperfect world.

Gospel people prayerfully and honestly reflect about continued participation. A gospel vision sees work as something that creates a better world. We cannot ignore the vision when it touches our pocketbook. Anyone can see the difficulty in resolving such issues.

Gospel people struggle with many questions in the work place. When unemployment strikes, how do we support or help the unemployed? How can we create more jobs so people can get honest work? What action can gospel people take in dealing with discrimination on the job? What can we do about a company which makes unconscionable profits while dehumanizing the employees?

What can we do about lazy or indifferent employees who turn out shabby products? How can we "redeem" these situations?

Gospel people will search for answers. The search for answers may be part of our "work."

Underlying these questions is the gospel attitude toward work. We make a commitment to deal with any issue that touches people and creation. We continue our efforts to create a world and a work place that conforms to Jesus' words to us. We cannot change everything. The Talmud has a realistic saying: "It is not incumbant upon you to complete the task, but neither are you free to desist from it."

Positively, the Rule offers a number of elements that are part of our attitude to work. They reflect the gospel approach to work.

1. Work is God's gift to us. We offer thanks to God for the gifts that we have.

2. Work allows us to share in God's continuing creation. We are partners with God in creating things and services that fill the needs of people.

3. Work helps us fulfill our role of caring for the earth and using the resources of the earth for the good of all people. God calls us to be faithful and responsible in our use of the earth's resources.

4. Work plays a role in making the earth a place that is livable for all people. Our concern is not only for the present generation, but for future generations as well. Conservation and environmental issues are part of this dimension of work.

5. Work enables us to meet the human needs of people. It is a global concern. We do not limit our work to how much profit we can make. Our priority is service to people. Reasonable profits are not evil, but they may not override our concern for people.

6. Our attitude to work is built on faith. God will help us develop attitudes that reflect the creative approach of God.

7. Our definition of work is a broad one. We acknowledge the creative power of prayer as work. We acknowledge the work of suffering and helpless people. They teach us how to deal with pain and powerlessness. Work is not ALL we do nor does it give us the only worth we have. But it is a sacred privilege.

> *The essential meaning of this "kingship" and "dominion" of man over the visible world, which the creator himself gave man for his task, consists in the priority of ethics over technology, in the primacy of person over things and in the superiority of the spirit over matter.*
>
> *... What is in question is the advancement of persons, not just the multiplying of things that people can use.*
> **Redemptor Hominis – John Paul II**
> **# 16**

Gospel people approach the challenge and problems of the work place with attitudes based on the gospel. We face complex and interconnected issues in our economic life. What we do in the USA touches poor people in South America. Business practices of many companies touch lives from Peoria, IL to peasants in Columbia, S.A. The banking system controls economic power worldwide. Our attempts to create a sensitive marketplace will not be received with open arms by all people. But we are committed to acknowledge that we are not "free to desist" from the effort. These are practical implications when we commit ourselves to follow the gospel.

On The Personal Side

In addition to consequences for the marketplace, gospel ideas of work also touch our personal lives. Each of us has gifts. We develop skills. Some things we do quite naturally. Some skills are in the arena of relationships.

We are sensitive to the needs of others. Some people listen well to the heart and with the heart. Others are skilled at healing. Their presence, prayer and touch enables others to deal with pain in a healthy way. Some have a gift of compassion, sensitively knowing when to speak and when to be silent. Some may write well, while others seem to have leadership skills. Whatever your gift(s), good self-awareness will allow it to be used wisely. Particular situations or people can reveal a gift of which we were unaware.

Knowing and developing our gifts allows us to use them freely in the service of others. Regular use sharpens gifts and skills. However we discover and use our gifts, they are part of our personal "work." This sort of work is not a burden but a delight. Yet persistent use of our skills and gifts in the service of others may not always be easy.

Crowning our work with love, in all kinds of situations, is no simple matter. To be gracious and compassionate can demand a good deal of energy. Engaging in ministry that fits our skills can also deplete our energy. Even when work is exciting it contains healthy stress. When gifts and skills are insufficient for someone's need, frustration takes its toll. The experience of powerlessness will call forth the gift of accepting reality – another name for humility. Many problems have no final answer. We may not even understand the "why" of it. Faith in Jesus demands that we work to serve our neighbor with a loving heart.

> *Come to me, all who are weary and whose load is heavy;*
> *I will give you rest. Take my yoke upon you, and learn*
> *from me, for I am gentle and humble-hearted; and you*
> *will find rest for your souls. For my yoke is easy to wear,*
> *my load is light.*
>
> **Matthew 11: 28-30**

St Francis And Work

St Francis was a practical person. He knew that work was important in our lives on earth. Laziness and idleness are enemies of God. They are quite different than leisure and solitude which actively respond to life and God. Listen to Francis' words:

> *And I used to work with my hands, and I still desire to*
> *work. I firmly wish that all my brothers give themselves*
> *to honest work. Let those who do not know how to work*
> *learn, not from the desire for receiving wages for their*
> *work, but as an example and in order to avoid idleness.*
> *When we are not paid for our work, let us have recourse*
> *to the table of the Lord, seeking alms from door to door.*
> *The Lord revealed to me a greeting, as we used to say"*
> *"May the Lord give you peace."*
>
> **Francis & Clare – Brady/Armstrong**
> **Paulist Press – Page 155**

Francis saved some of his harshest words for followers who were lazy. He grew angry with friars who always loved to eat but never lifted a hand to work. He called them "Brother Fly." If you find yourself being "lazy" about fraternity life, you might take these words to heart.

> *"Be off with you, Brother Fly, since you want to eat the*
> *labors of your brethren and be idle in the work of God.*
> *You are like a barren and idle drone, who gathers noth-*

ing and does no work but consumes the toil and gain of
the good bees!"
OMNIBUS OF SOURCES – Page 1150
Franciscan Herald Press

Leisure

All this talk about work could make workaholics of us all. A word of caution is in place. Anyone can make a fetish out of work. Work can so dominate our lives that there is room for nothing else. Family, friends and community simply cease to exist for us. We rationalize our addiction by buying things for those we love. But things cannot replace persons. Relationships need persons related directly to one another. Things can be an expression of real love, but they cannot substitute for personal contact. Family relationships do not deepen because bank books are balanced. Community life does not blossom because you contribute to the common fund – and little else! The rat-race attitude of society has led to the break-up rather then the strengthening of relationships. Some families need several jobs just to survive. We need to face this modern temptation head on. We cannot allow such a cancer to grow in our relationships.

But there is another factor to consider when we are diseased by workaholism. Workaholics tend to become less human. Friendships are neglected. Family time together becomes non-existent. Personal gospel growth may come to a screeching halt. Prayer becomes a casualty. Workaholics have little energy left for love-building. We must face such issues directly and honestly. Our lifestyle calls for putting people before profits, loved ones before loved work. This is "crunch time." We are committed to a gospel lifestyle. We must make decisions that accord with the gospel. Anyone who has dealt with such situations knows how frightening they can be. If present financial needs keep us apart, the COMMON FUND of the fraternity might be used to help out. The community needs to deal honestly with this issue. The community is called to help people live the gospel lifestyle. DO IT!

True leisure allows us time to re-create our spirit. It is NOT meant to be another intense form of work. Some folks recreate so intensely they are worn out by their "leisure." That is not what we mean by leisure.

Of all the commandments, many of us find "keeping holy the Sabbath" a difficult one to follow. We do all the "work" we can't get done during the week. Rather than a time of relaxation, it contributes to our stress quotient. Work and leisure need one another. We need time to talk to one another. We need time to celebrate without watching the clock. We need time, in silence, to free our minds and hearts from the beat of the rat-race.

> *Thus the heavens and the earth and everything in them were completed. On the sixth day, God brought to an end all the work he had been doing; on the seventh day, having finished all his work, God blessed the day and made it holy, because it was the day he finished all his work of creation.*
>
> **Genesis 2: 1-3**

Reflection Questions

How would you define "work?" How does your "work" follow a gospel lifestyle? What attitude do you have toward your self-image? How important is it for you to work? Why? List some signs of the disease of workaholism! How many of them apply to you? What are you going to do about it? How does workaholism affect relationships? What does it do to your ability to pray? What kind of stress is healthy? Which is worse – laziness or workaholism? Why? What insights does a gospel person bring to the work place? How responsible are we for changing inhuman conditions? If profit-taking is the only "bottom line" of a business, what does a gospel person bring to such a situation? Why is leisure important for humans? What role would a retreat or quiet time play in the life of a gospel person? What perspective does the SFO Rule give about work? Do you agree with it? Do you follow it? How well do you keep the sabbath (Sunday)? How well can you leave worries about work when you are relaxing or celebrating? How well do you listen to the people you love? Have you attempted to buy love with gifts rather than yourself? When does a gift become a true expression of love? How can a gospel community help you with work-related issues and/or problems? How do we discover our personal gifts? What do you do in order to sharpen your skills? Why is awareness of personal abilities, talents and gifts important for a gospel person? Does your work serve to enliven you or depress you? What can you do about it? How can we change work systems that take advantage of people or dehumanize them? How can we address issues in others countries when people are oppressed and exploited for their work? Can gospel people ignore such issues?

SECULAR FRANCISCAN RULE

24. To foster communion among members, the council should organize regular and frequent meetings of the community as well as meeting with other Franciscan groups, especially with youth groups. It should adopt appropriate means for growth in Franciscan and ecclesial life and encourage everyone to a life of fraternity. This communion continues with deceased brothers and sisters through prayer for them.

25. Regarding expenses necessary for the life of the fraternity and the needs of worship, of the apostolate and of charity, all the brothers and sisters should offer a contribution according to their means. Local fraternities should contribute toward the expenses of the higher fraternity council

Rule – Chapter 3 # 24-25

The Council has the responsibility of finding creative ways of sustaining and encouraging fraternity growth. The community gathering is a special time. Such meetings should be regular and frequent. Once a month would be the bare minimum for gathering the community. Smaller groups within a fraternity certainly might meet more frequently. The council is responsible to see that these meetings are organized. A good council will involve other members in planning meetings. Working with other members, the meetings can be made both growthful and social.

Meetings can focus on many different areas. Among the elements that might be part of a meeting are these:

1. The meetings may provide programs for a deeper sharing of our gospel life. It might include reflections on HOW people fulfill the gospel in their lives.

2. The meetings may offer input on scripture or time for sharing scriptural prayer. A better understanding of scripture can help in gospel living.

3. The meetings might offer time to share personal experiences in living the Franciscan life. Individuals might share their way of living the gospel – in their personal lives / at work / in their prayer life. It may also be a time to share problems that arise because of our gospel commitment. Some mutual sharing might uncover fresh ways of dealing with such problems.

4. The meetings might offer insights into the issues of peace and justice. It can be a time to offer support, both personally and for the ministry.

5. The meetings might offer opportunities for exploring different forms of prayer.

6. The meetings might become a learning situation into various forms of ministry in the fraternity, parish, neighborhood, city or diocese.

7. Some meetings might simply take time for people to get to know one another better. Allowing meandering time for people to share a bit of their lives with one another. Some ice-breakers or other programs might help this process.

8. The Council may use the meeting to report on their responsibilities. They may explain a new ministry or introduce new people to the fraternity. Formation needs may be shared or a new project explained. Communication is important. The meetings can be a good place to get immediate feedback and/or answer questions about fraternity life.

9. Outside speakers may address the fraternity at these meetings. Local, national and international issues in society and church might be topics for such a meeting. If the fraternity is partner-in-ministry with other groups, they could be invited to share experiences at a meeting.

10. Some meetings can be simple celebration times. Birthdays, profession days, anniversaries, accomplishments, can be celebrated at a meeting.

11. Sometimes the meeting may take on the nature of a retreat. Lent and Advent might offer opportunities for attention to our growth by an afternoon or evening of reflection. Franciscan feasts may call for special kinds of celebration.

12. Gathering to celebrate Eucharist may be the focus of a meeting. Good participation and real celebration could be a source of nourishment for the fraternity. Good liturgical preparation and shared ministries should be part of a fraternity celebration of Eucharist.

13. Tradition is important in any group. A fraternity might have a memorial day (meeting) when people share the history and happenings of the fraternity. Or people may share a bit of the life of Franciscans who have died. Create traditions that contribute to drawing people together.

14. There are many good films and videos that might be a part of a meeting. Franciscan communications produces much good material (1229 S. Santee St – Los Angeles CA 90045) There is plenty of good material available. Use it.

15. Sometimes a fraternity meeting might be replaced by having everyone share in some ministry. Visit nursing homes. Have people visit homebound individuals. Then gather together to share the experience at a meeting and/or take time to pray for the needs of the people visited.

Allow your creativity full reign. Meetings are meant to be sources of inspiration and support. If they are consistently boring and useless for growth, people will begin to absent themselves. The Council has a serious responsibility to design good meetings. Whether they take charge of it or, better, involve fraternity members, make the meeting life-giving. We need to come together frequently. We are often alone between gatherings, trying to follow the gospel in tough situations. We need the support and encouragement of a good meeting with good people. When the members are actively engaged in planning and designing meetings, the more active the fraternity will be. When only a few councilors bear the whole load of planning and members are passive, the fraternity will be passive.

Young people are our future. We have much to offer them. But we will need to reach out to them. Solid planning and competent help is needed here. Don't be afraid to ask competent people to give you helps and hints. Be willing to engage in the process of offering our gospel life to young people. They will bring life, excitement, frustration and energy to a fraternity. What more could be needed to help people grow in patience, understanding and openness to God's work within another generation.

Finally, communion extends beyond Sister Death. Community members who have died rely on our prayers. We gather to pray for them. A scriptural wake service can offer us a chance not only to pray for a fellow Franciscan, but also do some evangelizing by sharing scripture at this precious time. At some wakes, people are asked to share a short reflection on the life of the deceased member. There are many beautiful ways to show our prayerful support for the living at the time of death. Our prayer for the dead is a natural gift we offer one another. Thus do we retain communion with those who have died.

Financial Support

Fraternities do not run on love alone. Humans need money in order to provide the materials and services our life requires. Consider the things needed that cost money. Rental of facilities for meetings – formation materials – publishing a bulletin – postage costs – supporting regional and higher councils – offering a stipend to the spiritual director – stipending speakers – cost for film/video rentals – Rituals for meetings – assistance to the needy – helping members in financial need – supporting needs of ministries – Phone costs – anniversary gifts – Pins and crosses that are signs of belonging to SFO – Stationary – special needs of fraternity members – brochures and publicity materials – sending members to conventions and other gatherings. A local fraternity may have still other costs. Obviously we need financial support in a Franciscan fraternity.

Each member is asked to give "according to his/her means." A fraternity can help people decide by publishing a report of financial expenses. If so much money is needed, people can assess what they will be able to give. Giving financial support to the fraternity is way of sharing. It is done with generosity rather than out of obligation. For gospel people it is an act of love to share what we can for the good of all. Fraternity monies are put in a COMMON FUND.

The Council is responsible and accountable for the collection and disposal of funds. Requests for donations from the common fund should be made in writing. In some cases individuals may wish to attend the Council meeting to explain the need. The Council may need to seek further information before spending money from the common fund. The Council is expected to act wisely in using the COMMON FUND. Expenditures should be in accord with the spirit of the Rule. It is a healthy practice for the fraternity Treasurer to make an annual and/or quarterly report to the fraternity membership. If respect for individuals requires that donating money be kept confidential, the Council may do that.

Fraternity business is conducted at Council meetings. Some of the discussions at a Council meeting may be confidential. In such cases the meeting is not open to all the members. However, this is rare. At other times the members may request to attend a meeting. This is especially true when issues of concern to an individual are being discussed. Most often people need be present only for that portion of the meeting that concerns them. Always having a Council meeting in the presence of the whole fraternity is not a good idea. The Councilors need the assurance that they can speak freely. The presence of a large group of people does not always create an atmosphere that allows for such free expression. A gentle balance between reporting to the fraternity and preserving confidentiality is needed. Most adults find such a balance most acceptable.

As you read this, realize the quality of trust Franciscans place in one another. Members trust the Council to act well. After all, they were elected because they were competent for the task. Councilors must trust the members by sharing their deliberations with them. Together, in trusting collaboration, the fraternity will grow. If suspicion enters in and trust departs, the fraternity is in big trouble. Violations of confidentiality are serious. But hiding things that need to be communicated is no better. Members and Councilors need the prayer and support of one another to contribute to building a vibrant fraternity. DO YOUR BEST for one another!

We must not be conceited, inciting one another to rivalry, jealous of one another. If anyone is caught doing something wrong, you, my friends, who live by the Spirit must gently set him right. Look to yourself, each one of you; you also may be tempted. Carry one another's burdens, and in this way you will fulfill the law of Christ.

Galatians 6: 1-26

FRANCISCAN FOCUS

Clare And Francis – A Meal Together

Francis often visited Clare when he was in Assisi. He was consoled by Clare's support and advice. Clare often asked Francis to eat a meal with her. But he refused. Some of the Friars confronted Francis: "Father, it seems to us that this strictness is not according to divine charity, that you do not grant the request of Sister Clare ... especially considering that she gave up riches as a result of your preaching!" So Francis changed his mind He suggested to Clare that they have a meal at St Mary of the Angels. She had been cloistered at San Damiano a long time. She would enjoy seeing the Portiuncula again.

Clare came and Francis walked with her until the meal was ready. As they sat down on the bare ground, Francis began to speak about God. Both he and Clare were rapt in God by the special grace given by God.

While they sat there in a rapture, the people of Assisi looked and thought St Mary of the Angels was on fire. They ran down to put it out. When they reached the place, however, nothing was on fire.

They found Francis and Clare rapt in God. Then they knew for sure that it had been a heavenly and not an earthly fire. It symbolized the love burning in the hearts of Francis and Clare. The people left them filled with great consolation at what they had seen.

When Francis and Clare came back to themselves, they felt so refreshed by the spiritual food that they hardly touched their meal. After the meal, Clare returned to San Damiano.

Paraphrased from: Omnibus of Sources
Franciscan Herald Press
Page 1332-1333

The bond of friendship between Francis and Clare was special. Their mutual support was important for both of them. Francis promised that his Brothers would always show care for Clare and her sisters. He asked that they be given the same love as the brothers showed for each other.

QUESTIONS

1. What struck you most forcefully about the relationship between work and spiritual growth?

2. In your personal work habits, where do you need the most improvement? Explain how you intend to improve?

3. What is St Francis' attitude to work? What is his view about the purpose of honest work?

4. Why is workaholism a problem? How would you help someone who is caught in workaholism?

5. How does leisure help our human growth? What value does it have for you? How does it help you to better your relationships? How does it affect your prayer? How does leisure make you healthier?

6. What do you find most difficult in serving others? How do you feel when someone serves you? How could you handle these situations more effectively as a gospel person?

7. Evaluate your fraternity. Use these questions as a help. How much celebrating does your fraternity do? Is the fraternity "workaholic"? How much balance of leisure and business do fraternity meetings have? What is most attractive about your fraternity? What would you want changed? How would you assess the devotional life of the fraternity? How well does the Council communicate with the membership? What does the Council do best? How could it improve its service to the community? What do you do to make your fraternity better? ... Such an evaluation is a love-action. It is meant to make the fraternity better. Do it with love!

8. How does the fraternity show its love and concern for deceased members? What would be some creative ways to keep their memories alive in the fraternity?

9. What is your financial responsibility to the fraternity? Who is responsible for collecting and disposing funds? How would you go

about getting money for a poor family from the common fund of the fraternity?

SCRIPTURE reading/reflection

✛ Wisdom ... Chapter 9
It might be helpful to read the book of Wisdom from Chapter 7 through Chapter 10. The writer praises Wisdom lavishly. The writer acknowledges a need for wisdom. She is the source of all hope. This is a beautiful text.

In New Testament theology wisdom is the Holy Spirit. She is powerful, beautiful and wise. She leads us to the truth.

After reading Chapter 9, share your reflections about how wisdom and work relate to one another. How do wisdom and leisure touch each other? What role does the Holy Spirit play in helping us discover our gifts?

CHAPTER 16

ME, YOU, US & JESUS

Some years ago someone offered me this bit of advice for mental/emotional health:

1. Get a daily adequate portion of love i.e good interpersonal relationships

2. Take time each day for relaxation

3. Have a daily measure of success

4. Have self-discipline. Allot time for tasks and stop even if they are un-finished.

No one has much real life unless he/she is loved. When we are ignored and uncared for, our inner life deteriorates. We need signs that say we are worth something. Love helps to fulfill that need. Overworked people may find #2 difficult. There is always something that has to be done. Guilt enters if they aren't busy every minute. Stuck with a need to prove themselves through busyness, relaxation is impossible. What a sad life!

I have found that a daily measure of success can be achieved by ordinary things. There are days when my only accomplishment is emptying the garbage. But I am a successful garbage-emptyer. Doing an ordinary thing and finishing it keeps some days from being a total flop. Using the self-discipline of #4 is not so easy. I want to finish what I start. I hate leaving something partially finished. But if I don't stop I neglect some other task that needs doing. Then I am behind again and the "have to" cycle starts all over. #4 is healthy but hard.

Some people say that "hugs" are essential to well-being. It is a way of receiving love and recognition. In a world that produces both Hitlers and a Francis of Assisi, we need loving personal relationships. Human beings become less human when they are deprived of love. Anger, loneliness, violence and aggressive behavior become normative for people who are unloved. Their behavior draws even more rejection. They are convinced of their uselessness. Striking out at people is one way to be somebody. Bullying, violence, raw use of power, inability to show compassion – these are some consequences of rejection and lack of love. People who lack faith or put faith only in power and domination reflect qualities St Paul speaks about.

> *Anyone can see the behavior that belongs to the unspiritual nature: fornication, indecency, and debauchery; idolatry and sorcery; quarrels, a contentious temper, envy, fits of rage, selfish ambitions, dissensions, party intrigues, and jealousies; drinking bouts, orgies and the like.*
>
> **Galatians 5: 19-21**

We spend millions of dollars dealing with the consequences of self-destructive behavior. The casual observer can see that we need fresh ideas to deal with an enormous problem.

St Francis faced the stress of expectations. His father expected him to be a knight and bring honor to the family. His friends concurred in this expectation. Francis thought it was a good idea. When he failed, he tumbled into a hole of depression and a sense of failure. His call from the Lord was not an immediate solution. It began a tough time of struggle. His life was turned upside down and he was not certain what to do. He felt alone and isolated. He began the climb out of this hole when he realized God's call had something to do with God's love for Francis. He found the strength to respond to the call. Response to the call gave him a sense of integrity. Integrity in turn brought peace.

Most conversions face a similar struggle. It would be wonderful if one "born again" experience could do the job, but conversion has lifetime implications. It is not a one-shot affair. As Francis began to know Jesus better, Francis walked the conversion-way more confidently. Jesus shared everything with Francis. Jesus gave Francis a new sense of the heavenly Father. The Father is an "Abba", "Daddy." Having such a loving Father, Francis understood that all people were his brothers and sisters. Since that is true, Francis' behavior toward people needed to change. Francis' experience with the leper showed him the change required by having one Father. Jesus was faithful to his Father even to

350

death on a cross. Such is the quality-love God asks of Francis. Faithfulness unto death is called for by God. Conversion is risky but life-giving business.

St Francis lived in this faith reality. It confronted any unfaithfulness to the gospel. Francis needed to change again and again. Change showed his loyalty to Jesus. Francis deepened his intimacy with Jesus. The gospel word became the way, the truth and the life for Francis. That commitment stretched him in ways that were previously unthinkable. Jesus and the gospel taught Francis how to surrender. Francis spent a lifetime discovering how much there was to surrender. Even his Order, his beloved Friars, had to be surrendered to God. While he watched parts of his dream being ignored by his followers, his task was to remain faithful – even in sadness. The Order belonged to Jesus and not to Francis. Listening to Jesus and the gospel, Francis learned joy in the midst of pain. How else explain the Canticle of Brother Sun being written in a period of blindness and great physical suffering?

The power of Jesus and his relationship with Francis was bigger than suffering. When St Francis faced apparent failure and sadness; when illness brought pain and suffering; when the stigmata brought helplessness – the Canticle of Brother Sun poured from the spirit of Francis. Francis speaks of the reality of relationship with all of creation. He shouts out the wonders of the Father of Jesus. His symphony of praise calls all people to praise the most high God.

Without the power of love, this is a senseless experience. To miss the love that burned in the heart of Francis would be to miss the source of the Canticle. The Canticle of Brother Sun is Francis at his best. It expresses a union with God that discovers God in all of creation. It is a poem of love and faith and praise. To miss the love-source would be to miss Francis. Without awareness of Francis' union with Cod, the Canticle becomes simply a nature lover's lullaby. When we perceive the faith that is its foundation, we see the reality of a man who is touched by God.

> For all who are led by the Spirit of God are sons of God.
> The Spirit you have received is not a spirit of slavery,
> leading you back into a life of fear, but a Spirit of
> adoption, enabling us to cry: "Abba! Father!" The Spirit

of God affirms to our spirit that we are God's children;
and if children, then heirs, heirs of God and fellow-heirs
with Christ; but we must share his sufferings if we are
also to share his glory!

Romans 8: 14-17

St Paul's words are written for someone like Francis. Intimacy with God is real for Francis. God is "Abba" for Francis. How well Jesus had led Francis to this union of love. How powerful is the gospel word that transformed Francis. With God all things are possible. How clearly the words of Francis call his followers to such union and praise.

Incline the ear of your heart and obey the voice of the
Son of God. Observe his commands with your whole
heart and fulfill his counsels with a perfect mind. Give
praise to him since he is good and exalt him by your
deeds, for he has sent you into the entire world for this
reason: that in word and deed you may give witness to
his voice and bring everyone to know that there is no one
who is all powerful except him. Persevere in discipline
and holy obedience and with a firm and good purpose
fulfill what you have promised to him. The Lord God
offers <u>himself</u> to us as to his children.

Francis & Clare – Brady/Armstrong
Paulist Press – Page 56

True love seeks union with the beloved. It walks through desert and over mountain to reach the beloved. It commits itself to a public expression of its love. It willingly counters values and attitudes that diminish loving union. It forgives in a way that allows growth for the beloved. It seeks the ways of justice for people because of the beloved. Its first act of justice is to give God what is due to God. Neither pain nor failure can deter it from seeking union. The lives of Francis and Clare, their struggle to preserve the gospel dream, their personal surrender to God – reveal the power of love at work. The words of Jesus after the resurrection are like a summary of gospel lives.

Then he opened their minds to understand the scrip-
tures. "So you see," he said, "that scripture foretells the
sufferings of the Messiah and his rising from the dead

352

> *on the third day, and declares that in his name, repentance bringing the forgiveness of sins, is to be proclaimed to all nations beginning from Jerusalem. You are to be witnesses to it all. I am sending on you the gift promised by my Father; wait here in this city until you are armed with power from above."*
>
> **Luke 24: 45-49**

We are today's witnesses. We have the gift of the Holy Spirit. We are loved by God. Francis and Clare offer clear examples of people who believe the gospel. They offer a model of the power of little people fired by God's love. They illustrate the price of gospel-living. They show the unexpected and unimagined life God gives to faithful people.

> *I pray that the God of our Lord Jesus Christ, the all-glorious Father, may confer on you the spiritual gifts of wisdom and vision, with the knowledge of him that they bring. I pray that your inward eyes may be enlightened, so that you may know what is the hope to which he calls you, how rich and glorious is the share he offers you among his people in their inheritance, and how vast are the resources of his power open to us who have faith...*
>
> *We are God's handiwork, created in Christ Jesus for the life of good deeds which God designed for us.*
>
> **Ephesians 1: 17-19 & 2: 10**

Some Deeds To Do

If love makes the world go 'round, Franciscans want to help keep the world going. Life offers opportunities for loving one another. It also tests the quality of love.

Two people getting married need more than definitions of fidelity and marriage. More is needed than a contract about who does what in the marriage. Romantic love is beautiful, but may not be enough for the long haul relationship of marriage. Getting married in Church is important, but it is no guarantee that love will blossom in a marriage. Nice feelings about one another is "nice" but hardly sufficient for the intimacy of marriage. Sexual compatibility is one element of marriage, but it will hardly keep it going if the relationship breaks down. People who choose to marry need a loving relationship that is open, communicative, real and able to handle difficulties.

Friends need to communicate. Communication requires the revelation of self to the other. It is the ability to listen without prejudice. It requires a listening that is not an "obligation" but a loving response to the other's need. Communication requires a loving honesty that looks to the good of the other. It is NOT a confrontational judgement made in anger. Self-revelation is not easy. Allowing a friend into the inner room of my heart may be scary. There is the risk that the real "me" may not be accepted. Sometimes I wear too many masks. I lose sight of who I really am. A good friend helps me reveal myself freely. Trust is a requirement for honest communication. Suspicion destroys honest and loving communication.

Suspicion destroys trust. Constant bickering and nit-picking can diminish the desire to communicate. The silent treatment – non-communication – can move a partner to find escape in work or alcohol or infidelity. There is always someone who really "understands." There are many ways to escape intimacy with a partner. The revelation of our inner self is an intimacy that is more difficult than the intimacy of physical nakedness. Refusal to share time with a partner is a subtle way of refusing love. Intimacy needs time, space and loving presence.

Couples who love each other are important to a healthy society. Parents who love each other are important for healthy family life. Healthy family life is important for learning the ways of love. For gospel-people, the earlier such lessons can be learned the better. This is not a magical, sure-fire process. But it certainly beats the opposite.

When people are free to share fears, problems, celebrations, loneliness and failure they learn a loving way to deal with the issues of life. The atmosphere created by loving people is an asset in dealing with the ups and downs of life. It allows communication without fear of reprisal.

Loving one another is a commandment of the gospel life. Coupled with such love is the ability to bridge gaps that come between us. We are imperfect and hurt each other. We learn the ways of forgiveness and reconciliation. We are imperfect and ignore human needs. We learn the ways of compassion. We make assumptions and burden others with unrealistic expectations. We listen more openly to real information about people. We grow tired and irritable. We find little things ruining our day. Crisis cast a shadow on life. Bills, broken legs, accidents, unexpected sickness or death have a way of absorbing our time and energy. How hard to love others when our own needs seem so great!

On the other hand we glow when someone compliments us. We are delighted when success meets our efforts. We dance when a loved one reaches a cherished goal. We cry together at good news about a lump that is not cancerous. We enjoy being with people who allow us freedom to be ourselves. We find quiet satisfaction in being left alone when we need solitude. We find reasons to "keep on keeping on" when a friend listens to the pain of our hearts. Love has a way of allowing growth and promoting it. Reflect on the reactions of others that brings you the most satisfaction. Love has a way of rewarding us.

It is a lie to say "I love you" if nothing in your behavior shows it. Whatever we say about loving one another applies to our relationship with Jesus. It is not enough to say the words: "I love you, Jesus" if our life doesn't offer proof of love. Gospel people seek to be genuine lovers, not phrase-makers.

> "Why do you call me 'Lord, Lord' – and never do what I tell you? Everyone who comes to me and hears my words and acts on them – I will show you what he is like. He is like a man building a house, who dug deep and laid the foundation on rock. When the river was in flood, it burst upon that house, but could not shift it, because it had been soundly built.
>
> **Luke 6: 46-48**

The Bible reveals a faithful God. When God's people were most unfaithful, God sought ways to draw them back. God's passionate anger springs from a heart deeply concerned about the people. Love could not tolerate infidelity but neither could it promote separation. God loves in many ways, but it is a love that seeks a return to intimacy. What powerful words are spoken in the prophet Hosea.

355

*How can I hand you over, Ephraim, how can I surrender
you, Israel? How can I make you like Admah or treat
you as Zeboyim? A change of heart moves me, tenderness kindles within me. I am not going to let loose my
fury, I shall not turn and destroy Ephraim, for I am God,
not a mortal; I am the Holy One in your midst.*

Hosea 11: 8-9

*I shall betroth you to myself forever, bestowing right-
eousness and justice, loyalty and love; I shall betroth you
to myself, making you faithful, and you will know the
Lord.*

Hosea 2: 19-20

God's covenant love cannot tolerate unfaithfulness. Neither can it
imagine separation. God seeks a creative way to bring the loved one
home. Like the prodigal father (LK 15:20), God waits and waits until
we "come to ourselves" and return home. St Francis discovered this
covenant love of God. The discovery moved Francis to commit himself
to the covenant. Francis tried to deal with God and God's people as
God had dealt with him. Faithfulness to the covenant was the way of
love. The gospel reveals the covenant love of Jesus. The gospel was
Francis' way of life.

Secure in God's love made visible in Jesus, Francis chose the gospel
way of life. It was a contest of love. The more Francis realized God's
love, the more he tried to respond to it. How often Francis revealed his
meager love: "Let us begin to do good, for until now we have done
nothing." For Francis, so much remained to be done. Better ways to
love God and people were being discovered until the day he died. The
spirit of seeking to do better is our goal too. We will find ways to imitate
God's love more perfectly. With Jesus, all things are possible.

*For the grace of God has dawned upon the world with
healing for all mankind; and by it we are disciplined to
renounce godless ways and worldly desires, and to live
a life of temperance, honesty, and godliness in the present age, looking forward to the happy fulfillment of our
hope when the splendor of our great God and Savior
Jesus Christ will appear. He it is who sacrificed himself*

for us, to set us free from all wickedness and to make us
his own people, pure and eager to do good.
Titus 2: 11-14

Reflection

We are special people. God has chosen to make a covenant of love with us. God is willing to deal with imperfect and inadequate people like ourselves. What God seems to detest is unfaithfulness to the covenant. There is much we must learn. Personal experience is a healthy thing. We can learn much from our experiences. Personal experience can be an unhealthy thing. It can keep us from fresh learning opportunities. Anger can be helpful or hurtful, giving energy to fight evil or energy to destroy people. The honesty of love is not always acceptable to others. Nor are attempts to dialogue always well received. Tough love can be labeled "no-love." If we cover up destructive behavior by calling it "love", we discover destructive consequences that help no one. Within fraternity life we find a need for creative styles of covenant love. Wisdom and prayer will be needed to know HOW to love in particular situations.

Clinging love can destroy friendships. Unexpressed love is useless for nurturing friendships. The support of a caring friend makes a difference to us. Lack of the human touch can turn us into cold, indifferent people. Isolation denies us communication with others, yet solitude teaches us how to relate to others. People who receive no expressions of love, who are uncared for, get sick in many ways. People who get an adequate portion of love are able to blossom as individuals. Our need for one another's love is obvious. The gospel speaks often of loving one another. The gospel also speaks of the consequences of real love – reconciliation, forgiveness, understanding, concern, walking-with, confronting faults, celebrating gifts, and many others. Franciscans embrace both love and its consequences as part of the gospel life. Sound fraternity life will support our efforts to grow in love.

"Anyone who has received my commands and obeys
them – he it is who loves me; and he who loves me will
be loved by my Father; and I will love him and disclose
myself to him."
John 14: 21

The lack of love has many consequences. Clinging to resentment and refusing to forgive diminishes our ability to resist some diseases. A tendency toward self-pity does the same. Anyone who finds long term relationships difficult is subject to illness. The opposite is also true. Love heals because it requires forgiveness. It releases tensions between people and avoids egoism. Love is life giving.

Dialogue/Feedback

When friends or couples dialogue, or when groups choose to do so, both need openness to one another in a number of ways:

1. Open to accepting one another in the areas where you may feel and think the same. This is not very difficult.
2. Open to one another in areas where you differ or where you are uncertain about "others"' feelings or ideas. It is not easy to listen when we disagree. Good dialogue invites us to listen without pre-judging the ideas/feelings.
3. Open to one another by allowing time for change. None of us changes quickly. Most often change will require time. True love expects us to change destructive, annoying behavior. But if there is no mutual desire to change, dialogue is a waste of time.
4. Dialogue among friends works best if you remember you are both on the same side. The issue to be resolved is the problem. Work together to deal with it. Confronting the issue in dialogue is a way to HELP each other, not defeat each other.

Disagreements among people are common. Good dialogue may not be so common. There are many tools to good dialogue. These few ideas offer some beginning tools. Seek others as the need arises. Dialogue can offer a tool for deepening a relationship. Even without problem-solving, good dialogue offers a way of strengthening the bonds of love. Use it wisely and well.

Another dimension of the dialogical experience is feedback. Good feedback needs to be honest and deal with reality. To affirm something artificial in another is useless. Feedback allows us to reveal our perception of another's behavior, words, attitudes etc. As with good dialogue, doing it with love makes it more effective.

1. Good feedback deals with OBSERVABLE behavior – not my interpretation of behavior. Neither is it my "feelings" about your observable behavior. Feedback should have a good tone of objectivity. Just the facts, please.

2. The more immediate and up-to-date the feedback, the better it is. Two week old feedback has little value. People can't remember what you're talking about!

3. Make your feedback concrete, explicit and specific. Abstractions are useless.

4. When you offer feedback to someone, make certain it is something that CAN be changed. Telling another person something that is impossible to change is no help at all.

5. Present the feedback as YOUR SPECIFIC, SUBJECTIVE idea. Use "I" not "We" when you share it. Don't share it as though it were an infallible decree.

6. When you have shared your feedback, ask the individual to tell you what was heard. It is a check to make certain you both "hear" the same thing.

7. Give feedback with a loving desire to help the person. Feedback becomes another cause for conflict when it is given with a "put-down" or "Gotcha" approach.

Reflection Questions

Why is love important for a good gospel life? What are some different definitions that you use for "love?" How does love contribute to building a better society? How does love help individuals to healthy inner growth? What are some consequences when love is lacking? How would you define "tough" love? How do you experience the passionate love of God? When disagreements and hurts enter into relationships, what does love require? What is the most important quality for good dialogue? How would you define "intimacy?" What are some obstacles to love? What personal experiences of love have helped you the most? What personal experiences of lack of love touched you most deeply? How did you deal with these experiences? What did you learn about God from the quotations from Hosea? What is the best way to help people with feedback? What do St Francis' experiences with the Order and with God teach you? What does unresolved stress and conflict do to the human body? How would a gospel life help us deal with stress and conflict? How do you respond to loving confrontation? How does prayer fit into our ability to relate to one another? What does good anger do for us? What does bad anger do for us? What is the difference between them? What words of the gospel best challenge us to love God and people?

SECULAR FRANCISCAN RULE

26. As a concrete sign of communion and co-responsibility, the Councils on various levels, in keeping with the Constitutions, shall ask for suitable and well-prepared religious for spiritual assistance. They should make this request to the superiors of the four religious Franciscan families, to whom the Secular Fraternity has been united for centuries.

To promote fidelity to the charism as well as observance of the Rule and to receive greater support in the life of the fraternity, the minister or president, with the consent of the Council, should take care to ask for a regular pastoral visit by the competent religious superiors as well as a fraternal visit from those of the higher fraternities, according to the norms of the Constitutions.

RULE – Chapter 3 #26

The Rule recognizes the need for collaboration between the various branches of the Franciscan Order. In this number of the Rule, it offers direction to the local fraternity in seeking a spiritual assistant. The mutual responsibilities are these:

1. The Secular Franciscan Council asks the superiors of one of the four Franciscan families for a spiritual assistant. Generally these superiors will be at the regional or provincial level.

2. The four religious Franciscan families have a responsibility to provide a spiritual assistant who is: A) well prepared B) Knowledgeable about the SFO C) Competent to fulfill the role of spiritual assistant.

3. This collaboration is a sign of the communion and co-responsibility of the four Franciscan families.

Priests, Brothers or Religious Sisters can fulfill this role of spiritual assistant. The key quality is their competency. It would be unfair to the local fraternity to provide a spiritual assistant who is not well prepared or knowledgeable about the SFO. It would be unfair to the spiritual assistant as well. These are times when collaboration in the Franciscan family is important. Together we have an opportunity to share our Franciscan charism with the world. Working together we can develop a lifestyle that reflects our Franciscan heritage. It is our responsibility to offer this gift to the Church and to the world.

The Councils at various levels are invited to work together. One of the ways to accomplish this is through the visit by members of a higher Council. This visit to the local fraternity is both pastoral and fraternal. It fulfills a number of fraternal responsibilities.

1. The visit can help promote a deeper fidelity to the charism of St Francis.

2. Such a visit can help the local fraternity live the SFO Rule with greater dedication and fidelity.

3. The visit can offer support to the local council as well as the fraternity members.

4. The visit offers an opportunity to evaluate the life of the fraternity. The visitor can reflect with the fraternity A) On its formation program B) On its ministries C) On the manner of conducting community gatherings D) On its care for the sick and homebound. E) Other areas of need

The visitor can share news from other fraternities as well as sharing international news. It is an opportunity to offer feedback to the Council as well as getting feedback from the Council. Very often both the regional/provincial Spiritual Assistant and President will visit the fraternity. Well-used, the VISITATION can be an important part of fraternity life.

On a practical level, it is important to prepare well for the Visitation. The local Council can help by sending in good reports to the higher Council. If particular issues need to be addressed, let the visitors know beforehand. If our collaboration is to be effective, good communication is necessary. The local Council can provide a schedule for the visitor that will assist an effective visitation.

The creative possibilities for a good visitation are many. Here are a few.

1. Schedule an evening or afternoon of reflection with the visitor(s). Such time could offer the Visitor time to share insights and inspiration.

2. Allow time for dialogue/discussion between the fraternity members and the visitor(s). The Council could schedule some special time with the visitor(s).

3. Use the occasion to gather as many members as possible. Try to get members to the meeting who are not ordinarily able to attend. Some special prayer time might be prepared. Reflection on the scripture might be incorporated.

4. Provide special time for the Visitor(s) to share information with the membership. Sharing what other Secular Franciscan are doing can help fraternity growth.

5. If feasible, the Visitor(s) may be willing to lead the fraternity in a weekend retreat. This would have to be settled before the Visitation is scheduled. It could be a special time for the fraternity.

6. The Council should schedule a good period of time to meet with the Visitor. Offer the Visitor(s) an insight into the workings of the fraternity. Discuss successful projects. Ask help in dealing with problems. Clarify issues that impact on the running of the fraternity. It can be a good learning time, especially if the local Council is recently elected. Have the books and records of the fraternity available for evaluation.

7. Take time to review the ministries and outreach of the fraternity. Perhaps the dialogue can improve the ministries or offer ideas for new ministries.

In short, be creative about the VISITATION. Expect it to be a solid spiritual boost for the fraternity. Show good Franciscan hospitality to the visitor(s).

✛ ✛ ✛ ✛

This concludes my commentary on the Rule. It is not an official commentary but a very personal one. The Rule offers special opportunities to become an Order with an impact on our times. We are trying to discover the ways and means to have such an impact. The Rule is a good support for our efforts. It is our common task to give flesh to the vision offered in the Rule. As we grow, so will our understanding of the richness of this Rule.

We are blessed with a call to follow the gospel way of life as Francis did. The response of St Francis is the model for our response. His response to God's goodness invites us to respond fully to God's covenant love. We will discover HOW to do this as long as we live. Out of turmoil, insights, failures, successes and suffering we will draw new ways to imitate God's love for us. To the world, we offer a God of love who reaches out through Jesus.

Evangelization – *living and sharing the gospel*

Part of our task is to evangelize i.e. share with others our knowledge and experience of God's love. Love finds expression in signs and symbols. We are often the sign for others. The presence of Jesus in our lives can bring others to know him. Evangelization is sharing the gospel. Our joy in living the gospel is a primary evangelical tool. Sad Christians make poor evangelizers. Evangelization is not so much convert-making as it is dialogue with others. True evangelization happens when the dialogue is concerned with the gospel and an openness to conversion. It sounds much like the Franciscan way of life in action!

Paul VI wrote a special letter on evangelization: "On evangelization in the modern world" (Evangelii Nuntiandi). Pope Paul VI writes that evangelizing means bringing the good news to every level of society. The goal is to transform society, moving it to a more gospel style. Such evangelizing affects the criteria by which we judge personal and social issues. It touches the values that influence individual lives and the life of society. Effective sharing of the gospel helps determine the sources of inspiration and the models for life.

Every Christian is called to be a witness. Our commitment to the gospel way of life makes evangelization part and parcel of our lives. True evangelization proclaims the life, teaching, promises and kingdom of Jesus Christ. That is our call. We do this even if others do not accept what we offer nor follow the witness of our lives. As followers of St Francis we are committed to evangelization by our Franciscan calling.

There are many methods and approaches to evangelization. Sometimes evangelization is done through home visits. Going two by two, people visit others in order to share the faith. Sometimes evangelization is done in social settings. Evangelization is sharing gospel reflections with one another. It is done through educational programs or outreach programs for the unchurched. It is wise to seek training in methodology so that your evangelization efforts are done with competence and confidence. Seek information and help before embarking on organized programs. Your ordinary sharing through daily contact may be the primary place of evangelization.

Persistence

However we do gospel-sharing, we WILL DO IT!! The gospel is our way of life. Gospel-love never gives up. Love maintains hope because Jesus is with us through his Spirit. All people will receive our love, but we shall have a special concern for God's little ones and the poor. We know we are weak. We realize we are good though imperfect. That keeps us striving to do better. We are not saviors. We have one savior and his name is Jesus.

As Franciscans, we walk confidently into a future already blessed by God. We walk humbly before our God. We seek justice for God's people. We show justice to God by acknowledging that all things and people belong to God. We build the ways of peace and seek patterns of gentleness. We will see-through artificiality and embrace the real. We are hopeful because the Holy Spirit is within and among us. Jesus remains with his people, so we are not afraid. We often experience weakness and human inadequacy. We need community to support us on our gospel journey. What a way to go!!˙

> With all this in view, you should make every effort to
> add virtue to your faith, knowledge to virtue, self-con-

trol to knowledge, fortitude to self-control, piety to fortitude, brotherly affection to piety and love to brotherly affection.

If you possess and develop these gifts, you will grow actively and effectively in knowledge of our Lord Jesus Christ. Whoever lacks them is wilfully blind; he has forgotten that his past sins were washed away. All the more then, my friends, do your utmost to establish that God has called and chosen you. If you do this, you will never stumble, and there will be rich provision for your entry into the eternal kingdom of our Lord and Savior Jesus Christ.

2 Peter 1 : 5-11

FRANCISCAN FOCUS

Francis And The Sultan

The Crusades of the middle ages often were a blemish on Christianity. They were a mixture of dedicated heroism and bloody cruelty. Francis lived at a time when Crusades to the Holy Land drew all kinds of people to fight for the freedom of the holy places. The Saracens saw their battle as a holy war against Christian infidels. Both sides were fighting for God – as they knew God. Many also fought for glory, plunder, gold and easy power.

Before the siege of Damietta, the Crusaders were divided by hatred and self-seeking. They were bogged down in bitter struggles for power as well as with conflicting plans for battle. Mutilation of captured Saracens was not uncommon. It was war at its worst and men at their worst. This was the scene that confronted Francis upon his arrival.

St Francis expected to be martyred by the Saracens. But his life was in jeopardy from the Crusaders as well. Francis could not bear to see the inhuman treatment given to prisoners. He spoke up for them. He observed the drunken brawls and prostituting of the Crusaders and confronted them. He was hardly a welcome sight among these warriors supposedly dedicated to Christ. The battles were going badly and Francis boldly predicted defeat for the Crusaders. He was fortunate not to get killed by so-called Christian men.

Francis chose a direct way to try to end the hostilities. He decided to visit the Saracen Sultan. Getting from one camp to the other was life-threatening. But Francis managed it. The forward sentries of the Sultan beat him unmercifully. But somehow he finally reached the Sultan. When Francis was asked who accredited him, his response was predictable: "No man, but God, has sent me across the seas to announce the good news of the truth." Then he proceeded to share the gospel with the Sultan. The Sultan, impressed by his fervor and boldness, invited him to stay.

But Francis challenged the Sultan to abandon the law of Muhammed for the law of Jesus. Francis even offered to walk barefooted on hot coals to prove his point. The Sultan refused the challenge. Instead he offered gifts to Francis. But Francis refused the gifts. He wanted to share Jesus and the gospel with the Sultan. If the Sultan accepted Jesus, it would be a way to peace. When his attempt fails, he departs. The Sultan is no longer an enemy but a person Francis respected.

This episode reveals Francis' way of dealing with conflict. He rejected military might for the power of the gospel. Killing, violence, plunder and the evils of war are abhorrent to Francis. He trusted in Jesus and the gospel as a more effective way to peace. Though he failed to stop the bloodshed, he would not abandon the gospel way to peace. He would be faithful to his commitment to the gospel even in the face of apparent failure.

QUESTIONS

1. Share your ideas/feelings on the importance of relationships in living a gospel style of life. Indicate what you believe is most important in keeping relationships healthy and moving to greater intimacy.

2. What qualities are most important to a good marriage? To a good friendship? After making your list, prioritize the order of importance as you see it. Explain your answer.

3. What does prayer do in the development of good relationships? How does relationship with Jesus affect the other relationships in life?

4. What are some of the consequences of Francis' intimacy with Jesus? What are some of the consequences of YOUR intimacy with Jesus?

5. What is the purpose of the VISITATION of a local fraternity? What preparations by the local fraternity can help the effectiveness of the VISITATION?

6. What is the value of collaboration among the various families of the Franciscan Order?

7. What is meant by "Evangelization?" Describe the ways in which you evangelize!

8. What part of the RULE is most important and inspiring to you? Why? What part of the RULE is most difficult or least helpful for you? Why?

SCRIPTURE reading/reflection

+ Romans 12: 9-21
   St Paul invites the Roman community to love one another affectionately and with fervor of spirit. Such love manifests the presence of Jesus among us. Paul asks us to bless enemies and let God handle their conversion. These words of Paul are strong in

their demands. They reflect Paul's understanding of the way of Jesus.

After prayerful reflection, share some ideas from this text that apply to relationships – in family life; in fraternity life; in our life with God.

CHAPTER 17

PRAISE & BLESS MY LORD

And we can say, with almost as deep a certainty, that the stars which passed above that gaunt and wasted corpse, stark upon the rocky floor, had for once, in all their shining cycles round the world of laboring humanity, looked down upon a happy man.
St Francis of Assisi – Chesterton
Image Books – Page 82

Chesterton describes the death of a special person, Francis of Assisi. This moment of death brings Francis a step closer to the intimacy he sought in life. Sister Death leads him to another dimension of life. It is a passing over, a paschal experience. It is a fitting adieu to life on planet earth and a beginning of life in heaven.

Like many people of great stature, legends and myths about Francis abound. Legends and myths are ways of sharing the truth in a special style. The truth is clothed in a story-like telling about the person. St Francis was a natural subject for such things. We do the same for family members. We create a myth about Uncle Harry, expounding on exploits that seem to grow with time. It is the truth, but told in ways other than historical narrative. Legends and myths are as truthful as history. They grasp the spirit of a person with greater accuracy than much historical information. There are legends and myths about St Francis that reflect his spirit. When you read them, pluck the truth from the story. It will usually be right on target.

Stories about Francis blossomed in the eyes of his contemporaries. After the death of Francis, it was easier to see the pattern of God's work. Francis was close to Jesus, so the events of Francis' life are colored by the stories about Jesus. One legend says that Francis was born in a stable. Another that his mother was told by a beggar that her son would be admired by many people. The stories truthfully reflect the intimacy between Francis and Jesus. The tale of the wolf of Gubbio speaks to the truth of the ability of Francis to reconcile people with one another. Many stories about Francis reveal the truth by using myths and legends. When you read them, listen with the ear of your heart. You will be rewarded with fresh insights into the spirit of Francis.

Francis loved Jesus. Jesus revealed the Father to Francis. Francis grew to love the Father. The Father of Jesus could be trusted. A Father, concerned about sparrows and flowers, cared much more for Francis. The Father loves us and can be trusted to care for us. Jesus trusted his Father. Francis could do no less. Quite naturally Francis broke into a song of praise for such a Father.

> *You are holy, Lord the only God, you do wonders!*
> *You are strong, you are great, you are most high.*
> *You are the almighty, kind ...*
>
> *You are love, charity. You are wisdom.*
> *You are humility. You are patience.*
> *... You are enough for us ... Great and*
> *wonderful Lord, God almighty,*
> *merciful Savior!*
> **Francis & Clare – Brady/Armstrong**
> **Paulist Press – Page 99-100**

Familiarity with the gospel changed the life of Francis. He saw the world and people through the eyes of Jesus. The deeper his love for Jesus, the deeper his trust in the Father of Jesus. Jesus is the special gift of the Father. Jesus reveals the Father to his disciples. Pouring out love through Jesus, the Father reveals riches greater than we could ask or imagine. Jesus is the way to discover the truth.

Jesus is not a distant God, reigning from some far off heaven. Jesus is God become human. A God speaking with a human voice and shedding human tears. Jesus is God enduring frustrations and experiencing human pain. Jesus is the revelation of God in human form. Jesus is always central on our journey to God. How humble of God to be like us. How elevating of human nature to be embraced by God.

We ... are citizens of heaven, and from heaven we expect our deliverer to come, the Lord Jesus Christ. He will transfigure our humble bodies, and give them a form like that of his own glorious body, by that power which enables him to make all things subject to himself. This, my dear friends, whom I love and long for, my joy and my crown, this is what it means to stand firm in the Lord.

Philippians 3:20 to 4:1

Consequences

Intimacy with the Father through Jesus, who shares his Spirit with us, is amazing. We listen to the gospel as the revelation of the Father through Jesus' life and words. The Franciscan commitment to the gospel has important consequences. They are the "charism" of our Franciscan life.

1. God is Father, Creator and One who loves us. This world and everything in it belongs to God. When Francis realized this, the conclusion was obvious. To claim anything as one's own is to act like a thief. Such a claim is out of touch with reality. If this world and its people belong to God, poverty is the acknowledgement of reality. Consider the impact on our lives.

We need food, clothing and shelter. We acquire many things – stereos, cars, houses, money, cosmetics, certificates of deposit, stocks, land, etc – and call them "our own." We work to pay for what we acquire. We consider them as our possessions. We consider our bodies as our own. We are free to do what we want with them. The earth is ours and we can use it to our advantage. The waters of the earth are used to generate power and we own these resources. We explore outer space and lay claim to areas first touched by our space explorers. As we go, we lay claim to ownership and "take possession" of things.

We organize a legal system to sort out arguments about ownership. We fight legal battles to preserve the right to do what we want with our own bodies. We design unions to protect us from unscrupulous owners or to learn ways of collaborating with the owners of production. We buy and sell things. We live in an economy where this is common and acceptable to most citizens. What we pay for we claim as our own. We have laws to protect us from robbery.

Without totally disrupting this system, a gospel viewpoint on possessions is quite different. We believe all things are God's. Francis saw this as a fundamental building block for attitudes about material things. This being so, God desires that all people on earth have the right to what they need for a human life. We are the stewards. Our task is to use things so that all people can live a dignified human existence. Our primary concern is not the acquisition but the sharing of material goods. Since we are part of the "people", we have a right to what we need to live in dignity as human beings. This perspective influences the way we design structures and systems in society. They are meant to serve people. If someone is in need, we design a system in a way that provides for his/her need. Whether it be educational opportunity or good housing, our perspective moves us to care for the people.

Stewards are accountable for the manner in which they use things. Francis felt that when we held possessions that went beyond real needs, they would be shared. No one is called to destitution nor is perfect economic equality the goal. But God's earth is for all of God's people. God has no desire that people starve or suffer from lack of medical help or forever be caught on unemployment lines or forever be a slave to an impersonal welfare system. It is not God's will that people suffer and starve and die in agony. In God's way all people would be cared for because people would care for one another. A selfish, possessive steward is an anomaly from God's perspective. Gospel people are not to act as thieves by becoming possessive.

> *As Jesus looked up and saw rich people dropping their gifts into the chest of the temple treasury, he noticed a poor widow putting in two tiny coins. "I tell you this," he said: "this poor widow has given more than any of them; for those others who have given had more than enough, but she, with less than enough, has given all she had to live on."*
>
> **Luke 21: 1-4**

> *"No slave can serve two masters; for either he will hate*

the first and love the second, or he will be devoted to the
first and despise the second. You cannot serve God and
money."

The Pharisees, who loved money, heard all this and
scoffed at him. He said to them: "You are the people who
impress others with your righteousness; but God sees
through you; for what is considered admirable in human
eyes is detestable in the sight of God."
Luke 16: 13-15

2. If everything belongs to God it deserves reverence and respect. St
Francis developed a reverence for everything. Many legends about
Francis reveal this reverence. Francis is careful not to step on a
worm. Francis buys lambs to keep them from being slaughtered.
Francis negotiates with a wolf that is terrorizing a town. Francis
speaks to birds and invites them to be faithful in their praise of God.

Lepers were special to Francis because he saw God in their eyes. The
poor were special to Francis because God seems to reverence them.
Walking among the poor, Francis is transformed. For Francis, everyone
is king and he is their servant. His delight was NOT in leprosy or
destitution, but for people loved by God. They deserved reverence
from Francis. Courtesy flowed from this belief. The dignity of others is
God-given, not earned. If one loves God the choice of loving God's
people is already made.

He (Francis) only saw the image of God multiplied but
never monotonous. To him a man was always a man and
did not disappear in a dense crowd any more than in a
desert. He honored all men; that is, he not only loved but
respected them all. What gave him his extraordinary
personal power was this: that from the Pope to the
beggar, from the sultan of Syria in his pavilion to the
ragged robbers crawling out of the wood, there was never
a man who looked into those brown burning eyes
without being certain that Francis Bèrnadone was really
interested in HIM; in his own inner individual life from
the cradle to the grave; that he himself was being valued
and taken seriously and not merely added to the spoils

of some social policy or the names in some clerical document.

St Francis of Assisi – Chesterton
Image Books – Page 96-97

3. The Eucharist was special for St Francis. Jesus comes to us in such simple signs. Such love calls for a direct response. Francis tried to let his life be the response to Jesus' loving presence in Eucharist. Francis embraced the gospel as the message of Jesus. Hearing it read and broken open at Eucharist called him to a sense of wonder at such love. The gospel was Jesus sharing the way to peace and light and life. Nothing less than a dedicated life was worthy of such love.

Francis wanted the Brothers to reverence the Eucharist. Whether in huge churches or small chapels, the Brothers were to keep things neat and clean. When Mass is celebrated, all else is put aside in order to participate in this marvel of Christ's love.

> *Therefore, kissing your feet and with all that love of which I am capable, I implore all of you brothers to show all possible reverence and honor to the most holy Body and Blood of our Lord Jesus Christ in whom that which is in the heavens and on the earth is brought to peace and is reconciled to the all-powerful God.*

> *... Let them (Priests at Mass) do this with reverence and with a holy and pure intention, not for any mundane reason or out of fear or out of love of some person, as if they were pleasing people. But let every wish be directed to God inasmuch as grace will help them, desiring thereby to please only the most high Lord, since he alone does these things as he pleases. Therefore as he himself says: "Do this in memory of me." (LK 22: 19 ... 1 Cor 11: 24)*

Francis & Clare – Brady/Armstrong
Paulist Press – Page 56-57

4. It would be difficult to live the gospel without promoting peace and reconciliation. Our heavenly Father calls us together as one people. "Grant that we, who are nourished by his body and blood, may be

filled with his Holy Spirit and BECOME ONE BODY, ONE SPIRIT IN CHRIST." (Eucharistic Prayer #3)

Disunity and factions among us disregard the gospel call to be one people. Grudges and anger, resentment and unforgiveness do not reveal or reflect the gospel of Jesus. We humans will experience such things. We are imperfect people. But we are called to deal with these issues in a way that promotes unity. Personal pain caused by another's actions are not easy to forget. We need to pursue the road of reconciliation in order to create peace and unity.

Jesus walks with us on the road to reconciliation. As prodigal sons and daughters we are welcomed by a loving Father. When we have wandered from the flock, we are brought back on the shoulders of the good shepherd. When we acknowledge unfaithfulness we are forgiven by Jesus. Gospel communities are the places where such things can happen. We need people who welcome us home with the hugs of forgiveness. Franciscans are gospel people. We are committed to the work of peace and reconciliation.

> *It is through faith that you are all sons of God in union with Christ Jesus. Baptized into union with him, you have all put on Christ like a garment. There is no such thing as Jew and Greek, slave and freeman, male and female; for you are all one person in Christ Jesus.*
> **Galatians 3: 26-28**

5. We are a new creation, formed and re-formed by the Spirit of Jesus. God is at work in us, creating us anew throughout our lives. At the end of life, Sister Death walks us through one dimension of life into another. Things do not end, they are transformed. Death is the sign of a new beginning. God's call to this new life is not a punishment but the way to deeper intimacy. When we are faithful and seek to implement the gospel in daily life, death is less fearful. We already know the God who calls us home. Even so, there is something unfamiliar about the end of life on earth. There may be some fear. But there is hope of being with the person we have learned to love. If we have been unfaithful and uncommitted to God or the gospel, we need to deal with some real fears. But even here, a creative God finds ways to reach into our hearts and convert them.

Set your troubled hearts at rest. Trust in God always; trust also in me. There are many dwelling-places in my Father's house; if it were not so I should have told you; for I am going to prepare a place for you. And if I go and prepare a place for you, I shall come again and take you to myself, so that where I am you may be also; and you know the way I am taking.

John 14: 1-4

With trust in Jesus and the Father, Francis did not fear Sister Death. The stories of the death of Francis are surrounded with joy and thanksgiving. He prays with the brothers as he is dying. He is not ashamed to ask for the almond cakes of "Brother" Jacoba. Aware of the approach of Sister Death, he asks that the gospel of John be read. He asks them to begin with the words: "It was before the Passover festival ..." (John 13: 1ff). He invited Sister Death to make its lodging with him: "Welcome, my Sister Death." Celano, in his second life, reports the death quite simply: "The hour therefore came, and all the mysteries of Christ being fulfilled in him, he winged his way happily to God." (Omnibus – FHP – Page 536) Gospel people accept Sister Death as a welcome relative.

A man might fancy that the birds must have known when it happened; and made some motion in the evening. ... Hidden in the woods, perhaps, were little cowering creatures never again to be so noticed and understood; and it has been said that animals are sometimes conscious of things to which man, their spiritual superior is for the moment blind. We do not know whether any shiver passed through all the thieves and the outcasts and the outlaws, to tell them what had happened to him who never knew the nature of scorn. But at least in the passages and porches of the Portiuncula there was a sudden stillness, where all brown figures stood like bronze statues' for the stopping of the great heart that had not broken till it held the world.

St Francis of Assisi – Chesterton
Image Books – Page 147

6. Francis was a person full of wonder. Wonder at the Father's love

for him. Wonder at the ministry of Jesus. Wonder at the gospel word of life. Wonder at the marvels of creation. Wonder at human love. Wonder at Clare and her dedicated friendship. Wonder at sun and moon and cloud and rain and fire and the rest of the family. Wonder that sprang from darkened eyes to praise the light of Brother Sun and Sister moon and stars. Wonder at being redeemed by Jesus. Wonder at being called to intimacy with Jesus. Wonder at brothers, called to follow the gospel. Wonder at Sister Death and her hidden surprises. Wonder that someone like himself could be so cared for by God. Wonder at the Eucharist. Wonder at the Church as she reflected the light of the gospel. Wonder as he struggled with illness. Wonder in the awesome intimacy of La Verna. Wonder at the sparrows and beloved friends.

From his mountain caves, Francis wondered as he saw the majestic sweep of the valleys of Italy. Wonder at the swamps and rivers, the rain and cold that filled this land. Wonder at how God had created such a place for people to live on. Wonder that God had made Francis a temple in which to dwell. Wonder at the community that gathered around him. The wonder of the miracle of life and all it meant. The wonder at the miracle of love and all it can accomplish. What a wonder to realize that someone as weak and miserable and imperfect as himself could be the dwelling place of the Holy Spirit.

Franciscans without wonder would be like streams without water. We bring to the world a breath of wonder. Wonder at the black holes of space. Wonder at the exploding understanding of the universe. Wonder at being able to walk around in a room called an airplane at 30,000 feet above the earth. Wonder at satellite dishes that transmit "presence" around the world. Wonder at communication and film and all the ways we share with one another. Ours is a world full of wonder. God has gifted us and we praise God for the wonders of creation. Above all, there is wonder that we too are temples of the Holy Spirit. Wonder that we too are privileged to proclaim the good news. Wonder that we too are called to gift the world with the gospel. Wonder that we are called to intimacy with Jesus on the La Vernas of our lives.

> *Let the wilderness and the parched land be glad, let the desert rejoice and burst into flower. Let it flower with fields of asphodel, let it rejoice and shout for joy. The*

379

*glory of Lebanon is given to it, the splendor too of Carmel
and Sharon; these will see the glory of the Lord, the
splendor of our God.*

*... Then the eyes of the blind will be opened, and the ears
of the deaf be unstopped. Then the lame will leap like
deer, and the dumb shout aloud; for water will spring
up in the wilderness and torrents flow in the desert. The
mirage will become a pool, the thirsty land bubbling
springs; instead of reeds and rushes, grass will grow in
country where wolves have their lairs.*

*... The Lord's people, set free, will come back and enter
Zion with shouts of triumph, crowned with everlasting
joy. Gladness and joy will come upon them while suffering and weariness flee away.*
Isaiah 35: 1-2 & 5-7 & 10

7. St Francis, in his reflection on God's love, focused on two special
    signs of that love, namely, the INCARNATION and the CRUCIFI-
    XION. For God to become human in the incarnation was proof
    positive of a deep love for us. God sent Jesus to reveal the way of
    life to a people who walked in darkness. Coming among us as a
    human being, God risked littleness for the goal of intimacy with us.
    God entered our world through a woman, Mary. This is not play
    acting but the reality of Emmanuel, God-with-us.

    *So the Word became flesh; he made his home among us,
    and we saw his glory, such glory as befits the Father's
    only son, full of grace and truth.*
    John 1: 14

    *While they were there the time came for her to have her
    baby, and she gave birth to a son, her firstborn. She
    wrapped him in swaddling clothes, and laid him in a
    manger, because there was no room for them at the inn.*
    Luke 2: 6-7

    *It was there from the beginning; we have heard it; we
    have seen it, and felt it with our own hands; our theme*

is the Word which gives life. This life was made visible;
we have seen it and bear our testimony; we declare to
you the eternal life which was with the Father and was
made visible to us. It is this which we have seen and
heard that we declare to you also, in order that you may
share with us in a common life, that life which we share
with the Father and his Son, Jesus Christ.

1 John 1: 1-3

When Francis looked to the end of the life of Jesus, he was again touched by God's love. Jesus chose the path of faithful love and obedience even to death. There was no backing away from the price of intimacy with the Father. Jesus struggles but remains faithful to his Father. The cross is a sign that nothing can defeat the power of this love. No wonder Francis asked to experience such love in his own heart. The request on La Verna is but the echo of a heart seeking union with the Beloved. The crucifixion, for Francis, was clearly a sign of love. The good shepherd loves his sheep. He dies for them that life may be theirs. Francis felt that life itself, lived as Jesus taught, is the only adequate response to such love.

The word of God is alive and active. It cuts more keenly
than any two-edged sword piercing so deeply that it
divides soul and spirit, joints and marrow; it discrimi-
nates among the purposes and thoughts of the heart.
Nothing in creation can hide from him; everything lies
bare and exposed to the eyes of him to whom we must
render account.

Since therefore we have a great high priest who has
passed through the heavens, Jesus the Son of God, let us
hold fast to the faith we profess. Ours is not a high priest
unable to sympathize with our weaknesses, but one who
has been tested in every way we are, only without
sinning.

Let us therefore boldly approach the throne of grace, in
order that we may receive mercy and find grace to give
us timely help.

Hebrews 4: 12-16

Jesus, beyond the crucifixion, is raised from the dead because he was faithful. The risen Lord, Jesus Christ, continues to give life. Jesus sent the Holy Spirit that we might be a new creation and remember all that he had taught us. The Spirit is sent into our lives to enable us to share life with others. We are little less than the angels and we are held in God's palm with tender love. The gentleness of God, the creativity of God, the embrace of God, the Spirit of God, is given to us. It seems too good to be true. But it IS the gospel truth.

> *How can any human being learn what is God's plan? Who can apprehend what is the will of the Lord? The reasoning of mortals is uncertain, and our plans are fallible, because a perishable body weighs down the soul, and its frame of clay burdens the mind already so full of care. With difficulty we guess even at things on earth, and laboriously find out what lies within our reach; but who has ever traced out what is in heaven? Who ever came to know your purposes unless you had given him wisdom and sent your holy spirit from heaven on high? Thus it was that those on earth were set on the right path, and mortals were taught what pleases you; thus were they kept safe by wisdom.*
> **Wisdom 9: 13-18**

We are a Spirit-filled people. The Spirit continues the process of conversion within us. We are an unfinished people who are being reformed by the power of the Holy Spirit. For Franciscans, the Holy Spirit is a compelling influence for gospel living. Unafraid of such strong influence, we freely embrace the way of the Spirit. We are not slaves, walking in lock-step to some conformist propaganda. We are unique individuals, allowing the Spirit to call forth new expressions of our gifts. In such a life-giving response both we and God's people benefit from a responsible sharing of our uniqueness.

> *I am free and own no master; but I have made myself everyone's servant, to win over as many as possible. To Jews I behaved like a Jew, to win Jews; that is, to win those under the law I behaved as if under the law, though not myself subject to the law. To win those outside the law, I behaved as if outside the law, though not myself*

*outside God's law, but subject to the law of Christ. To
the weak I became weak, to win the weak. To them all I
have become everything in turn, so that in one way or
another I may save some. All this I do for the sake of the
gospel, to have a share in its blessings.*

1 Corinthians 9: 19-23

*So when we preach, we do not curry favor with men; we
seek only the favor of God, who is continually testing
our hearts. We have never resorted to flattery, as you
have cause to know nor, as God is our witness, have our
words ever been a cloak for greed. We have not sought
honor from men, not from you or from anyone else,
although as Christ's own envoys we might have made
our weight felt; but we were as gentle with you as a nurse
caring for her children. Our affection was so deep that
we were determined to share with you not only the
gospel of God but our very selves; that is how dear you
had become to us! You remember, my friends, our toil
and drudgery; night and day we worked for a living,
rather than be a burden to any of you while we proclaimed to you the good news of God.*

*... we appealed to you, we encouraged you, we urged
you, to live lives worthy of the God who calls you into
his kingdom and glory.*

1 Thessalonians 2: 4-9 & 12

We are a people in love. While law places limits on the demands that
can be made, love has no limits. People in love do not think in terms of
the minimum required but of the maximum that can be given. The
Spirit of Jesus, dwelling within us, prompts us and nudges us to new
horizons of love. What begins in the heart finds expression in the world.
We are guided by the Spirit to get to the heart of things. With singleness
of heart we proclaim:

*"The Spirit of the Lord is upon me because he has
anointed me; he has sent me to announce good news to
the poor, to proclaim release for prisoners and recovery
of sight for the blind; to let the broken victims go free, to*

proclaim the year of the Lord's favor."

Luke 4: 18-19

John, who was in prison, heard what Christ was doing,
and sent his own disciples to put this question to him:
"Are you the one who is to come, or are we to expect
someone else?" Jesus answered: "Go and report to John
what you hear and see: the blind recover their sight, the
lame walk, lepers are made clean, the deaf hear, the dead
are raised to life, the poor are brought good news – and
blessed are those who do not find me an obstacle to faith."

Matthew 11: 2-6

Such gospel words are what prompted Francis' way of life. We are the proclaimers for our world and our time. Jesus has given us his own Spirit. What might seem impossible to weak human beings is possible with God. Go and proclaim the good news!

8. Francis was a "heart" person. The transformation of the heart will lead to transformation of the person. It is simple hypocrisy to claim that our heart has undergone a radical conversion if it doesn't show on the outside. If God took flesh to be visible to us, the love in our hearts must take flesh to be visible to others. Body and heart are partners in proclaiming the gospel.

From this perspective Francis saw two things as especially destructive to a gospel life.

A) Sin ... to choose something that diminishes or destroys our relationship with God, self or neighbor. It is the opposite of union and communion that is the gift of the Spirit. Unfaithfulness to gospel responsibilities is not life-giving. Whatever diminishes gospel-life must be dealt with, head-on, by a Franciscan.

B) Blindness ... refusing to see with the insight of faith. A blinded heart condemns us to wander in circles, refusing the light that could restore our sight. Francis mourned for those who refused to see the goodness of God. What sorrow he had for those who allowed sin to separate them from "communion."

They are blind because they do not see the true light, our

Lord Jesus Christ. They do not have spiritual wisdom
because they do not have within them the Son of God
who is the true wisdom of the Father.
Francis & Clare – Brady/Armstrong
Paulist Press – Page 72

Separation and blindness have consequences. Loneliness and isolation become companions. Stumbling and failure often accompanies those who refuse to see. Even success finally fades when it is built on the sand of greed and acclaim. We long for intimacy and companionship, for hope and a dream to fulfill our hope. Sin and blindness deprive us of cherished human needs. Francis gives a clear-cut call not to be deceived but to walk in the light of Jesus.

Coupled with sin and blindness is our search for independence. What begins as a healthy search for individuality can end in the isolation of individualism. When we are concerned only with ourselves; when our actions serve only ourselves; when we use freedom with only our own needs in mind; when we accumulate wealth only to satisfy ourselves – individualism has gone haywire.

Dependence is not something we seek. Neither does it lack dangers of its own. We can renege on responsibility through unhealthy dependence. We can surrender our lives to cultish leaders and follow them blindly. But there is an inter-dependence on God and people that is healthy. We listen to Jesus to learn values for living. We allow the Spirit the freedom to prompt our actions. We freely acquiesce to the call of God as we understand it. Such inter-dependence brings us sound growth.

When we embrace healthy "inter-dependence" our vision is expanded. Breaking free of the narrow confines of individualistic vision, we "see" with the grand vision of faith. No longer stooped over and seeing only our small plot of earth, we stand straight and see the "whole" world. Such is the way of inter-dependence. Chesterton expresses it well.

> *If a man saw the world upside down with all the trees*
> *and towers hanging head downwards as in a pool, one*
> *effect would be to emphasize the idea of DEPEND-*
> *ENCE. ... It would make vivid the Scriptural text which*

*says that God has hung the world upon nothing. If St
Francis had seen, in one of his strange dreams, the town
of Assisi upside down, it need not have differed in a
single detail from itself except in being entirely the other
way round. But the point is this: that whereas to the
normal eye, the large masonry of its watchtowers and
its high citadel would make it seem safer and more
permanent, the moment it was turned over the very
same weight would make it seem more helpless and more
in peril. It is but a symbol; but it happens to fit the
psychological fact. St Francis might love his little town
as much as before, or more than before; but the nature of
the love would be altered even in being increased. He
might see and love every tile on the steep roofs or every
bird on the battlements; but he would see them all in a
new and divine light of eternal danger and dependence.
Instead of being merely proud of his strong city because
it could not be moved, he would be thankful to God
Almighty that it had not been dropped.*

St Francis of Assisi – Chesterton
Image Books – Page 74-75

Reflection

These ideas on the charism of St Francis are quite incomplete. Yet they
may stimulate your own search to give flesh to the gospel in YOUR life.
We cannot follow Francis and ignore his perspective on life. Part of the
attractiveness of Francis is the way he does impossible things with such
a sense of humor. He may not have planned everything that happened
to him. But he was alert to God and responded with graciousness and
dignity. He might well be known as a fool, but being a fool became his
banner. Jesus was the savior and leader. Francis was the "fool" who felt
confident in following Jesus.

The world may not move beyond the "birdbath Francis." The price of
doing so is expensive. There is something about Francis that gets under
our skin. His life says that the gospel is possible. His life says that
following the gospel brings joy. His life says that praising God is a
normal stance for human beings. His life says that faithfulness is

primary and perfection is a gift only God can give. His life says that the heart yearns for intimacy and God grants it through Jesus. His life says that fear and pain and suffering and failure do not have more power than the love of Jesus Christ. His life proclaims that the Holy Spirit continues to build, within and among us, the kingdom of God. To all of which we can only say: AMEN!

Reflection Questions

What elements of the charism of Francis are especially attractive to you? Which one(s) do you find hardest to accept and/or implement? Why is the incarnation and crucifixion of Jesus important for Franciscans? How would you evaluate your sense of wonder? Why is a "sense of wonder" important for a Franciscan? What is the role of the Holy Spirit in our gospel life? How would you define "poverty"? How would you assess your practice of "poverty?" How strong is your sense of possessiveness? How would you describe a healthy "dependence?" Why is the Eucharist important for our spiritual development? What is your image of God the Father? How does it help or hinder your relationship with God the Father? If inner holiness is insufficient for gospel people, what else is needed? Why would gospel people be expected to work for peace and reconciliation? How does blindness and sin hinder genuine gospel living? How would you define "sin" and "blindness?" Why is individualism dangerous for the gospel life? How would you define gospel freedom? What are the consequences of healthy inter-dependence?

FRANCISCAN FOCUS

The Friends Of Francis

Francis had good friends among his companions. They walked with him, suffered with him, wondered with him and tried to be faithful to his dream. Angelo, Rufino, Giles, Leo and many others formed a nucleus of friends. Juniper was his delightful clown, simple and perceptive. Leo was a faithful secretary and traveling companion. They touched Francis with their loyalty and love. Only a few have left us a written legacy. Among them is Giles.

Brother Giles once asked a lay judge: "Do you think God's gifts great?" The lawyer answered: "I certainly do!" Brother Giles said: "I'll show you that you don't think so," and he insisted. "How much are all your possessions worth?" "Maybe a thousand dollars." "And would you trade them all for ten times that?" The man answered" "Yes, most willingly." Brother Giles said: "It's certain that all this world's goods are worthless compared to heavenly things. Why, then, don't you trade the lot for these?" The judge retorted: "Do you think that a man acts on all that he believes?" Brother Giles answered: "Holy men and women have always tried to act out in real life whatever they could. Whatever their efforts could not reach they still thirsted after with the longing of a lover. What was lacking in deeds they made up for in desires. If a man had whole faith he would arrive at such a grade. He would be gifted with absolute certainty. And so, if you really believe, you should set to work right away."

Golden Words – Ivo O'Sullivan
Franciscan Herald Press – Page 49-50

Three things in life are very deep and truly useful. He who grasps them will not lose himself. First, endure peacefully, for the love of God, all the troubles that come your way. Secondly, become more unassuming with the many things you do and all the talents you acquire. Thirdly, keep a steadfast heart for those good things unseen by human eyes.

IBID – Page 48

Don't harm people. If a man harms you, take it patiently so that you may love God more and obtain pardon for your sins. It is much better to accept one single injury without resentful complaint than to feed a hundred people for weeks while you yourself fast daily far into the night. It does not help you to give your body a hard time with fasts, prayer, vigils and penances, if you cannot tolerate a snub from your fellow man. The reward for forbearance is greater than any you could earn through the afflictions you think up for yourself. To feel resentment only shows that your hidden pride is wounded!

IBID – Page 60

Brother Giles gives witness to good influence by Francis. May the life and words of Francis have a similar effect in our lives.

QUESTIONS

1. What elements of the Franciscan charism are most attractive to you? Which ones do you find most difficult to embrace and implement in your life? Explain both answers.

2. How does society's stress on individual freedom impact on the gospel life? Explain why it helps or hinders that life!

3. What attitude are we expected to have in regard to the resources of the earth? What is the basis for such an attitude?

4. How would you describe the spirit of "wonder?" What connection is there between wonder and prayer?

5. Why are the incarnation and crucifixion so important to Francis and Franciscans?

6. Give yourself prayerful reflection time on this question. At this point of your formation, write your description of the Franciscan charism. Lots of words come to mind: Lady Poverty – Gospel – Jesus – Cross – Incarnation – Wonder – Clare – Reconciliation – Justice – Praise – Blindness – Eucharist – Penance – Conversion – Joy. This question is meant to help you personalize the charism of Francis. So let it be your very own reflection and not someone else's.

SCRIPTURE reading/reflection

+ 2 Corinthians 8: 1-15
  St Paul spends time sharing his ideas on generosity. Everyone is called to offer assistance to others. No one should lack what is needed for life. Even more, Paul speaks of the riches of faith that should be shared.

  Reflect on this text. Share your ideas on why generous love is important to community life. Try to spell out practical ways of showing such generosity in the fraternity and in your own life. Don't hesitate to dialogue with others in discovering the ways generosity might find expression.

Woodcut by John Aloysius Uboldi

CHAPTER 18

CATCHING THE RAINBOW

Since the time of Noah, when a rainbow appeared after forty days of rain, the rainbow has been a sign of hope. God used it as a sign of the covenant with Noah.

> *God said: "For all generations to come, this is the sign*
> *which I am giving of the covenant between myself and*
> *you and all living creatures with you:*
>
> > *My bow I set in the clouds*
> > *to be a sign of the covenant*
> > *between myself and the earth.*
> > *When I bring clouds over the earth,*
> > *the rainbow will appear in the clouds.*
>
> *... Whenever the bow appears in the cloud, I shall see it*
> *and remember the everlasting covenant between God*
> *and living creatures of every kind on earth.*
> **Genesis 9: 12-14 & 16**

For Franciscans the rainbow is a reminder of a God who is faithful to the covenant. Franciscans look at Jesus and realize again the faithfulness of God. God sent Jesus that we might be saved and live. Jesus shares with us everything the Father has told him. In the ongoing revelation of the scriptural word, God continues to speak to us.

St Francis believed this so strongly that following the gospel seemed the only adequate covenant response. God's presence is discovered in Francis' caves of darkness and fear. The sign of God's presence is discovered in the love and dedication of Clare. The sign of God's presence is discovered in the lepers of his life. Even in his weaknesses, Francis discovered a faithful God who forgave and offered new life. God heals and strengthens a broken spirit. Francis found God in Pope Honorius who approved his Rule. Francis discovered God when it seemed God had disappeared and the storms in the Order raged around him. In the storm Francis discovered that it was but preparation for the covenant-sign of the rainbow. God is with us.

Profession as a Secular Franciscan invites you to enter the same journey of discovery. There is no end to the opportunities for change and growth. We are never quite finished with the search. Maturity is not a one-time happening but an everyday process. We trust in the covenant promise of our God. We profess to be faithful in our response to this covenant with God. Our storms will be uniquely our own. The lightning and thunder of storms will touch our lives, perhaps often. But they are prelude to the rainbow, the reminder of God's covenant.

> ... this is the word of the Lord, the word of your creator, of him who fashioned you, Israel; Have no fear, for I have redeemed you. I call you by name, you are mine. When you pass through water, I shall be with you; when you pass through rivers, they will not overwhelm you; walk through fire, and you will not be scorched, through flames, and they will not burn you.
>
> ... You are more precious to me than the Assyrians; you are honored, and I love you. ... Have no fear, I am with you.
>
> **Isaiah 43: 1-2 & 4 & 5**

Such is the covenant-promise of God. God is faithful and will be with us. Over and over God repeats that covenant. Finally, God seals the covenant through the life and death of Jesus, God-made-flesh. The faithfulness of God is signed loud and clear through the passion and death of Jesus. The faithfulness of God to Jesus is signed loud and clear when God raised Jesus from the dead. The Franciscan way of life is one way to be faithful to our covenant with God.

Following Jesus

Jesus is an honest leader. He does not double-talk us into following him. He does not minimize the cost of being his disciple. Jesus clearly points out that suffering and persecution are a part of discipleship. He offers clear proof of the power he gives us. The power of Jesus does not rest on possessions. In fact, he invites us to take nothing with us on the journey. We need only the power he gives and it will be enough. In his own travels Jesus exhibits the rhythm of prayer and action, of strong words and gentle responses and a fierce loyalty to the way of his Father. He faced the pain and apparent defeat of Gethsemane and Calvary and is raised from the dead by his loving Father.

Jesus often spoke of commitment to himself. Followers of Jesus are asked to prefer Jesus to anyone else. Only total commitment allows the disciple freedom to follow the whole gospel. We need to know whom we will serve. When we make this basic commitment, we apply gospel-love to the other people in our lives. There is a challenge to our integrity to do what Jesus asks. It may seem counter to human wisdom. The result of a genuine response to the gospel is the joy that Francis knew.

> *No one is worthy of me who cares more for father or mother than for me; no one is worthy of me who cares more for son or daughter; no one is worthy of me who does not take up his cross and follow me. Whoever gains his life will lose it; whoever loses his life for my sake will gain it.*
>
> **Matthew 10: 37-39**

> *Jesus said to him: "If you still wish to be perfect, go, sell your possessions, and give to the poor, and you will have treasure in heaven; then come and follow me." When the young man heard this, he went away with a heavy heart; for he was a man of great wealth.*

> *Jesus said to his disciples: "Truly I tell you, a rich man will find it hard to enter the Kingdom of heaven. I repeat, it is easier for a camel to pass through the eye of a needle than for a rich man to enter the kingdom of God." The disciples were astonished when they heard this, and exclaimed: "Then who can be saved?" Jesus looked at them and said: "For men this is impossible; but everything is possible for God."*
>
> **Matthew 19: 21-26**

> *Jesus called them to him and said: "You know that*

among the Gentiles the recognized rulers lord it over
their subjects, and the great make their authority felt. It
shall not be so with you; among you, whoever wants to
be great must be your servant and whoever wants to be
first must be the slave of all."

Mark 10: 42-44

Calling the twelve together, he gave them power and
authority to overcome all demons and to cure diseases,
and sent them out to proclaim the kingdom of God and
to heal the sick. "Take nothing for the journey," he told
them: "neither stick nor pack, neither bread nor money;
nor are you to have a second coat. When you enter a
house, stay there until you leave the place. As for those
who will not receive you, when you leave their town
shake the dust off your feet as a warning to them." So
they set out and travelled from village to village, and
everywhere they announced the good news and healed
the sick.

Luke 9: 1-6

"If your brother does wrong, reprove him; and if he
repents, forgive him. Even if he wrongs you seven times
in a day and comes back to you seven times saying: 'I
am sorry,' you are to forgive him."

Luke 17: 3-4

"I do not look to men for honour. But I know that with
you it is different, for you have no love of God in you. I
have come accredited by my Father, and you have no
welcome for me; but let someone self-accredited come,
and you will give him a welcome. How can you believe
when you accept honor from one another, and care
nothing for the honor that comes from him who alone is
God?"

John 5: 41-44

The gospel word is clear. Gospel people know that Jesus is their source
of strength: "For God all things are possible." Jesus tells us that he is
strength and nourishment for the journey. With sensitive sharing Jesus

points out how much the Father and he wish to share with us.

> *"I am the bread of life. Whoever comes to me will never be hungry and whoever believes in me will never be thirsty. ... All the Father gives me will come to me, and anyone who comes to me I will never turn away. I have come down from heaven, to do not my own will, but the will of him who sent me. It is his will that I should not lose even one of those he has given me, but should raise them all up on the last day. For it is my Father's will that everyone who sees the Son and has faith in him should have eternal life; and I will raise them up on the last day."*
>
> John 6: 35-40

> *This is how we know that we dwell in him and he dwells in us; he has imparted his Spirit to us. Moreover, we have seen for ourselves and we are witnesses, that the Father has sent the Son to be the savior of the World. If anyone acknowledges that Jesus is God's son, God dwells in him and he in God. Thus we have come to know and believe in the love which God has for us.*
>
> 1 John 4: 13-16

These are the revelations Jesus gives us. As gospel people they become our way of life. Nothing can keep God from being faithful to the covenant. Nothing will hinder Jesus from being faithful to his gospel promises. By PROFESSION in the Secular Franciscan Order we make a public commitment to the gospel as our way of life. It is a possible commitment for the same reason Francis could commit himself. Jesus has given us his Spirit.

Our intellectual understanding, our personality, our good feelings may assist us in keeping the commitment. But the reason we can be gospel people is because of Jesus. Profession in the SFO is our way to gift God with the life God has given us. The commitment is for a lifetime. The journey will last till then. Until Sister Death calls us home, radical change will continue to touch our lives. Walking with us, covenanted to us, loving us – is Jesus.

The folly of God is wiser than human wisdom, and the weakness of God stronger than human strength. My friends, think what sort of people you are whom God has called. Few of you are wise by any human standard, few powerful or of noble birth. Yet to shame the wise, God has chosen what the world counts folly, and to shame what is strong, God has chosen what the world counts weakness. He has chosen things without rank or standing in the world, mere nothings, to overthrow the existing order. So no place is left for any human pride in the presence of God. By God's act you are in Christ Jesus; God has made him our wisdom and in him we have our righteousness, our holiness, our liberation. Therefore in the words of scripture, "If anyone must boast, let him boast of the Lord."

1 Corinthians 1: 25-31

Be bold in living the Franciscan lifestyle. Be strong in following the example of St Francis. Be joyful in the wonder of God's call to you. Be full of praise as you realize how God loves you. Let no one and nothing deter you from the path you have chosen. Follow nothing that would draw you to mediocrity. The gracious power of our God is able to take poor clay vessels and mold them into vessels that give glory to God. From the weak of the earth God chooses faithful followers to confound the strong. How we need God and one another to persist in our commitment!

For that is the full and final spirit in which we should turn to St Francis; in the spirit of thanks for what he has done. He was above all things a great giver; and he cared chiefly for the best kind of giving which is called thanksgiving. If another great man wrote a grammar of assent, he may well be said to have written a grammar of acceptance; a grammar of gratitude. He understood down to its very depths the theory of thanks; and its depths are a bottomless abyss. He knew that the praise of God stands on its strongest ground when it stands on nothing. He knew that we can best measure the towering miracle of the mere fact of existence if we realize that but for some strange mercy we should not even exist. And something of that larger truth is repeated in a lessor form in our own relations with so mighty a maker of history. He also is a giver of things we could not have even thought of for ourselves; he also is too great for anything but gratitude. From him came a whole awakening of the world and a dawn in which all shapes and colors could be seen anew.

St Francis of Assisi – Chesterton
Image Books – Page 156-157

In the hands of the Father, I am a vessel molded for peace and love. I will attempt to replace hatred and doubt, despair and darkness, moping and sadness with love and hope, faith and light, forgiveness and joy.

I need the power of the Father and Jesus and the Holy Spirit. But I also need the power of a community that loves me. I need Brothers and Sisters with skin on, to walk with me and talk with me. I need them as a place of refuge and support and acceptance when life has trampled on me. I need you to be quiet with me and listen even if you cannot understand my ways. I need you to create for me the space and the heart where I can feel "at home."

Whatever I ask of you, I will also try to give. Thus we will create an atmosphere where each of us can be always on the way to greater wholeness. For this we have been called by the Lord. Amen. Alleluia.

Reflection Questions

What does the word "covenant" mean to you? Share some of the ways you have experienced God's covenant-love. What areas of your life least respond to the gospel call? What/Who is the source of power that enables us to follow the gospel? Which scriptural text in this chapter struck you most forcibly? Why? How would you explain why Jesus expects us to love him more than we love sons, daughters etc? Does that mean we are excused from loving others? If not, explain why not! In a few words explain what is the basic belief of our faith that will bring us to God? Share your ideas about the role of Jesus in the gospel life of a Franciscan. Why is "thanksgiving" so important for a Franciscan?

FRANCISCAN FOCUS

<u>*THE TRANSITUS* "*The passing of Francis*"</u>

While, therefore, the Brothers were weeping bitterly and grieving inconsolably, the holy father commanded that bread be brought to him. He blessed and broke it and gave a small piece of it to each one to eat. Commanding also that a book of the gospels be brought, he asked that the gospel according to St John be read to him from the place that begins: "Before the feast of passover ..." He was recalling that most holy supper which the Lord celebrated as his last supper with his disciples. He did all of this in reverent memory of that supper, showing thereby the deep love he had for his brothers.

Then he spent the few days that remained before his death in praise, teaching his companions, whom he loved so much, to praise Christ with him. He himself, as far as he was able, broke forth in this psalm: "I cried to the Lord with my voice; with my voice I made supplication to the Lord." (Ps 141) He also invited all creatures to praise God, and by means of the words he had composed earlier (Canticle of Brother Sun) he exhorted them to love God. He exhorted death itself, terrible and hateful to all, to give praise, and going forth joyfully to meet it, he invited it to make its lodging with him. "Welcome," he said: "my Sister Death." To the doctor he said: "Tell me bravely, Brother Doctor, that death, which is the gateway to life, is at hand." Then to the Brothers: "When you see that I am brought to my last moments, place me naked upon the ground just as you saw me the day before yesterday. And let me lie there after I am dead for the length of time it takes to walk a mile unhurriedly."

*The hour, therefore, came and all the mysteries of Christ
being fulfilled in him, he winged his way happily to God.*
Omnibus of Sources – (Celano)
Franciscan Herald Press – Page 536

✝ ✝ ✝ ✝

St Francis died on a Saturday evening, October 3, 1226. He was
canonized two years later on July 16, 1228. The feast of St Francis is
celebrated on October 4.

Many Franciscan places celebrate what is called the TRANSITUS or the
"passing on" of St Francis. It offers a special opportunity to honor
Francis. If possible, it is celebrated on the evening of October 3rd. There
are a variety of rituals that can be used for the Transitus Service.
Franciscans are free to design their own.

St Francis was buried in Assisi. Upon the completion of the Basilica of
St Francis his body was buried in the lower level.

One final note. The "Peace Prayer" has been attributed to St Francis. It
certainly reflects his spirit. However, research indicates that it was
written in the early part of the 20th century. But his "Canticle of Brother
Sun" deserves widespread publicity. It is written by St Francis and
contains much of the spirit of Francis.

✝ ✝ ✝ ✝

Postscript

You have completed your initial formation. After profession you face
the challenge of continuing what you have begun. You may be called
to service within the fraternity. You may be called to ministry. You may
be called to deeper prayer. Whatever you can do to make the Frater-
nity-community a familiar home for gospel growth -do it! Whatever
you can do to bring life to people in your daily life – do it! Whatever
you can do to grow in intimacy with Jesus`– do it! Search out the ways
of supporting others. Learn the ways of loving confrontation and
affirmation. Know your gifts and skills and use them well. You have a
covenant with Jesus. Keep it with all your heart!

Now to him who is able, through the power which is at work among us, to do immeasurably more than all we can ask or conceive, to him be glory in the Church and in Christ Jesus from generation to generation for evermore! Amen.

Ephesians 3: 20-21

a view of the Medieval Citadel in Assisi.

QUESTIONS

This concludes "Catch me a rainbow." My suggestion would be this ... Take special time to write a statement on what this time of formation has done for you. You might include:

1. What does a gospel lifestyle mean to me?

2. In all the things I have learned, what has done the most to change my life?

3. What issues have I been able to address better because of this time of formation?

4. What new ideas have I gained in regard to what makes a good community?

5. How has my prayer life been helped?

6. How do I view social justice issues at this point in my life? How has the formation period helped me in this area of life?

7. How do I view relationships? With God? With Jesus? With myself? With others?

8. What is the most important personal thing I have learned during this time of initial formation?

These questions are simply reflection "starters." Feel free to share whatever you think is important. Writing some of these things can help to clarify your expectations and responsibilities as you move to profession.

SHALOM

The Canticle of Brother Sun

Most High, all powerful, good Lord
Yours are the praises, the glory, the honor
and all blessing
To you alone most High, do they belong,
and no one is worthy to mention your name.

Praised be you, my Lord, with all your creatures,
especially Sir Brother Sun, who is day
and through whom you give us light.
He is beautiful and radiant with great splendor
and bears a likeness of you, most high One.

Praise be you, my Lord, through Sister Moon and Stars
In heaven you formed them, clear and precious and
beautiful

Praised be you, my Lord, through Brother Wind, and through
the Air, cloudy and serene, and every kind of weather
through whom you give sustenance to your creatures

Praised be you, my Lord, through Sister Water, which is
very useful and humble and robust and strong.

Praise be you, my Lord, through Brother Fire
through whom you light up the night
He is beautiful and playful, robust and strong

Praised be you, my Lord, through our Sister, Mother Earth
who sustains and governs us and who produces
varied fruits with colored flowers and herbs

Praised be you, my Lord, through those who give pardon
for your love and bear infirmity and tribulation
Blessed are those who endure in peace,
for by you, most High, they shall be crowned

Praised be you, my Lord, through our Sister, Bodily Death
from whom no living person can escape
Woe to those who die in mortal sin
Blessed are those whom death shall find in your holy will,
for the second death shall do them no harm.

Praise and bless my Lord and give him thanks
and serve him with great humility.